Eve's Enlightenment

Eve's Enlightenment

Women's Experience in Spain
and Spanish America, 1726–1839

Edited by CATHERINE M. JAFFE
and ELIZABETH FRANKLIN LEWIS

LOUISIANA STATE UNIVERSITY PRESS ❈ BATON ROUGE

This publication was made possible in part by a grant from the Program for Cultural Cooperation between Spain's Ministry of Culture and United States Universities.

Published by Louisiana State University Press
Copyright © 2009 by Louisiana State University Press
All rights reserved
Manufactured in the United States of America
FIRST PRINTING

DESIGNER: *Amanda McDonald Scallan*
TYPEFACE: *Whitman*
PRINTER AND BINDER: *Thomson-Shore, Inc.*

Library of Congress Cataloging-in-Publication Data

Eve's Enlightenment : women's experience in Spain and Spanish America, 1726-1839 / edited by Catherine M. Jaffe and Elizabeth Franklin Lewis.
   p. cm.
  Includes bibliographical references and index.
  ISBN 978-0-8071-3389-7 (cloth : alk. paper) 1. Women—Spain—History—18th century. 2. Women—Spain—Intellectual life. 3. Women—Latin America—History—18th century. 4. Women—Latin America—Intellectual life. 5. Enlightenment—Spain. 6. Enlightenment—Latin America. 7. Spanish literature—Women authors—History and criticism. 8. Latin American literature—Women authors—History and criticism. 9. Women and literature—Spain. 10. Women and literature—Latin America. I. Jaffe, Catherine Marie, 1958- II. Lewis, Elizabeth Franklin, 1964-
  HQ1693.E84 2009
  305.40946—dc22
                                                2008029225

The paper in this book meets the guidelines for permanence and durability of the Committee on Production Guidelines for Book Longevity of the Council on Library Resources. ∞

Contents

Acknowledgments vii
Introduction 1
CATHERINE M. JAFFE AND ELIZABETH FRANKLIN LEWIS

PART I. WOMEN AND THE REPUBLIC OF LETTERS 15

1. Women of Letters in Eighteenth-Century Spain
Between Tradition and Modernity 17
MÓNICA BOLUFER PERUGA

2. Enlightenment Experience in the Life and Poetry of Sor María Gertrudis de la Cruz Hore 33
FRÉDÉRIQUE MORAND

3. Reasons for Education
New Echoes of the Polemic 51
ISABEL MORANT DEUSA

4. Margarita Hickey's Guide to the Traps of Love 62
MARÍA A. SALGADO

5. Illustrating Sainthood
The Construction of Eighteenth-Century Spanish American Hagiography 84
ELISA SAMPSON VERA TUDELA

PART II. WOMEN'S LIVES
Material and Social Practices 101

6. Women in Society in Eighteenth-Century Spain
Models of Sociability 103
MARÍA VICTORIA LÓPEZ-CORDÓN CORTEZO

7. The Wife, the Maid, and the Woman in the Street 115
REBECCA HAIDT

8. Women Alone in Enlightenment Spain 128
MARÍA JOSÉ DE LA PASCUA SÁNCHEZ

9. An Enlightened Perspective on Hysteria in Eighteenth-Century Mexico 143
BEATRIZ QUINTANILLA-MADERO

PART III. REPRESENTATIONS OF WOMEN
Between Rational Equality and Sensibility 159

10. The Enlightenment Origins of Cuba's Iconic *Mulata* 161
LUCY D. HARNEY

11. Doña Leonora's Library
Women's Reading from the Spectator *(1711) to* El Semanario de Salamanca *(1795)* 178
CATHERINE M. JAFFE

12. "Virtue in Distress" in the Spanish Sentimental Novel
An Unsustainable Model of Rational Sensibility 197
ANA RUEDA

13. Mothers, *Majas*, and *Marcialidad*
Faces of Enlightenment in Spain 218
JANIS A. TOMLINSON

Contributors 237

Index 241

Acknowledgments

An undertaking as complex as this collection of essays could not have come about without the help and advice of many colleagues and friends. We would first like to thank our contributors for their hard work, their trust in us, and their patience throughout the long process of editing this book. David Gies helped us to find translators from among his graduate students in the Department of Spanish and Portuguese at the University of Virginia. We are grateful for his help and advice and for the translators' hard work. We would like to recognize the financial support provided by the Department of Modern Languages at Texas State University-San Marcos and the Program for Cultural Cooperation between Spain's Ministry of Culture and United States Universities. And finally, many thanks go to our families, who supported us in so many ways as we were working on this project.

Introduction

CATHERINE M. JAFFE AND ELIZABETH FRANKLIN LEWIS

The second example [of why women are the cause of all evil in the world], if it proves that women in general are worse than men, also proves that the Angels in general are worse than women: because since Adam was induced to sin by a woman, woman was induced by an Angel. Until now it has not been determined who sinned most gravely, Adam or Eve; because the Fathers of the Church are divided. And in truth the excuse that Cayetano [St. Cajetan, 1480–1547] gives Eve, that she was deceived by a creature of superior intelligence and sagacity, a circumstance that did not occur with Adam, makes his sin greater in comparison to the sin of Eve.
—BENITO JERÓNIMO FEIJOO, "Defensa de las mujeres"

Eve did not resist these temptations; first she persuaded her husband, and he sinned out of condescension what she had begun out of curiosity. Detestable curiosity for certain, but curiosity tends to be an indication of talent.
—JOSEFA AMAR Y BORBÓN, "Discurso en defensa del talento de las mujeres"

To write about how Spanish and Spanish American women experienced the Enlightenment is to try to bring into focus a doubly effaced realm of history. Studies of the European Enlightenment have generally shown little concern for even the outstanding exponents of Enlightenment thought in Spain, such as the Benedictine friar and prolific essayist Benito Feijoo (1676–1764). Even within Hispanic studies the Enlightenment movements in Spain and Spanish America have received little attention and until recently have been considered by most to be of little importance to the overall development of Hispanic culture.[1] To this lack of attention to the Spanish and Spanish American Enlightenment both outside and within Hispanism must be added the further neglect of the category of gender. Classic and even relatively recent studies of the Hispanic Enlightenment often make no reference to the particularity of women's history or to the important contributions that women authors such as Josefa Amar y Borbón, Margarita Hickey, María Gálvez, and María Gertrudis Hore made to cultural production.² The historian Mónica Bolufer Peruga, in her landmark study *Mujeres e Ilustración: La construcción de la feminidad en la España del siglo XVIII* (1998), notes the paucity of studies of women's history in Spain for all periods, especially the Enlightenment period. Prior to the 1980s only three book-length studies on Spanish women's history had appeared (22).³ Important scholarship about eighteenth-century Spanish and Spanish American women's history has often been published in Spanish and so has not been available to the broader community interested in women's history and gender studies. The pioneering work of Spanish women historians, beginning with Carmen Martín Gaite and Paula Demerson and followed by the work of María Victoria López-Cordón, Isabel Morant Deusa, and Mónica Bolufer Peruga, along with Asunción Lavrin for Latin America,⁴ among others, has made remarkable progress in shedding light on this blind spot of history, as the increasing amount of scholarship devoted to the issue in the past decade shows.⁵

In his incisive critique of the neglect of the Enlightenment's legacy in Spain, Eduardo Subirats defends what he describes as Spain's "insufficient Enlightenment" and calls for a more objective study of the "limitations and deficiencies" of the *Ilustración* (24). Such a project can only be attempted with a broad understanding of the Enlightenment as an opening to a modern "program of secularization of thought and artistic manifestations, of openness to and development of sciences, arts, and technology . . . and a search for a conscious and controlled agreement between culture and power," according to Jesús Pérez Magallón, who also reminds us that each culture should be studied in its own context and without imposing unrelated values and paradigms (14, 51).⁶ It is precisely through the study of gender, and particularly through new ways of constructing gender relations that developed during the long eighteenth century, that we may more fully understand the significance and legacy of the Enlightenment in Spain and Spanish America to modern Hispanic culture. As Theresa Smith has asserted, "[Gender] debates were central to reconfiguring Spain as an enlightened nation. In the eyes of those who witnessed it, redefining gender identities was critical to Spain's political, social and economic modernization" (7).

During the Enlightenment—a broad process of intellectual and cultural change that propelled Western societies toward modernity between the late seventeenth and early nineteenth centuries—the interrogation of the practices, understanding, and ideologies of gender invariably accompanied the period's critique of traditional social, philosophical, political, scientific, and religious systems, as recent scholarship has made clear.⁷ In the Enlightenment, a movement characterized by its contradictions as much as by its widely diffused currents of thought,⁸ debates regarding women's appropriate place in society were no less contentious in Spain and Latin America than in the rest of Europe and North America. Like their sisters across the Atlantic and over the Pyrenees, Spanish and Spanish American women who breathed these supposed winds of change nevertheless continued to confront traditional stereotypes founded on their inherent inferiority. Nowhere was this more evident, especially in the strong Catholic tradition of Hispanic culture, than in the interpretation and application to women's situation of the biblical story of Eve. Eve had had a long and vigorous cultural tradition as a potent symbol of women's moral inferiority, as we see in the *Cantigas de Santa María*, no. 60, by Alfonso X el Sabio (1221–84):

> Entre Av' e Eva
> gran departiment'á.
> Ca Eva nos tolleu
> Parays'e Deus.

> Between Ave [the Virgin Mary] and Eva
> there is a great difference.
> For Eva took us away
> from heaven and from God.

Eve was often invoked as a justification for women's consequent inferior role in society, but for Enlightenment advocates of women's rights, such as Benito Feijoo and the essayist and intellectual Josefa Amar y Borbón (1749–1833), Eve became a symbol of women's potential. As the epigraphs to this introduction show, while Feijoo defends Eve in his groundbreaking 1726 essay "Defense of Women," six decades later Josefa Amar muses upon Eve's experience when she is tempted by the serpent, seeing in Eve evidence of women's abilities and intellectual curiosity. Amar thus cleverly reevaluates a traditionally pejorative sense of "curiosity" when applied to women, ascribing to them instead the positive sense of a scientific, inquiring, and critical *modern* spirit.⁹

The title of the present volume, *Eve's Enlightenment*, suggests the conflicts and contradictions produced when traditional stereotypes used to explain, understand, and categorize women met the broad cultural shift in the direction of secularism, empiricism, and skepticism toward authority that occurred during the Enlightenment period. The transformation of inherited ideas about women's nature, the theorizing of gender itself and of women's role in society, "la ilustración de Eva," is one of the period's significant contributions to modern thought. With some distinctive differences because of their societies' strong Catholic tradition, women in Spain and Spanish America experienced this transformation along with women in the rest of Europe and North America. As the essays in this volume show, these women acted as writers, intellectuals, philanthropists, artists and patrons of the arts, leaders of fashion, and nuns; they made up a new class of readers who wielded power in the literary marketplace and were influenced by new literary models; they performed their duties as mothers and wives influenced by new conceptions of the family and the maternal role; they lived as women served by Enlightenment pedagogical reforms and medical theories; and they survived as part of the urban or rural underclass or as women of color affected by new interpretations of matrimony, race, civic responsibility, and nationalism. How did women in Spanish America and Spain "experience" the Enlightenment? How was their experience represented? Were there gaps between women's experience and representations of it, or between Enlightenment philosophies and women's lived experience? These are a few of the questions that these essays address by drawing on the insights of literature, history, art history, and psychology.

Given the empirical orientation of the Enlightenment, experience was integral to its epistemology. As John Locke had in his 1690 *Essay Concerning Human Understanding,* Enlightenment thinkers abandoned received notions of human knowledge being formed by innate ideas and instead began to conceive of the mind as a tabula rasa, a blank slate, that was "written" upon by sensory experience.[10] The Spanish *ilustrado* (enlightened reformer) Gaspar Melchor de Jovellanos wrote in his treatise on public education, *Memoria sobre educación pública* (1802), that experience is crucial for the development of human reason: "But the necessity that this directing reason has of instruction is more evident regarding itself, that is, regarding the intellectual faculties of man, because it is clear that these are developed with use, and they increase and improve with habit and observation" (282). This emphasis on experience led many Enlightenment thinkers, as it did Jovellanos, to see education as the key to improving the lives and minds of men and women. Although most *ilustrados* did not advocate education for all, regardless of class or gender, some, such as Benito Feijoo, attributed women's lack of intellectual acumen to their lack of education, pointing out that "[n]o one knows more than what he studies, which could lead one to infer, although it would be a barbarous conclusion, that ability does not extend beyond one's application" (par. 9). Although Feijoo's logical objections to the conventional belief in women's intellectual inferiority reflected the Enlightenment tendency to question all inherited systems of thought, other influential intellectuals in Spain, Spanish America, and throughout Europe and America would begin to form a new conception of women's abilities based on the category of radical gender difference.

Many European and American philosophers and scientists in the eighteenth century believed that women's experiences, as felt through their bodies, especially the "debilitating reproductive history men did not experience," were fundamentally different from those of men, as the historian G. J. Barker-Benfield has observed (26). This supposed delicacy of women's bodily experience, or their "sensibility," increasingly led to a definition of women's social and gender roles as radically "different" from and complementary to those of men. Jean-Jacques Rousseau advised in *Émile* (1762) that one should "[c]onsult the women's opinions in bodily matters, in all that concerns the senses; consult the men in matters of morality and all that concerns the understanding" (qtd. in Kramnick 569). For Immanuel Kant, in *Observations on the Feeling of the Beautiful and the Sublime* (1764), women were associated with beauty, while men were linked with noble feelings of the sublime: "Women have a strong inborn feeling for all that is beautiful, elegant, and decorated. . . . In short, they contain the chief cause in human nature for the contrast of the beautiful qualities with the noble, and they refine even the masculine sex" (qtd. in Kramnick 581). Despite contemporary social and political discussions of liberty, equality, and "inalienable" rights, women were considered by even the most radical thinkers as inferior to men physically, morally, and intellectually. Rousseau's influential conception of "natural" gender roles proscribed women's intellectual efforts and exalted (and limited) her influence to the domestic sphere: "Women are what they ought to be, they will keep to what they can understand, and their judgment will be right; but since they have set themselves up as judges of literature, since they have begun to criticize books and to make them with might and main, they are altogether astray" (qtd. in Kramnick 569).[11] The subsequent polarization of men's and women's experience contrasted logically with the Enlightenment understanding of human nature as universal, an irony that was not lost on eighteenth-century feminists.

Perhaps no other author writing during Spain's Enlightenment was as concerned with women's experience as was Josefa Amar. In her controversial 1786 essay "Discurso en defensa del talento de las mujeres" (Discourse in Defense of the Talent of Women), in which she advocated for women's admittance into the Economic Society of Madrid, Amar commented on women's limited and conflicted experiences, which she blamed on men: "On the one hand, men seek out women's approval, they pay homage to them that they would never pay to one another; they do not permit them command in public, but they concede absolute reign in private; they deny women instruction, and then they complain that women are not educated" (145). Josefa Amar dedicated her life's work to exposing the inequities of women's lives in Enlightenment Spain and to improving their experience through education. Unfortunately Amar's plans for women's education and her contributions to the debate over women's participation in the Spanish Enlightenment were largely forgotten until the early part of the twentieth century, when Manuel Serrano y Sanz included an entry on her life and works in his monumental *Apuntes para una biblioteca de escritoras españolas desde el año 1401 al 1833* (Notes for a Library of Spanish Women Writers from 1401–1833), first published in 1903. Seven decades later, another Spanish woman of letters, the historian and novelist Carmen Martín Gaite, saw connections between the preoccupations and concerns of women of her own generation and the experiences of eighteenth-century women like Amar, which she detailed in her 1972 study *Usos amorosos del dieciocho en España (Love Customs in Eighteenth-Century Spain)*.

The present collection proposes to expand the understanding of women's history and cultural activities during the Enlightenment in Spain and Spanish America with essays from scholars working in diverse disciplines within eighteenth-century gender studies.[12] These essays, which not only examine those women who joined the public sphere as writers and intellectuals but also consider how women were affected by evolving legal, social, and medical norms and the way women and the Enlightenment were represented in art and literature, point to the crucial importance of gender in the Hispanic Enlightenment. The studies in this collection of both real women and literary and artistic representations of them underscore the Enlightenment's contribution to modern gender ideology; at the same time they point out its inherent contradictions.

One way to understand women's Enlightenment experience is through the writings of women themselves. Women writers who "inscribed themselves in the lacunae of Enlightenment ideology" (Bannet 6) help us to understand how the Enlightenment affected women's lives. Moreover, writing was crucial to women's participation in the Enlightenment project of modernity, because through writing they too could exercise critical reasoning and "moral self-governance" (Hesse x–xvi, 155). Still, as Dorinda Outram argues, women (much like the poor or non-European peoples) were difficult to accommodate in Enlightenment universalizing conceptions of human nature. Because women during the eighteenth century implicitly began to claim social and political authority by writing, they "affected who and what the Enlightenment thought it was" (89). In other words, by claiming Enlightenment experience as their own, women in turn affected the very notion of enlightenment. For example, as Elizabeth Lewis has suggested, one of the primary human goals identified during the Enlightenment—the pursuit of happiness—might be conceived of very differently when considered from a woman's viewpoint. Indeed, much of what we consider to be "changes associated with modernity—such as the separation of the family from wider kinship groups, the separation of the household and economy . . . and the emergence of the modern state—are all *gendered* processes" (Marshall 9). The studies in this volume begin with a concept of "the subject as an *embodied* subject" (Marshall 103) and contend that the full implications of "embodying" Hispanic Enlightenment, as Rebecca Haidt has also argued, have still to be fully explored.

Yet the legacy of gender constructions from the eighteenth century is contradictory and problematic, as the essays that follow show. English women, writes Phyllis Mack, "did have an Enlightenment of sorts, but the impact of Enlightenment values on the world of women was at least partly negative" (9). Similarly, Mónica Bolufer Peruga finds that gender differences conceived during the Spanish Enlightenment have bequeathed an ambivalent inheritance to modernity, "a crossroads that led to several opposing paths" (400). By considering how traditional thought about women was transformed during the Enlightenment, how this process affected intellectual, social, political, and cultural experiences in women's lives, how "Eve" was "enlightened," this volume hopes to explore and map some of these "opposing paths."

One such path that the essays explore, and that the volume's title also acknowledges, is the overcoming of traditional stereotypes used to classify and delimit women and their unique, individual experiences. "Eve" as the morally weak culprit responsible for mankind's post-Edenic existence is one symbol that writers alternately invoked or countered, as we have seen. Beatriz Quintanilla-Madero shows in her essay how women's physical illness was attributed to Eve's, and therefore to all women's, weak moral nature. Among the impossible examples that were held up to women was the biblical *mujer fuerte* (strong woman), the extraordinary, talented woman, which Mónica Bolufer Peruga examines in her essay. Real women who studied or who had a modicum of instruction also had to counter the negative connotations of the *bachillera*, the woman who talks too much about her knowledge, an affront to feminine decorum and gender distinctions. In Spanish America, race also classified women, as Lucy Harney's essay on the iconic Cuban *mulata* shows; in this case, the *mulata* is cast as a victim who falls to a seducer owing to her lack of education and the irresponsibility of the upper class. Woman as victim of the male libertine is a stereotype perpetuated in the rhetoric of sensibility in novels that presented a dubious moral example for readers, according to Ana Rueda.

Types could also be deliberately assumed by women to perform or to challenge their social role, as in the case of the *petimetra* (a French-influenced fashionable woman) or her nationalistic counterpart, the *maja* (a typical lower-class Spanish woman), as Janis Tomlinson explains. Catherine Jaffe shows that the romantic woman reader was a stereotype often used to counter and devalue women's intellectual activities, and Quintanilla-Madero studies how the traditional mistrust of witches and demonic possession led to an often misunderstood medical stereotype, the hysteric.

Just as certain inherited stereotypes were alternately invoked or contested, traditional discourses could be employed in a spirit of subversion, as several of the essays show. Women writers had to challenge traditional discourses that excluded women's voices through rhetorical means such as humility or utility in order to establish their literary credentials, according to Mónica Bolufer Peruga. María José de la Pascua Sánchez contends that "women alone" (living without a man) employed legal discourse regarding the marriage contract to defend their rights and to assert their autonomy, and María Victoria López-Cordón Cortezo cites the subtle rhetorical discourse that women had to master to join civil society. Even a realm of expression often viewed with mistrust by the Enlightenment trend toward secularization, mystical discourse, could be turned to a woman's advantage. Elisa Sampson Vera Tudela shows how an eighteenth-century Mexican nun invoked traditional spiritual discourse and the passionate expression of emotion to record her experience during a period of conventual reform. María Salgado finds that the poet Margarita Hickey countered what she considered the deceptive baroque discourse of love with an enlightened, feminist discourse in her poetry.

Another "path" followed by these essays is that of the interrogation of the purpose and validity of the records that can be used as a window into women's experiences. For example, Rebecca Haidt defends a particular material record, textiles, as an important historical category that can reveal women's work inside and outside the home, women's often unseen contributions to the economy, relations between classes, and a wealth of information on the minutiae of daily life. María José de la Pascua Sánchez studies census records and transcripts of legal proceedings to find authentic expressions of women's agency. María Victoria López-Cordón Cortezo analyzes social practices of court society, such as the *tertulia* (a social gathering where men and women talked and mingled), the emphasis on polite conversation, meals shared by the consorts, and the arrangement of domestic spaces, and finds that they gradually influenced the practices of the lower classes as well. For Quintanilla-Madero, an eighteenth-century Mexican periodical provides data regarding health and sanitation issues, medical views of women, and preoccupations regarding social practices in Mexican society. While texts authored by women are often considered key to revealing women's experiences, Janis Tomlinson warns that using artistic images, such as Goya's portraits, to analyze women's experience must only be undertaken with an understanding that they represent the projected desires of the sitter, the patron, and the artist's interpretation. Frédérique Morand cites Gertrudis de Hore's poetry as a window into her historical dilemma: an intellectual woman buoyed by new practices of sociability and education who became a poet yet was undone by an honor code that punished women's marital infidelity.

A theme that runs through many of the essays is the conflict between the Enlightenment reformers' demands for rational equality for men and women (an issue generally conceded by the century's end) and the increasing emphasis on sentiment and passion as a defining characteristic of the feminine sex. Bolufer Peruga finds that sentimental rhetoric stressing gender complementarity (fundamental difference) between men and women took hold by the end of the eighteenth century. As Isabel Morant Deusa shows, Josefa Amar was at pains to counter the example of Rousseau's "natural" woman, Sophie, in her own discourse on education. Ana Rueda's study of sensibility and the sentimental novel shows the crucial changes that occurred after the French Revolution and the Spanish War of Independence. Sensibility as a moral faculty came to be viewed with suspicion, and the sentimental heroines' virtue that excited sexual passion was considered too ambivalent an example for the novels' readers. That these patterns were presented to a new class of female readers as models of behavior attests to the moral scrutiny given to women's developing literacy. Several essays mention Josefa Amar's distrust of the effect on women of the shift from rationality to passion: she believed that women's interests, including happiness and long-term stability, were not well served by an insistence on the predominance of passion. Elisa Sampson Vera Tudela, however, shows that the Mexican nun Sor Sebastiana invoked her passions and emotions to validate her mystical experiences as a means to spiritual illumination.

The echoes of social, economic, and political history are repeatedly heard throughout these essays. The Bourbon dynasty that arrived with the eighteenth century opened the country up to new ideas, fashions, reforms, and social practices, as López-Cordón discusses, making possible the *petimetra,* for example, and inspiring the reforms of Carlos III, the efforts of economic societies, and the Junta de Damas. But the resistance to foreign influence came to be seen after the French Revolution as a patriotic response, and Janis Tomlinson shows how the nationalistic, reactionary *maja* countered the *petimetra.* Trade and emigration to the Indies brought Enlightenment ideas and knowledge of medical advances to its colonies, as we see in Quintanilla-Madero's study of the Mexican physician José Ignacio Bartolache, but they also affected women who were left alone to survive and to defend their honor, as María José de la Pascua Sánchez's study of women from the port city of Cádiz shows. Also in Cádiz, a husband's emigration and his wife's entering the convent could be solutions to a failed marriage and business partnership, observes Frédérique Morand. Tomlinson and Rueda cite the Spanish War of Independence as a galvanizing event that allowed women to act and be represented, in novels and in Goya's series of etchings *Los desastres de la guerra,* or *The Disasters of War,* as authentic heroines, agents of autonomy who could fight and defend themselves and their families. Just as these heroines characterized the growing nationalism in Spain after the war, the *mulata,* Harney's essay tells us, became the defining symbol of Cuban nationalism, fraught with questions of race, class, and gender.

This volume makes available for the first time in English an interdisciplinary perspective on women in the Spanish and Spanish American Enlightenment and brings together the work of Anglo-American scholars and that of scholars from France, Spain, and Spanish America. The essays and authors represented here contribute a richness and depth to our understanding of women's Enlightenment experiences in the Hispanic world, despite the challenges of uniting them in a coherent way. Not only do we speak different languages in the linguistic sense (and several of these essays have been translated from Spanish) but we speak different disciplinary and academic languages as well, and as editors we have tried as far as possible to preserve the diversity of approaches present in these essays. Yet all of these essays point to the same broad conclusion: that women in Spain and Spanish America were part of the social and cultural transformations taking place during the eighteenth and early nineteenth centuries and that not only were they themselves changed by these forces but they exerted their own power and influence on the path that the Spanish-speaking world took toward modernity. Although this process was troubled, and women continued to struggle for access to intellectual life and for social and political equality throughout the nineteenth and twentieth centuries, we agree with Theresa Smith when she concludes that "remnants" of the activity of eighteenth-century women of Spain—and, we would add, Spanish America—"would remain for new waves of emerging female citizens to revive and revise." It is our aim that this collection will help to overcome the geographical, cultural, and linguistic boundaries that have sometimes hindered the understanding of the interdependence of women's experience and culture between the North and the South and between Europe and the Americas during the long period of social transformation known as the Enlightenment.

NOTES

1. See Aldridge.
2. See, e.g., Sarrailh; and La Rubia Prado and Torrecilla.
3. The studies are Oñate; Demerson; and Martín Gaite.
4. See López-Cordón Cortezo; Morant Deusa; and Lavrin.
5. Other recent Spanish and English monographs that have brought to light the contribution of women to the Spanish Enlightenment include Fernández Pérez; Kitts; Morand; Lewis; Palacios Fernández; and Smith. In addition to these, several modern editions of texts by Josefa Amar y Borbón, María Rosa Gálvez, and the Marquise of Fuerte-Híjar have been published recently.
6. See Carlos Rincón's nuanced study of the changing understanding of the *Ilustración* in Spain in the eighteenth century.
7. See Bannet; Barker-Benfield; Goodman; Hesse; Kleinbaum; Knott and Taylor; Mack; Marshall; Outram; Scott; and Spencer.
8. As Sarah Knott and Barbara Taylor have recently observed in their collection of essays on women and the Enlightenment, the period was "a powerful movement of innovatory thought and practice whose tributaries and counter-currents demand . . . no less attention than its would-be orthodoxies" (xvii).
9. Amar's positive interpretation of women's curiosity aligns them with Pérez Magallón's sense of the Enlightenment's "modern curiosity" (46–51).

10. "Let us then suppose the mind to be, as we say, white paper, void of all characters, without any ideas: How comes it to be furnished? Whence comes it by that vast store which the busy and boundless fancy of man has painted on it with an almost endless variety? Whence has it all the materials of reason and knowledge? To this I answer, in one word, from EXPERIENCE." Locke, bk. 2, ch. 2, pt. 2.

11. Both J. R. Spell and Mónica Bolufer Peruga have demonstrated the important influence of Rousseau even though he was banned in Spain and Spanish America by the Inquisition. His book on education, *Émile*, was hugely influential in the articulation of a gendered and differentiated education that fitted young ladies for motherhood (Bolufer Peruga 125–26). Josefa Amar even mentions him, albeit in an attempt to dispel his influence on her ideas about female education.

12. This is done with an understanding of feminist history as "a way of critically understanding how history operates as a site of production of gender knowledge" (Scott 9–10), underscoring that history, cultural production, and conceptions of gender are intertwined.

WORKS CITED

Aldridge, A. Owen. "Introduction: The Concept of the Ibero-American Enlightenment." In *The Ibero-American Enlightenment,* ed. A. Owen Aldridge, 3–18. Urbana: University of Illinois Press, 1971.

Alfonso X el Sabio. "Entre Av' e Eva." *Cantigas de Santa María,* no. 60. http://brassy.club.fr/PartMed/Cantigas/CSMtext/c60.html (accessed 14 April 2008).

Amar y Borbón, Josefa. "Discurso en defensa del talento de las mujeres y de su aptitud para el gobierno y otros cargos en que se emplean los hombres." Ed. Carmen Chaves Tesser. *Dieciocho* 3.2 (1980): 144–59.

Bannet, Eve Tavor. *The Domestic Revolution: Enlightenment Feminisms and the Novel.* Baltimore: Johns Hopkins University Press, 2000.

Barker-Benfield, G. J. *The Culture of Sensibility: Sex and Society in Eighteenth-Century Britain.* Chicago: Chicago University Press, 1992.

Bolufer Peruga, Mónica. *Mujeres e Ilustración: La construcción de la feminidad en la Ilustración española.* Valencia: Diputació Alfons El Magnànim, 1998.

Demerson, Paula. *María Francisca de Sales y Portocarrero, condesa de Montijo: Una figura de la Ilustración.* Madrid: Editora Nacional, 1975.

Feijoo, Benito Jerónimo. "Defensa de las mujeres." Discourse 16 in *Teatro crítico universal: Discursos varios en todo género de materias, para desengaño de errores comunes,* vol. 1. Biblioteca feijoniana del Proyecto Filosofía en español. Madrid: Ibarra, 1778. http://www.filosofia.org/bjf/bjft116.htm (accessed 23 May 2006).

Fernández Pérez, Paloma. *El rostro familiar de la metrópoli: Redes de parentesco y lazos mercantiles en Cádiz, 1700–1812.* Madrid: Siglo XXI, 1997.

Goodman, Dena. *The Republic of Letters: A Cultural History of the French Enlightenment.* Ithaca, NY: Cornell University Press, 1994.

Haidt, Rebecca. *Embodying Enlightenment: Knowing the Body in Eighteenth-Century Spanish Literature and Culture.* New York: St. Martin's, 1998.

Hesse, Carla. *The Other Enlightenment*. Princeton, NJ: Princeton University Press, 2001.
Jovellanos, Gaspar Melchor de. *Memoria sobre la educación pública o Tratado teórico-práctico de enseñanza*. In *Poesía, teatro, prosa*, ed. José Luis Abellán, 259–356. Madrid: Taurus, 1979.
Kitts, Sally-Ann. *The Debate on the Nature, Role, and Influence of Women in Eighteenth-Century Spain*. Lewiston, NY: Edwin Mellen, 1995.
Kleinbaum, Abby R. "Women in the Age of Light." In *Becoming Visible: Women in European History*, ed. Renate Bridenthal and Claudia Koonz, 217–35. Boston: Houghton Mifflin, 1977.
Knott, Sarah, and Barbara Taylor. Introduction to *Women, Gender, and Enlightenment*, ed. Sarah Knott and Barbara Taylor, x–xxi. New York: Palgrave Macmillan, 2005.
Kramnick, Isaac, ed. *The Portable Enlightenment Reader*. New York: Penguin, 1995.
La Rubia Prado, Francisco, and Jesús Torrecilla, eds. *Razón, tradición, y modernidad: Re-visión de la Ilustración hispánica*. Madrid: Tecnos, 1996.
Lavrin, Asunción. *Latin American Women: Historical Perspectives*. Westport, CT: Greenwood, 1978.
Lewis, Elizabeth Franklin. *Women Writers in the Spanish Enlightenment: The Pursuit of Happiness*. Burlington, VT: Ashgate, 2004.
Locke, John. *An Essay concerning Human Understanding*. New York: Institute for Learning Technologies Digital Classics, 1995. http://www.ilt.columbia.edu/publications/Projects/digitexts/locke/understanding/chapter0201.html (accessed 23 May 2006).
López-Cordón Cortezo, María Victoria. *Condición femenina y razón ilustrada: Josefa Amar y Borbón*. Zaragoza: Prensas Universitarias de Zaragoza, 2005.
Mack, Phyllis. "Women and the Enlightenment: Introduction." In *Women and Enlightenment*, by Margaret Hunt, Margaret Jacob, Phyllis Mack, and Ruth Perry, 1–11. New York: Haworth, 1984.
Marshall, Barbara L. *Engendering Modernity: Feminism, Social Theory and Social Change*. Cambridge: Polity, 1994.
Martín Gaite, Carmen. *Usos amorosos del dieciocho en España*. Madrid: Siglo XXI, 1972. Translated by María G. Tomsich as *Love Customs in Eighteenth-Century Spain* (Berkeley and Los Angeles: University of California Press, 1991).
Morand, Frédérique. *Doña María Gertrudis Hore (1742–1801): Vivencia de una poetisa gaditana entre el siglo y la clausura*. Alcalá de Henares: Premio de Investigación María Isidra de Guzmán, 2004.
Morant Deusa, Isabel. *Historia de mujeres en España y Latinoamérica*. 2 vols. Madrid: Cátedra, 2005.
Oñate y Pérez, María del Pilar. *El feminismo en la literatura española*. Madrid: Espasa-Calpe, 1938.
Outram, Dorinda. *The Enlightenment*. Cambridge: Cambridge University Press, 1995.
Palacios Fernández, Emilio. *La mujer y las letras en la España del siglo XVIII*. Madrid: Ediciones Laberinto, 2002.
Pérez Magallón, Jesús. *Contruyendo la modernidad: La cultura española en el Tiempo de los Novatores (1675–1725)*. Madrid: Consejo Superior de Investigaciones Científicas, 2002.
Rincón, Carlos. "Sobre la noción de Ilustración en el siglo XVIII español." *Romanische Forschungen* 83.4 (1971): 528–54.
Sarrailh, Jean. *La España ilustrada en la segunda mitad del siglo XVIII*. Trans. Antonio Alatorre. México: Fondo de Cultura Económica, 1957. Originally published as *L'Espagne eclairée de la seconde moitie du XVIIIe siècle* (Paris: Nationale, 1954).

Scott, Joan Wallach. *Gender and the Politics of History.* New York: Columbia University Press, 1988.

Serrano y Sanz, Manuel. *Apuntes para una biblioteca de escritoras españolas desde el año 1401 al 1833.* Biblioteca de autores espanoles, 268-71. 2 vols. in 4. 1903. Facsimile ed., Madrid: Atlas, 1975.

Smith, Theresa Ann. *The Emerging Female Citizen: Gender and Enlightenment in Spain.* Berkeley and Los Angeles: University of California Press, 2006.

Spell, Jefferson Rea. *Rousseau in the Spanish World before 1833: A Study in Franco-Spanish Literary Relations.* Austin: University of Texas Press, 1938.

Spencer, Samia. *French Women and the Age of Enlightenment.* Bloomington: Indiana University Press, 1985.

Subirats, Eduardo. *La ilustración insuficiente.* Madrid: Taurus, 1981.

PART I
WOMEN AND THE REPUBLIC OF LETTERS

The essays in this first part examine how women writers asserted their presence as active participants in a literary world in which they had historically played only a marginal role. Mónica Bolufer Peruga describes how intellectual women and women writers reshaped the cultural icon of the woman of letters "to fit their needs of self-assertion and cultural authority." She sees a "coalescence" between women's experience and Enlightenment thought, because their experiences, collective and individual, were interpreted through the values of a changing society. Women writers had to discover and fashion their own voices through rhetorical strategies while countering the opprobrium of the traditionally masculine republic of letters. Many of the issues Bolufer raises are echoed and elaborated in the other essays of this part. Frédérique Morand contends that Sor María Gertrudis de la Cruz Hore's life as poet, wife, mother, and cloistered nun embodies the contradictions experienced by intellectual women during the Enlightenment. She finds in Hore's poetry evidence of women's experience of both the optimistic promise of the Enlightenment and the bitter limitations still set on women's moral behavior. Isabel Morant Deusa describes the innovative pedagogical project in Josefa Amar y Borbón's book on women's education, the *Discurso sobre la educación fisica y moral de las mujeres* (1790). More than merely repeating the ideas of other thinkers, Amar y Borbón makes her own contributions to the heated international debate concerning women's proper education, which crossed boundaries of time as well as place. María Salgado finds evidence of women's experience in the poetry of Margarita Hickey, who cautioned women about the "traps of love" in her work and contrasted what she claimed to have learned from experience to the false representations of love in traditional and contemporary male-authored love poetry. Elisa Sampson Vera Tudela explores the implications of the Enlightenment for the life and work of Sor Sebastiana Josefa de la Santísima Trinidad, whose confessional letter and its recasting by her confessor as a hagiography document women's lives and writing practices in early eighteenth-century New Spain and expand our definition of the Enlightenment. Sampson raises the issue of multiple enlightenments, especially in the context of eighteenth-century Mexico, following J. G. A. Pocock, David Sorkins, and Eduardo Subirats, whose works point out the tensions between secularization and the role of religion during this period. Sampson contests the exclusion of mystical experience from traditional interpretations of the Enlightenment in order to "recover the precise language of an eighteenth-century debate about religion, subjectivity, and gender in colonial Spanish America."

1

Women of Letters in Eighteenth-Century Spain
Between Tradition and Modernity

MÓNICA BOLUFER PERUGA

There is no cultivated nation which cannot present a considerable number of learned or studious women.
—*Memorial literario de Madrid*, June 1785

Recent research on women's writing and intellectual activity has been making increasingly visible how women in Spain, as in the rest of Europe, became relevant agents in the cultural landscape of the eighteenth century. In their own time, literary critics and journalists tended to welcome what they considered a development characteristic of the Enlightenment, the new prominence attained by "women of letters," and to celebrate their achievements. However, their diplomatic praises worked at the same time to draw limits that would contain women's intellectual activity: their reading and writing (in genre and content, pedagogical and moral works were most often recommended to them); their declared aims (preferably moral and utilitarian); their approach to publishing (apparently reluctant and modest, rather than ambitious); and their public presence in the republic of letters (which was prescribed to be discreet and secondary).

Eighteenth-century women writers and intellectuals developed their activity in a context marked by both tradition and modernity. They had not only to make their own way against commonplace misogyny (popular as well as learned) but also to take advantage of, and at the same time distance themselves from, certain traditions. These traditions, revived and reshaped during the eighteenth century, tended to celebrate women of letters, but only in certain circumstances and under strict conditions. In fact, the "learned woman" was in early modern culture not only a negative archetype but also quite a celebrated one, very often intertwined with the *querelle des femmes*, the debate about the moral and intellectual capacities of women. However, because of its ambivalence, its implications were not always straightforward for women. That is, celebrating a woman of learning did not always mean, in fact rarely meant, assuming intellectual equality as a general principle; it could even mean just the opposite by stressing exceptionality in regard to the norm. But even so, the imposing image of the learned woman was a powerful reference for real early modern women of letters, especially writers, one that they incorporated into their works and reshaped to fit their needs of self-assertion and cultural authority.

The Learned Woman as a Cultural Icon

The celebration of learned women was part of a venerable tradition with classical roots and a particular flourishing between the fifteenth and eighteenth centuries: that of "famous women" or "women of merit" (Rang). In Spain as in the rest of Europe, this genre developed and went through significant changes during the Renaissance, the baroque period, and the Enlightenment. It would die out, or at least be dramatically altered, in the nineteenth century, when modern societies based on liberal principles of equality became less likely to tolerate exceptions on the grounds of status and the model of the domestic woman outshined that of the "strong woman," with which the woman of letters was very often associated (Bucci; Bolufer Peruga, "Galerías").

Catalogs or encyclopedias of women of merit were made up of short biographies *(vitae)*, or rather portraits or evocations of famous women (historical, biblical, or mythical), usually falling into very fixed categories—"arms," "letters," and "government"—to which were often added various other categories from the classical tradition, such as "chastity," "conjugal love," and "the keeping of secrets," or from the Christian tradition, such as "religious faith" and "loyalty." Plutarch's *Mulierum virtutes* and Giovanni Boccaccio's *De mulieribus claris* (ca. 1360) set the foundations of a genre that followed rather rigid conventions. Throughout early modern Europe local authors gave their versions a distinctive national turn by incorporating with the classical examples those of their fellow countrywomen (Rang). Boccaccio's *De mulieribus claris* was translated into Spanish in 1494, exerting a deep influence on subsequent Spanish works against or in defense of women, including catalogs of famous women. In 1790, in her *Discurso sobre la educación física y moral de las mujeres* (Discourse on Women's Moral and Physical Education),

Josefa Amar y Borbón, a writer and reformer with an already established intellectual reputation, recognized that "[t]his kind of work exists in all languages." It was, in fact, an international tradition, made up of works in Latin and in all the major European languages, which circulated and were cited and used from country to country. Josefa Amar herself, as well as some of her contemporaries, mentioned many French and Italian texts, ancient and modern (Plutarch, Christine de Pisan, Paolo Ribera, Hilarion de la Coste, Lucrezia Marinelli, Anna Maria Schurmann, Madeleine de Scudéry). In their turn, Spanish works would nourish the pool of a European tradition of learned women, from which other writers would continue to draw. However, it is in conquering new spaces and audiences that the genre shows its vitality. By the end of the eighteenth century, biographies of famous women (particularly, but not only, women of letters) had become a standard feature of the periodicals that addressed a wide public of polite and cultivated although not necessarily learned or erudite men and women. An additional and crucial example of how this tradition was used and reformulated in the eighteenth century was the visible and highly publicized rituals in which girls from aristocratic families were celebrated for their learning.

It would be too simple to read the eighteenth-century celebration of the learned woman as a direct reflection of and an incentive to contemporary developments in women's education, writing, and participation in cultural sociability. The aims, implications, and ambivalences of this figure were manifold, and therefore it could be given different meanings and displayed for many diverse and sometimes contradictory uses. First, it is important to note that learned women of the past as well as the present were very often presented as exceptions that did not undermine the general limits set for their sex. Second, learned women were very often displayed to make a case for something that had very little to do with women's reason or education. Public examinations were solemn acts, social ceremonies that paid homage to the power and prestige of their families, all of whom belonged to the nobility or were on their way to social promotion and prided themselves on taking interest in the education of their offspring. The celebration of extremely young women performing incredible displays of erudition connected both with the early modern fascination with wonders and prodigies and with the Enlightenment's stress on education that favored pedagogical experiments of intellectual stimulation. Third, learned women were also exhibited as a token of national pride. In 1758 the journalist Mariano Nifo noted that Enlightenment Europe was characterized by the development of philosophy and the sciences, and particularly by women's contribution to them.[1] Therefore, during the polemics concerning Spanish contributions to European culture, writers and politicians used Spanish women's alleged merits to make patriotic statements and to show their loyalty to the Bourbon dynasty. All this illustrates a growing assumption that women's learning was an index to a country's intellectual status and degree of civilization; thus, if Spain wanted to be admitted into the restricted circle of enlightened countries, examples of learned women had to be recovered from the past and appreciated in the present.

Building on Tradition, Claiming Modernity: Eighteenth-Century Women of Letters

The writings of women, particularly religious women but also lay women in court society, were common in Golden Age literature; some of these women, such as María de Zayas, earned considerable fame and success in their own time (López-Cordón, "La fortuna"). And women readers made significant contributions to the success of some genres, such as humanist moral and religious essays, chivalric and pastoral novels, and baroque short stories (Bouza). However, during the eighteenth century there were relevant changes in the modes of women's participation in a republic of letters that was widening its limits and exerting a stronger influence on public opinion. To some extent, in order to build their respectability, they would have to reinvent themselves as writers because the tradition of women writers of the previous century no longer was an acceptable model, and the most popular among them, María de Zayas, was scorned not only for her baroque style and her open treatment of amorous matters but also for the sharp critiques on women's condition found in her narratives.

The contemporary term *woman of letters* captures more broadly than *learned women, women writers,* or *intellectuals* the many different aspects of women's (real or perceived) relation to intellectual activity in Spain as in the rest of Europe (Clarke). It refers not only to writers who had a sustained relation to the world of print but also to those who failed to publish or never intended to publish their own works. It can include women who showed a determination to have a public presence in the republic of letters through other cultural activities, such as patronage, polite, cultivated conversation, or institutional debate, as well as those who valued reading and study as a private pleasure (Bolufer Peruga, "Escritura"; Bolufer Peruga and Morant Deusa). Those new intellectual ambitions of women can be represented by *La sabia indiscreta*,[2] one of the two comedies written by the

Marquise of Fuerte Híjar to be represented in her private theater, which plays on a clever irony: if the heroine finally gives up the joys of erudition for those of love and marriage, under the conventional disguise of the *bachillera* she implicitly stands as a positive model of women's intellectual and moral autonomy (Bolufer Peruga, "Escritura"; Jaffe, "Of Women's Love"; Acereda).

Women in the eighteenth century gradually became, in Spain as in the rest of Europe, an increasing and influential part of an ever-expanding reading audience (Bolufer Peruga, *"Espectadores," Mujeres e Ilustración*, ch. 7, and "Mujeres de letras"; Urzainqui, "Nuevas propuestas"). They figured prominently among subscribers to didactic and moral works, including translations of such novels and pedagogical treatises as Mme Le Prince de Beaumont's *La nouvelle Clarice (La Nueva Clarisa)* and *Lettres de Mme de Montier (Cartas de Mme de Montier)* and Mme de Genlis's *Les veillées du château (Las veladas de la Quinta)*, and were a targeted audience for journalists, who competed to secure women's support for their periodicals (Bolufer Peruga, *"Espectadores"*; Larriba; Urzainqui, "Los espacios"). They also became a focus for moral exhortation to choose the "right" reading material among a rising number of publications addressed to them (Bolufer Peruga, *"Espectadores"* and "Second 'Rise'"; Jaffe, "Suspect Pleasure"). In fact, the transformation of the catalog of women of merit shows how it expanded its audience, as dedications to aristocrats such as the Countess of Amayuelas (Cubié), the Duchess of Pópoli (Thomas), and the Duchess of Osuna (Le Moyne) started to give way to more general reference to women readers. Thus, if Alonso Álvarez justified his work as a response to the demands of a (probably fictitious) cultivated lady, whom he represented in his preface, "A Lady's Reasoning to an Eighteenth-Century Erudite on the Need to Write the Memoirs of Spanish Heroines," Vicente del Seixo addressed his 1801 essay quite simply "To The Ladies."

Women wrote and published in greater numbers as they took advantage of the increasing dimensions of the literary market and the wider range of publishing opportunities available to them. Some women (and also several men under female pseudonyms) collaborated in periodicals, one of the newest and most dynamic fields of eighteenth-century literature. The enigmatic "Beatriz Cienfuegos" (*La Pensadora gaditana*, 1763–64) and "Escolástica Hurtado" (*La Pensatriz salmantina*, 1777) took on the guise of "female spectators" to address a public composed of both men and women (Sullivan, "Gender"; Canterla; Urzainqui, "Un enigma"). Many other women sent occasional contributions (letters, essays, and poems) to the press, thereby constituting a public presence that consolidated in the last decades of the century, and although this female presence was in many cases fictional, it contributed to the trend to "normalize" the figure of the woman writer and at the same time to establish its conventions (Bolufer Peruga, "*Espectadores*"). Women's works also circulated semipublicly in circles of cultural sociability or enlightened reformism such as salons. For instance, the poets María Gertrudis de Hore and Margarita Hickey apparently shared discussions and readings at the *tertulias* of Antonio de Ulloa in Cádiz and Agustín Montiano in Madrid, respectively, and the translator Inés Joyes y Blake entertained in her home in Vélez-Málaga.[3] Another public space for debate and writing was philanthropic societies, such as the Junta de Damas de Honor y Mérito, attached to the Economic Society of Madrid, and other provincial institutions, whose members composed and discussed reformist essays on education, luxury, textile production, and social assistance (Demerson; Fernández Quintanilla; Bolufer Peruga, *Mujeres e Ilustración*, 371–88; Smith, *Emerging Female Citizen*, ch. 5).

The number of women who wrote and published in Spain, while far behind the number in France and Britain, where a more dynamic print culture stimulated the rise of the woman writer, increased considerably during the eighteenth century, with an estimated 170 to 180 authors.[4] Among eighteenth-century women writers, not only the traditional figures of the aristocratic learned woman and the cultivated nun but also women of the lower nobility *(hidalguía)* and the middle classes figured prominently. Moral and pedagogical works, followed by poetry and reformist essays, were among the most cultivated genres, both because they were understood as "proper" for women and because of their connection to public or semipublic spaces (*tertulias*, reformist societies, etc.) that could provide women with a stimulus, and an alibi, for writing. However, in a country where novels were subject to moral suspicion—unlike in France and Britain—women very rarely wrote in that genre (García Garrosa; Bolufer Peruga, "Second 'Rise'"). Women also made themselves a place in the world of translation, where women of the upper and middle classes put to use their newly acquired education, which usually included foreign languages (mostly French), to win access to writing for the market and to gain some intellectual prestige, insofar as translation implied, to some extent, active intervention in the text. They skillfully played with the possibilities of speaking through the voices of others while at the same time writing in the margins of their translations (in prefaces, footnotes, dedications, and other added materials) their own personal views.[5] Other women writers, rather than using those new resources, followed the well-established tradition of religious writing (mostly of spiritual autobiographies, religious poetry, chronicles of a convent or a religious order), which for centuries had represented the immense majority of women's writing in Spain and its American possessions and which took its authority from divine inspiration, mystical experience, and obedience to superiors and confessors.

How did these women writers place themselves in relation to the strong but often ambiguous celebration of women's learning? Could they use it in any helpful way in a period in which women's intellectual activity (in particular going public through print) involved "a large measure of self-definition and self-justification" (Goldsmith and Goodman 3)? As we have seen, the learned woman could be displayed as a cultural icon whose exceptionality was very often stressed and which was used for purposes of affirming social status, political authority, or national pride. But this does not exhaust all its potential: it was also a powerful image used particularly by women to give authority to their claims for education and writing. It was, in fact, a woman, Josefa Amar, who translated Lampillas's essay on Spanish literature (originally written in Italian) in 1782–84, with a second revised and expanded edition in 1789, to which she contributed extensive corrections and footnotes and, especially, a preface directing the attention of her potential women readers to the merits of women, which were included in the fourth volume. She also displayed historical examples of women of letters in her own original works, such as the 1786 "Discurso en defensa del talento de las mujeres" (Discourse in Defense of Women's Talent), a contribution to the debate about the admittance of women to the Economic Society of Madrid, and her later, major work, the *Discurso sobre la educación física y moral de las mujeres*.[6] For her, these examples seem to have been powerful arguments in favor of women's intellectual equality and of their right to be admitted into Enlightenment public space. They were also attractive models with whom she identified in order to build her own identity as a writer and a classical erudite and to present and authorize herself in the public eye.

All this is not to say that putting on the respectable clothes of the learned woman was not without tensions for real women. This icon could be confidently displayed only as far as conventions were respected and invisible yet very clear limits were not violated. One of these unwritten rules was that the "woman of merit" discourse could be flatteringly displayed and even overstated but not used in the first person. In 1803 the famous playwright María Rosa Gálvez, when protesting to the censors who would not allow the staging of two new plays, represented herself as a woman whose literary talent could well rival that of her most distinguished European contemporaries: "[T]o this may be added the wish to make public a work unequaled by any other woman or in any other nation" (qtd. in Serrano y Sanz 1:449). This was just too much. The permit was not allowed, and we might well think that the censors did not appreciate her statement as an act of cultural patriotism but considered it an improper self-assertion, at odds with true femininity as well as with the particular humility that was expected from a woman from the middle classes. In presenting herself as a national glory, she did no more (and no less) than to appropriate the rhetoric that unvaryingly praised exceptional women as an "honor to their sex" as well as to their country and that had been used to describe her by Vicente del Seixo, who included María Rosa Gálvez among the "examples deserving no less glory" than learned women of the past (Seixo 128). However, the learned woman would do better to wait modestly to be praised by others rather than show any ambition or appear proud of her own intellectual achievements.

Other individual examples show a wide range of strategies by which women worked to place themselves within the protective walls of tradition while at the same time incorporating the new language of Enlightenment morality and utility and reaching out to grasp the new opportunities available for intellectual activity and public presence. María Rosario Cepeda, who as a gifted child was exhibited by her family and city as a local glory, managed to develop in her adult life a more solid career as a woman implicated in Enlightenment reformist and intellectual circles; she served as secretary of the Junta de Damas (Álvarez de Miranda). The poet María Gertrudis de Hore combined in her personal and literary identity the venerable tradition of the religious writer, the many practical duties and occupations of a woman in the cloister, and new literary forms and spaces. Although forced by personal circumstances to enter the convent, she continued to be a genuine enlightened woman who kept her taste for comfort and elegance in her surroundings, had a busy correspondence, and sent contributions to the periodical press (Lewis; Morand).

In enlightened women aristocrats, an acute sense of the traditional values of rank and lineage went hand in hand with a new consideration of the importance of education and personal talent. Many showed a remarkable, almost arrogant confidence in their own entitlement to write and publish. This was the case with Cayetana de la Cerda, Countess of Lalaing, the translator of Mme de Lambert, who was denied permission to publish her translation of Mme Le Prince de Beaumont's *Les Américaines*, a dialogue that aimed at proving the truth of Christianity on the sole basis of reason but was deemed capable of inducing doubt among impressionable and candid readers, particularly women (Bolufer Peruga, "Pedagogía"). Not resigned to accepting a negative answer, the countess initiated a long polemic with the censors. She not only defended the work's orthodoxy, showing her remarkable erudition on divinity and moral theology, but also dared to question the censors' criteria and asked for a second report from the *inquisidor general* himself.[7] Although her plea was finally turned down, her words and attitude rang with a defiance linked both to a traditional (implicit) consciousness of her rank in relation to that of her opponents and to a "modern" emphasis on merit—her own, as a learned woman and author, and that of cultivated women readers.

A few steps down the social scale, the issue of merit, personal as well as female, was of dramatic importance for women who could not rely on hierarchy to ensure respect and who would not accept gallant condescension from male colleagues when going public as writers. Respectability, together with personal preferences and education, seems to have worked as an incentive for women like Josefa Amar and Margarita Hickey to cultivate an austere image of themselves as intellectuals who made a point of despising other women's "frivolous" literary taste. Margarita Hickey preceded her *Poesías varias* (1789) with a general preface and several shorter presentations in which she justified her most polemic decisions, such as risking a "masculine" genre like the epic. Both her words and her eloquent silences (the absence of any apologetic tone) make obvious her determination to be treated as an equal by her (mostly male) colleagues. For this reason, she strategically reproduced a letter written to her by the influential man of letters Agustín Montiano, secretary to the Royal History Academy, who at the beginning of her career had shown his enthusiastic approbation of her work, together with some minor criticisms, which underlined even more, to the readers' eyes, how seriously he must have taken this young writer (Hickey). Josefa Amar, out of personal taste but also conditioned by a powerful model, that of the solid scholar at ease with rare editions and profound works rather than the despised eighteenth-century *erudito a la violeta* (pedant) and his female nonsymmetric counterpart, the *bachillera*, made every effort to transmit to her readers the sound foundations of her thought and was very critical of what she and many of her contemporaries considered light, superficial reading, particularly novels (*Discurso sobre la educación* 185).

Obscure writers of lower social position found themselves, in a different way, between the requirements of tradition as far as the position of the writer was concerned and the new opportunities opened by the expanding print culture. They had either to display the modesty attached to their gender and social position to plead for protection from aristocrats or the royals and humbly accept any negative criticism or to appeal to the public as a new mode of authorizing their public speech. We are just beginning to reconstruct these women's strategies and the operations by which they made their way, more or less successfully, into the republic of letters through personal contacts, social and intellectual relations, and publishing opportunities (Bolufer Peruga, "Las mujeres en la España del siglo XVIII"). Among them, Mercedes Gómez de Castro was the author of *Pintura del talento y carácter de las mujeres* (Painting of the Talent and Character of Women), for which she requested a publishing license in 1797. When her text was pointed to by the censors as a quite transparent plagiarism (or rather a clumsy, unacknowledged adaptation) of Antoine-Léonard Thomas's very popular work (already translated into Spanish in 1773), she pleaded guilty. In a most traditional way, she begged the censors' benevolence, representing herself, not as a writer, but as a destitute widow and mother—of men, she rushed to add, with no proper reward for their services to the monarchy—who desperately needed to earn some money from occasional scribbling and who would humbly make any change or correction in order to obtain a publishing license.[8] Her dubious writing, full of errors, suggests that her ambitions were economic rather than literary; she perceived the new opportunities opened up by widening audiences and was ready to grasp them, but the heavy restrictions in Spain on women's writing for money must have conditioned her self-presentation, not as a professional writer (even an occasional one), but, more conventionally, as a petitioner.

A different case is that of María Rosario Romero Masegosa y Cancelada, the translator in 1792 of Mme de Graffigny's *Lettres d'une péruvienne*. She carefully constructed a literary persona, that of an enlightened and virtuous woman who, under the guidance of her brother, had given up the pleasurable and frivolous reading of her youth (novels and plays by Calderón, María de Zayas, and "others of that sort") in favor of moral, solid works (Romero Masegosa y Cancelada; Bolufer Peruga, *Mujeres e Ilustración* 326; Smith, "Writing out of the Margins" and *Emerging Female Citizen*, ch. 6). In this guise, she could safely allow herself generous modifications of Mme de Graffigny's text (in her footnotes, preface, and even an added letter) and a public attack on a rival translator of the same work).[9] Cayetana de Aguirre innovated by dedicating her translation of *Virginia, la doncella cristiana* (1806) to the "Unwed maids of Spain" and by manipulating the work—a pious novel—to present it in her preface as an appeal to women's autonomy (Bolufer Peruga, "Escritura"). She had previously failed to dedicate it to the queen, who found completely improper and almost scandalous the critique of marriage and the appeal to lay celibacy included in the preface, an addition at odds with the more conventional spirit of the original novel.[10] In a similar tone, in 1789 Margarita Hickey tried to anticipate and defuse any negative criticism she might receive from men of letters because of her gender by seeking the reader's complicity and claiming to accept no other authority but that of public opinion (140), although, as we have seen, she combined this rhetorical appeal with an effort to place herself firmly within the institutionalized republic of letters.

Inés Joyes y Blake, the author of a vibrant "Apología de las mujeres" (1798), can serve as a final example of how women outside the aristocratic sphere of power and patronage grasped the new opportunities connected to the expansion of a cultivated audience and to the proliferation of spaces for cultural conversation. A member of a dynasty of Irish merchants long established in Spain, she seems to have benefited from a polyglot education and managed to combine her duties as a wife, prolific mother, and precocious widow with a knowledge of European Enlightenment debates, including the debate on gender (Bolufer Peruga, "Traducción" and "Inés Joyes"). Her essay, titled "Carta de la traductora a sus hijas" (Letter to her daughters) and dedicated to the Duchess of Osuna, was attached to her translation of Samuel Johnson's *Rasselas, Prince of Abissinia*, with which it had no evident connections, probably as a strategy to downplay the radical nature of her message and to ease her going public as a writer. Deliberately nonerudite and fluid, Joyes's "Apology" acknowledges some debt to Feijoo's "Defensa de las mujeres," but above all it reveals its author as a mature woman who has gained, through experience, conversation, and social observation, a knowledge of relationships and conflicts in women's lives. The fact that one of the most lucid and vehement texts on women's condition in eighteenth-century Spain was written by a woman who led a rather obscure and provincial life suggests that critical reflection on those issues, far from being limited to the most brilliant and exclusive circles, could be the result of a coalescence between experience (the "common" experience of a middle-class woman's life) and Enlightenment values and thought, through which this experience was interpreted.

Women writers and intellectuals in the eighteenth century, then, had to negotiate to place themselves and to build their careers and self-images while confronting models of representation and self-representation of the woman of letters that were undergoing significant changes in their time—from an emphasis on the exceptionality of the "illustrious woman," that icon of *ancien régime* culture and society; to the Enlightenment problematic handling of the learned woman (half-praised, half-feared, ridiculed and employed for political purposes); to the incipient development of the professional woman writer (a still very rare figure, in Spain more than in France or Britain, by the end of the eighteenth century). They were heavily conditioned by their diverse social status and cultural background. Aristocrats and middle-class women, well educated or not, lay and religious, court-based and provincial, faced very different opportunities for reading, writing, and participation in the republic of letters through publishing, conversation, and other cultural activities. However, the more we know about them, the more we become aware that Enlightenment women of letters displayed a wide range of strategies that included, in various combinations, aristocratic patronage and appeal to the public; recourse to the century-old genealogy of women of merit and an emphasis on rational equality between genders; religious inspiration and a grounding in secular values; the use of traditional genres and participation in new forms of circulating ideas, such as translations and the periodical press; the topoi of modesty and self-effacement and a consciousness of themselves as fully entitled intellectuals and writers. In accommodating their individual and collective experience to the new conditions of a society immersed in a process of change and with the values, priorities, and judgments of the Enlightenment, they wove the threads of tradition and modernity in ways that challenge our inclination as historians to establish clean-cut divisions between those categories.

NOTES

Earlier versions of the ideas contained in this essay have benefited from presentation and discussion at the conferences "Bluestockings: Women, Writing, and the Politics of Sociability" (Eighteenth-Century Studies Centre-University of York, 10 March 2001) and "Eleventh International Congress on the Enlightenment" (University of California–Los Angeles, 3–10 August 2003). I am grateful to Jane Rendall, Harriet Guest, Joanna de Groot, and Kate Davies; to Elizabeth Lewis, Catherine Jaffe, Rebecca Haidt, and David T. Gies for their comments; and to Norma Clarke, for many enjoyable and productive conversations on women of letters in Britain and Spain.

1. *Diario noticioso* (Madrid), 1 February 1758.
2. See Acereda.
3. See Frédérique Morand's discussion of Hore in chapter 2 of this volume and María Salgado's of Hickey in chapter 4.
4. The identification of eighteenth-century Spanish women writers is often difficult and tentative,

which explains why numbers offered by different scholars differ slightly. See Sullivan, "Las escritoras"; Palacios Fernández; Bolufer Peruga, "Representaciones" and "Las mujeres en la España"; and Smith, *Emerging Female Citizen*, 114.

5. See Rípodas Ardanaz; López-Cordón, "Traducción"; Bolufer Peruga, "Escritura," "Inés Joyes," *Mujeres e Ilustración*, "Pedagogía," and "Traducción"; and Smith, *Emerging Female Citizen*, ch. 6, and "Writing out of the Margins."

6. See Isabel Morant's discussion of Amar's *Discourse* in chapter 3 of this volume.

7. Archivo Histórico Nacional, Madrid, Consejos, 5556/35.

8. Ibid., 5562/4. A different reading of Gómez's negotiation with censorship is that offered in Smith, *Emerging Female Citizen*, 117–21.

9. See *Correo literario de Murcia* 6 (1794): 30–32, 249–55.

10. Archivo Histórico Nacional, Madrid, Estado, 3234/11.

WORKS CITED

Acereda, Alberto. *La marquesa de Fuerte-Híjar, una dramaturga de la Ilustración: Estudio y edición de "La sabia indiscreta."* Cádiz: Universidad de Cádiz, 2000.

Aguirre, Cayetana. Preface to *Virginia, la doncella cristiana: Historia siciliana, que se propone, por modelo a las señoritas que aspiran a la perfección*, by Michel Ange Marin. Trans. Cayetana Aguirre. Madrid: Repullés, 1806.

Álvarez, Alonso. *Memorias de las mugeres ilustres de España.* Vol. 1. Madrid: Sancha, 1798.

Álvarez de Miranda, Pedro. "¿Una niña en la Academia?" *Boletín de la Real Academia Española* 82.285 (2002): 39–45.

Amar y Borbón, Josefa. "Discurso en defensa del talento de las mujeres . . ." (1786). In *La educación popular en España en la segunda mitad del siglo XVIII*, by Olegario Negrín Fajardo, 162–76. Madrid: Universidad Nacional de Educación a Distancia, 1984.

———. *Discurso sobre la educación física y moral de las mujeres.* Ed. María Victoria López-Cordón. Madrid: Cátedra, 1994.

Bolufer Peruga, Mónica. "Escritura femenina y publicación en el siglo XVIII: De la experiencia personal a la 'república de las letras.'" In *Género y ciudadanía: Revisiones desde el ámbito privado*, ed. Margarita Ortega, Cristina Sánchez, and Celia Valiente, 197–223. Madrid: Universidad Autónoma de Madrid, 1999.

———. "*Espectadores* y lectoras: Representaciones e influencia del público femenino en la prensa del siglo XVIII." *Cuadernos de Estudios del Siglo XVIII* 5 (1995): 23–57.

———. "Galerías de 'mujeres ilustres,' o el sinuoso camino de la excepción a la norma cotidiana." *Hispania: Revista Española de Historia* 60/1, no. 204 (2000): 181–224.

———. "Inés Joyes y Blake: Una ilustrada, entre privado y público." In *Mujeres para la Historia: Figuras destacadas del primer feminismo,* ed. Rosa M. Capel, 27–55. Madrid: Abada Editores, 2004.

———. "Mujeres de letras: Lectoras y escritoras en los siglos modernos." In *Relaciones de género, sociedad y cultura en el ámbito mediterráneo.* Málaga: Universidad de Málaga, forthcoming.

---. "Las mujeres en la España del siglo XVIII: Trayectorias de la investigación y perspectivas de futuro." In *Imagen y palabra de mujer: La mujer en la literatura española*. Valladolid: Instituto de la Lengua de Castilla y León–Universidad de Valladolid, forthcoming.

---. *Mujeres e Ilustración: La construcción de la feminidad en la España del siglo XVIII*. Valencia: Institució Alfons el Magnànim, 1998.

---. "Pedagogía y moral en el Siglo de las Luces: Las escritoras francesas y su recepción en España." *Revista de Historia Moderna: Anales de la Universidad de Alicante* 20 (2002): 251–91.

---. "Representaciones y prácticas de vida: Las mujeres en la España del siglo XVIII." *Cuadernos de Ilustración y Romanticismo* 11 (2003): 3–34.

---. "The Second 'Rise' of the Novel in Eighteenth-Century Spain." In *Remapping the Rise of the European Novel, 1500–1800*, ed. Nicholas Cronk, Barry W. Ife, and Jenny Mander. Oxford: Voltaire Foundation, forthcoming.

---. "Traducción y creación en la actividad intelectual de las ilustradas españolas: El ejemplo de Inés Joyes y Blake." In *Frasquita Larrea y Aherán: Europeas y españolas entre la Ilustración y el Romanticismo*, ed. Gloria Espigado Tocino and María José de la Pascua, 137–55. Cádiz: Ayuntamiento del Puerto de Santa María–Universidad de Cádiz–Junta de Andalucía, 2003.

Bolufer Peruga, Mónica, and Isabel Morant Deusa. "On Women's Reason, Education and Love: Women and Men of the Enlightenment in Spain and France." *Gender and History* 10.2 (1998): 183–216.

Bouza, Fernando. "Memorias de la lectura y escritura de las mujeres en el Siglo de Oro." In *Historia de las mujeres en España y América Latina*, ed. Isabel Morant Deusa, vol. 2, *El mundo moderno: España y América colonial*, 169–91. Madrid: Cátedra, 2005.

Bucci, Susanna. "La produzione letteraria dedicata alle donne illustri: Pubblico e autori nel clima polemico del dibattito sui diritti del sesso femminil." In *La condizione della donna nel XVII e XVIII secolo*, ed. Fiorenza Tariccone and Susanna Bucci. Rome: Carucci, 1983.

Canterla, Cinta. "El problema de la autoría de *La Pensadora gaditana*." *Cuadernos de Ilustración y Romanticismo* 7 (1999): 29–54.

Clarke, Norma. *The Rise and Fall of the Woman Writer*. London: Hambledon, 2004.

Cubié, Juan Bautista. *Las mugeres vindicadas de las calumnias de los hombres, con un catálogo de las Españolas que más se han distinguido en Ciencias y Armas*. Madrid: Antonio Pérez de Soto, 1768.

Demerson, Paula. *María Francisca de Sales y Portocarrero, condesa de Montijo: Una figura de la Ilustración*. Madrid: Editora Nacional, 1975.

Diario noticioso (Madrid), February 1758.

Feijoo, Benito Jerónimo. "Defensa de las mujeres." Discourse 16 in *Teatro crítico universal; o, Discursos varios en todo género de materias, para desengaño de errores comunes*, vol. 1. Madrid: Francisco de Hierro, 1746.

Fernández Quintanilla, Paloma. *La mujer ilustrada en la España del siglo XVIII*. Madrid: Ministerio de Cultura, 1981.

García Garrosa, María Jesús. "Mujeres novelistas en el siglo XVIII." In *Actas del I Congreso Internacional sobre novela del siglo XVIII*, ed. Fernando García Lara, 163–83. Almería: Universidad de Almería, 1998.

Goldsmith, Elizabeth, and Dena Goodman. Introduction to *Going Public: Women and Publishing in Early Modern France*, ed. Elizabeth Goldsmith and Dena Goodman, 1–9. Ithaca, NY: Cornell University Press, 1995.

Hickey, Margarita. *Poesías varias sagradas, morales y profanas o amorosas: Con dos poemas épicos en elogio del Capitán General D. Pedro Cevallos; Obras todas de una dama de esta Corte.* Madrid: Imprenta Real, 1789.

Jaffe, Catherine. "Of Women's Love, Learning, and (In)Discretion: María Lorenza de los Ríos's *La sabia indiscreta* (1803)." *MLN* 119 (2004): 270–89.

———. "Suspect Pleasure: Writing the Woman Reader in Eighteenth-Century Spain." *Dieciocho* 22.1 (1999): 35–59.

Joyes y Blake, Inés. *El Príncipe de Abisinia: Novela traducida del inglés por doña Inés Joyes y Blake; Va inserta a continuación una Apología de las mujeres en carta original de la traductora a sus hijas.* Madrid: Sancha, 1798.

Lampillas, Xavier. *Ensayo histórico-apologético de la literatura española.* Trans. and ed. Josefa Amar y Borbón. 2nd ed. Madrid: Pedro Marín, 1789.

Larriba, Elisabel. *Le public de la presse en Espagne à la fin du XVIIIe siècle (1781–1808).* Paris: Honoré Champion, 1998.

Le Moyne, Pierre. *Galería de mujeres fuertes.* Madrid: Benito Cano, 1794.

Lewis, Elizabeth Franklin. "Mythical Mystic or *Monja Romántica?* The Poetry of María Gertrudis Hore." *Dieciocho* 16.1–2 (1993): 95–109.

López-Cordón, María Victoria. "La fortuna de escribir: Escritoras de los siglos XVII y XVIII." In *Historia de las mujeres en España y América Latina,* ed. Isabel Morant Deusa, vol. 2, *El mundo moderno: España y América colonial,* 193–234. Madrid: Cátedra, 2005.

———. "Traducción y traductoras en la España de finales del siglo XVIII." In *Entre la marginación y el desarrollo: Hombres y mujeres en la historia,* ed. Cristina Segura and Gloria Nielfa, 89–112. Madrid: Ediciones del Orto, 1996.

Morand, Frédérique. *Doña María Gertrudis Hore (1742–1801): Vivencia de una poetisa gaditana entre el siglo y la clausura.* Alcalá de Henares: Ayuntamiento de Alcalá, 2004.

Palacios Fernández, Emilio. *La mujer y las letras en la España del siglo XVIII Madrid.* Madrid: Ediciones del Laberinto, 2002.

Rang, Brita. "A 'Learned Wave': Women of Letters and Science from the Renaissance to the Enlightenment." In *Perspectives on Feminist Political Thought in European History from the Middle Ages to the Present,* ed. Tjitske Akkerman and Siep Stuurman, 50–66. London: Routledge, 1998.

Rípodas Ardanaz, Daisy. "Una ignorada escritora en la Charcas finicolonial: María Antonia de Río y Arnedo." *Investigaciones y Ensayos* 43 (1993): 165–207.

Romero Masegosa y Cancelada, María Rosario, trans. *Cartas de una peruana, escritas en francés por Mme. de Graffigny.* Valladolid: Viuda de Santander e hijos, 1792.

Seixo, Vicente del. *Discurso filosófico y económico-político sobre la capacidad o incapacidad natural de las mugeres para las ciencias y las artes.* Madrid, 1801.

Serrano y Sanz, Manuel. *Apuntes para una biblioteca de escritoras españolas (desde el año 1409 a 1833).* Biblioteca de autores españoles, 268–71. 2 vols. in 4. 1903. Facsimile ed., Madrid: Atlas, 1975.

Smith, Theresa Ann. *The Emerging Female Citizen: Gender and Enlightenment in Spain.* Berkeley and Los Angeles: University of California Press, 2006.

———. "Writing out of the Margins: Women, Translation, and the Spanish Enlightenment." *Journal of Women's History* 15.1 (2003): 116–43.

Sullivan, Constance. "Gender, Text, and Cross-Dressing: The Case of 'Beatriz Cienfuegos.'" *Dieciocho* 18 (1995): 29–54.

———. "Las escritoras del siglo XVIII." In *Breve historia feminista de la literatura española (escrita en castellano)*, ed. Myriam Díaz-Diocaretz and Iris Zavala, vol. 4, *La literatura escrita por mujer desde la Edad Media al siglo XVIII*, 305–30. Barcelona: Anthropos, 1997.

Thomas, Antoine-Léonard. *Historia o pintura del caracter, costumbres y talento de las mugeres en los diferentes siglos*. Trans. Alonso Ruiz de Piña. Madrid: Miguel Escribano, 1773.

Urzainqui, Inmaculada. "Los espacios de la mujer en la prensa del siglo XVIII." In *Del periódico a la sociedad de la información*, ed. Celso Almuiña and Eduardo Sotillos, 53–79. Madrid: Sociedad Estatal España Nuevo Milenio, 2002.

———. "Nuevas propuestas a un público femenino." In *Historia de la edición y de la lectura en España (1472–1914)*, ed. Víctor Infantes, François Lopez, and Jean F. Botrel, 481–92. Madrid: Fundación Germán Sánchez Ruipérez, 2003.

———. "Un enigma que se desvela: El texto de *La Pensatriz salmantina* (1777)." *Dieciocho* 27.2 (2004): 129–55.

2

Enlightenment Experience in the Life and Poetry of Sor María Gertrudis de la Cruz Hore

FRÉDÉRIQUE MORAND

*B*efore her twenty-three-year stay at the Santa María del Arrabal convent in Cádiz, Sor María Gertrudis de la Cruz Hore was called Doña María Gertrudis Hore y Ley (1742–1801). This unusual "married" nun, of late vocation (1778), unofficially administered the accounts of her monastery. She was the convent secretary and "medical escort" during at least two three-year periods during the 1790s.[1] Her fascinating life and poetic writings provide a unique glimpse into women's experience during Spain's Enlightenment period. The only daughter of the Irishman Miguel Hore and his wife María Ley, María Gertrudis de la Cruz Hore came from a family that for generations had been dedicated to commerce. She married Esteban Fleming, her father's business partner, in an arranged marriage, a typical practice at the end of Spain's *Antiguo Régimen*. Hore was barely twenty years old when she married. She lived in relative solitude owing to her husband's profession, even though she had nine servants and one slave in her service. She enjoyed the freedom that Cádiz, the "City of Hercules," provided her, and she attended prominent events in the city during the 1770s. At that time, when she was still a wealthy and respected laywoman, her contemporaries dubbed her *Hija del Sol* (Daughter of the Sun) for her beauty and erudition.

Although I do not consider the work of this poet a true reflection of her life, I cannot completely disassociate her personal history from her poetry. One might reject my autobiographical reading of Hore's poems, but according to Luis Cernuda, eighteenth-century lyric poetry corresponds to "a poetry of consciousness, conceived as social communication," while that of the nineteenth century, "poetry of the unconscious, of individual inspiration," corresponds to another epoch (36).

Translated by David Vassar

Literature, including poetry, is a system of codes in which Hore exercised her desire to transmit a "literary message," relying on a cultural and historical foundation. In the words of Roland Barthes, as quoted by Angelo Marchese and Joaquín Forradellas, "[W]riting is a function: it is the relationship between creation and society, it is literary language transformed by its social destiny, the form captured in its human intention and in that way united to the great crises of History" (139). In her poetry Hore was also able to unite her personal experience and women's social experience of the Enlightenment in Spain.

Toward the end of the 1770s, while living with her husband at the Puerto de Santa María, Hore had one of her first experiences as a woman of the Enlightenment. Most likely, she went to the Puerto de Cadiz in order to attend the "performance" of young Rosario Cepeda at her public examination on 19, 22, and 24 September 1768. María del Rosario Cepeda, a girl of twelve years, answered all of the questions asked her by a panel of scholars in such disparate areas as translation, astronomy, literature, and geography. In the room with her were more than three hundred residents who had been invited to observe as the child prodigy displayed her intellectual aptitude. María Gertrudis Hore attended at least two of the three days of the young girl's assessments.

The Hija del Sol stood out not only because she attended the assessments but also because she dedicated several poems to Cepeda that were later published, along with those of sixteen others, by the authorities of Cádiz.[2] Hore decided to publish her first poetic creations under the veil of anonymity, referring to herself as "una dama adoptiva de Febo, y como tal, mejor Thalia" (an adopted lady of Phoebus, and as such, best named Thalia) in a poem that begins "Sabia afrenta del hombre" (Wise affront to men).[3] Opposite the first poem, in the script of one of her copyists, is written "La de Hore" (The Lady of Hore). The second text—"¿Dónde Minerva, las Lechuzas tristes?" (Where, Minerva, the sad owls?)—which is explained as being "From the same queen of the Muses who wrote the laments addressed the day of the First Act," also leaves no room for doubt as to its author. Hore had come to attend the public exam of the girl she called her "amiga" in order to communicate her feelings and emotions as a clear and committed "lady of letters."[4] At twenty-six years of age she praised her twelve-year-old companion in arms while at the same time warning her of the dangers that awaited her simply because of her gender. Hore would always maintain a critical view of Cepeda's examination. In the second poem mentioned above, after Hore reflects upon the repercussions and real meaning of the public examination of the young Cepeda, she does not seem quite so enthusiastic: "¿A dónde el premio está, que le destinas,

/ Al Alumno feliz que vas buscando?" (Where is the prize that you destine / to the happy student for whom you are searching?). As Hore recognized, the occasion was extraordinary, less because the protagonist was a young child than because of her gender. She knew, without a doubt, that the epithet *bachillera*[5] threatened any woman that possessed learning and culture, for which reason she preferred to maintain her anonymity:

> (Soy) la que nunca sabrás;
> (Tú) ya muy de corazón;
> (Fina) en cualquiera ocasión;
> (Amiga) y fiel me hallarás.
>
> (I am) the one whom you'll never know;
> (Your) heartfelt supporter;
> (Fine) in any occasion;
> (Friend) and faithful you'll find me.

In the words of Mónica Bolufer Peruga, the hypothetical merit of these precocious young women in such circumstances was "hidden by the rhetorical verbiage of the elegies . . . that were very difficult to appreciate behind the veil of highly conventional descriptions" ("Galerías" 215–16). In this case, Hore transcends literary hypocrisy in order to convey and to share sincerely her womanly judgment of Cepeda's examination:

> Y permite a mi afecto que repita
> Aquel aviso; pues gustosa hallo,
> Que licencia me da para este asunto,
> Ser de tu Sexo, y el tener más años.
> Guárdate, como digo de Cupido,
> Pues su alevoso, su engañoso trato,
> Enemigo mortal de los ingenios,
> Acaba en ocio, si empezó descanso.
> Repara en Safo, y en Medea, y Circe,
> Estudios, y sosiego abandonados,
> Y un Faón, un Jasón, con un Ulises,
> Primeros instrumentos de su daño.
> —("¿Dónde, Minerva, las Lechuzas tristes?" 40)

> Permit my affection to repeat
> That advice; since I happily find
> That being older and of your same sex,
> Gives me license in this matter.
> Beware, as I say, of Cupid,
> Since his arrogant and deceiving dealings
> Are the mortal enemies of the intelligent,
> That which began as rest, ends up as leisure.
> Take notice of Sappho, or Medea and Circe,
> Studies and peace abandoned,
> And a Phaon, a Jason, together with a Ulysses,
> Were foremost instruments of their doom.

Hore does not hesitate to blame men for women's misfortunes in the academic realm, and she makes use of her knowledge of mythology in order to warn Rosario Cepeda of the danger. Her criticism of men is similar to that of her contemporary Margarita Hickey.[6] However, Hore does not seem to blame women for the unjust situation, as her compatriot Inés Joyes y Blake did, accusing them of encouraging, agreeing to, and maintaining their deplorably unequal condition.[7] Both conscious of her boldness and at the same time cautious, Hore would have preferred to continue in anonymity. However, this desire does not appear to have been fulfilled, as the concluding acrostic to the above poem shows:

> (Tuya) de ti me despido;
> (Soy), la que has sabido ya;
> (Y)nfinito lo he sentido;
> (Seré) quien lo negará,
> (Siempre) que llegue a mi oído.
> —(41)
>
> (Yours) from you I bid farewell;
> (I am) the one you've already known;
> (And) infinitely I've felt it;
> (I will be) the one who'll deny it,
> (Always) when I hear it.

In "Sabia afrenta del hombre" the Hija del Sol informs the reader of her own frustrated desire:

> Siendo Mujer que nunca,
> A pesar de mi anhelo,
> Para estudios tan dignos,
> Ni permiso logré, ni tuve tiempo.
> —(34)

> Being a woman that never
> Despite my desire
> Has achieved permission or time
> For such dignified studies.

Because of her gender, she was not allowed to study at the university. However, Hore was able to take advantage of her familial and geographical environment, which were favorable to her intellectual development. Since she was surrounded by cooks, servants, and a slave, she never had to fulfill the domestic role reserved for the women of her time, although, like any woman of the elite, she had to act as if she did. She made visits, frequented theaters, and walked the busy streets of Cádiz, Puerto de Santa María, the Isla de León, and Madrid.

Approximately ten years before entering the convent, María Gertrudis Hore attended the *tertulias* of Antonio de Ulloa, who, alongside Jorge Juan, accompanied French astronomers and scholars to the ends of the earth in order to do away with the old Copernican system. In this circle of intellectuals, and in the company of some ladies, she enjoyed the intimate presence of Gonzalo de Cañas, professor of astronomy and mathematics at the Royal Observatory in Cádiz. This friend of Jorge Juan's was also a member of the Real Compañía de Caballeros de Guardias Marinas and epitomized the select nature of Ulloa's company.[8] In my judgment, these meetings were not incidental to Hore's intellectual development. They might have taken place in the Pópulo neighborhood, where Antonio de Ulloa had his bookstore, which was filled with musical scores and operas (Rivas Pérez 3). Perhaps she chose the poetic name Fenisa—the literary name given to one of the two constellations near the North Pole, either Ursa Minor or Ursa Major—during one of these *tertulias*.[9] A series of three manuscript poems, likely written between

1769 and 1775, testify to her participation in Ulloa's meetings and reveal a mysterious trip to Madrid. The first, "No me culpéis de ingrata," begins:

> No me culpéis de ingrata,
> mis amables amigas,
> si anoche al despedirme
> oculté mi dolor a vuestra vista.
> . . . .
> Cuidaba de mis ojos,
> de quienes más temía,
> que incautos descubriesen
> de mi silencio el cauteloso enigma.
>
> Do not accuse me of being ungrateful
> My dear friends
> if last night upon bidding you farewell
> I hid my pain from your sight.
> . . . .
> I was guarding my eyes
> from those I most feared,
> who carelessly would discover
> in my silence the cautious enigma.

We know that Hore was familiar with the latest scientific findings and the new ways of viewing the world, no longer solely through Christianity's conceptual prism. She was aware of the new ideas being developed, ideas that called into question the religious beliefs on which the understanding of the universe had been based. She lived during a century in which philosophy allowed for the belief in the progress of science as the essential transformative element within society. Without a doubt, her poetry was the fruit of her learning, a reflection of her firm understanding of both the classics and her contemporaries.

Hore's unpublished poems, which were less likely than her poems published in contemporary journals to show the effects of male censorship,[10] offer another view of the Spanish Enlightenment woman's amorous experience. During the 1760s not only was she conscious of the educative "traps" that the so-called enlightened society offered her but she reclaimed her right as a woman to love and be loved:

> El campo piso apenas
> cuando con alegría
> a recibirme amante
> Mirteo se anticipa.
> ¡Con qué placer le veo!
> ¡con qué gusto me mira!
> ¡ah amor! ¿quién a tu imperio
> le llama tiranía?
> —("Luego que de la corte")

> I hardly step into the countryside
> when with happiness
> Mirteo hurries
> to receive me lovingly.
> With such pleasure I see him!
> With such happiness he looks at me!
> Oh, love! Who can call your empire
> A tyranny?

In the following manuscript ode the poet appears neither to distrust love nor to denounce extramarital passion; nor does she worry herself with moral condemnations. In this idyll of a pastoral nature, "Zagal el más bello," the poetic voice clearly reflects the joy found in the pleasures of love without hesitation or even denial of romantic passion:

> Zagal, el más bello
> de cuantos zagales
> esparcen iguales
> al aire el cabello;
> En mi verso amante
> aún más celebrado,
> que el barquero amado
> de Safo constante;
> Por benigna estrella
> de mi tan querido
> cual lo fue Cupido
> de su Psiquis bella.

> Shepherd, the most handsome
> of all shepherds
> who equally toss
> their hair in the wind;
> In my loving verse
> even more celebrated
> than the beloved boatman
> of the faithful Sappho;
> By the benevolent star
> so loved by me
> as it was with Cupid
> by his beautiful Psyche.

Hore not only insists on the intensity of her love, surpassing even that of Mitilene, but also confesses her joy:

> Hasta que con cuidado
> mis ojos examinan
> que el amado Mirteo
> por el monte venía.
> ....
> Y en Mirteo me ofrece
> cuanto mi afecto estima,
> cuanto mi gusto anhela,
> cuanto mi amor aspira.
> —("Cuando huyendo las sombras")[11]
>
> Until carefully
> my eyes see
> that the beloved Mirteo
> was coming over the mountain
> ....
> And in Mirteo I offer myself
> everything that my affection esteems
> everything that my pleasure desires
> everything that my love aspires.

Hore's lyric production is marked by its abandonment to passion.

It seems to me that although María Gertrudis Hore developed an awareness of her own independence, she ended up facing the opposite result: her desire to design and carry out her own plans was dashed by the customs and laws of the day concerning arranged marriages and the punishment of adultery. In fact, she appears not to exalt marriage, but rather to hate the institution as merely an arranged social connection. In one of her odes, "Bellísima Diana" (Beautiful Diana), her disapproval of prearranged unions is summed up in two words: "tálamo odioso" (odious nuptial bed). Let us examine this violent rhetorical figure. Hore joined two opposite meanings in order to express with an oxymoron, which in turn was also reduced to a synecdoche, two words that seem to be mutually exclusive, thereby juxtaposing the marital bed and the hate it engenders.

In another poem, "Zagal, el más bello," she writes to her lover invoking the prophesy of relationships for love: "Si tu amor seguro / y el mío contemplo, / seremos ejemplos / al tiempo futuro" (If your certain love / and mine too I contemplate, / we will be examples / to future times). But soon new oppressions would arise, as seen in this line from the sonnet "Soberbio bruto que de instinto ajeno" (Ignorant pride that from distant instinct), which was written after her mysterious stay in Madrid, in 1774 or 1775: "Siento que lo que no fue / ejemplo sea escarmiento" (I'm sorry that that which was not / an example might now be a punishment). It seems to me that she traveled to the capital in order to attend her divorce trial, or "separation of table and bed," according to ecclesiastic terminology.[12] Canonical separation was the only way that Fleming could free himself of his wife (their business had shut down in 1771) and still preserve his honor despite the behavior of this "free woman."

In the following poem, "Luego que de la corte," she writes to a friend after leaving Madrid:

> Luego que de la corte
> dulce amigo me aparte
> la obligación gustosa
> de ver mi madre amada
> y volver al sosiego
> de mi tranquila casa
> a esperar mi fortuna
> o llorar mi desgracia;
> Then pleasant obligation
> separates me sweet friend

> from the court
> from seeing my beloved mother
> and from returning to the peace
> of my tranquil house
> to wait for my fortune
> or weep for my disgrace.

Her destiny does not seem terribly clear. Again she employs an oxymoron to express her stay in the house of her mother as something between imposition and delight: "obligación gustosa."

In another manuscript poem, most likely written soon after her entry into the convent, she begins: "¿Quién dijera que una ave / su libertad perdiera / mil veces más dichosas / fuera por ser cautiva?" (Who could have said that a bird / who had lost its freedom / would be a thousand times luckier / because she was captive?). She contrasts the freedom of the bird (her state of happiness) with the privation of her freedom, her captivity.[13] If we look at private correspondence from the poet to her friend Gerarda—the poem that Cueto in his edition preferred to entitle "Meditación"—we find the tracks of her personal "tragedy":

> y este corto consuelo, rigurosas
> leyes de esta república me privan
> por un espacio, que cual siglos cuento,
> aunque los cuenten todos como días.
> —("Los dulcísimos metros que tu pluma")

> and rigorous laws of this republic
> deprive me of this the brief consolation
> for a period that I count like centuries,
> although everyone else counts them as days.

In this manuscript version Cueto replaces the original word "presan" (hold captive) with the less forceful "privan" (deprive). If Hore's contemporaries Margarita Hickey and Inés Joyes exhorted women to flee from love, if they warned them against romantic language and its dangerous deceptions that could harm their reputation, Hore experienced firsthand "the most dangerous of the passions"[14] and lost her freedom, it seems, because of adultery. Was the decision to take on the veil her own? Was she forced to enter into a perpetual regimen of cloister? In another poem, classified as one of Hore's "mystic poems," she writes to the Virgin Mary:

> ayudad compasiva
> mis ruegos repetidos.
> Haced que de mis culpas
> se borre el negro libro;
> Aunque quedan las notas
> en ser para el castigo
> Que yo sabré gustosa
> sufrir lo merecido
> —("A vos padre amoroso")

> compassionately help
> my repeated pleas.
> Assure that my faults
> are erased from the black book;
> Although notes remain
> to be for the punishment
> I'll know how to happily
> suffer what I deserve

In the collection of her poems published in the series *Biblioteca de Autores Españoles* by Leopoldo Augusto de Cueto the lines "Aunque quedan las notas / en ser para el castigo" do not appear; they were censored by Cueto. A close reading of her poems reveals a real coherence in her work, expressing an existence made up of both pleasure and resignation. Most critics, since Fernán Caballero's account, remembered the Hija del Sol as a repentant religious woman.[15] Unlike Fernán Caballero, I do not think that she decided to enter the cloister; rather, I think she was a "forced" nun, removed from society by both civil and religious authorities. It is hard to believe that if the Hija del Sol lived through the traumatic experience of a solemn profession as her punishment (according to the rules in force for adulterers), it did not influence her lyrical poetry written at the time of her "hypothetical trial" (1773?–1775?), as well as the poetry written after she entered the convent (1778).

Castilian law punished female adultery. Punishment for adulterous women can be found in the *Fuero Real* and in the Roman laws of the medieval King Alfonso X's *Partidas* (4 and 7), according to which they were forced into perpetual reclusion in a monastery.[16] In the eighteenth century a couple could choose from only three legally recognized means of separation: by sentence; by ordinary decree; or by private authority, but only in cases in which the adulterer was recognized as guilty and the case was "morally clear" (Bernárdez Cantón 71–73). In order to provide for the separation of property, which is what took place in this case, there was no alternative but to go before the appropriate tribunal in order to obtain a divorce.[17] A private separation sworn and carried out before a notary was not sufficient. Additionally, according to canonical law, only separation for adultery could be perpetual, whether it conveyed by sentencing or by a private authority, because in all other cases only by exception or in extraordinary cases can perpetual divorce result (Aguilar Jiménez 17). Could this have been the case of the "adulterous" poetess of Cadiz? Only if the Hija del Sol was able to extricate herself from the judicial web of marital separation.

Upon entering the convent, María Gertrudis Hore did not completely abandon her routines. She decorated her cell with memories from her previous life: mahogany furniture, icons, and books. Some titles listed in her inventory at her death, such as her Moreri and Castillian language dictionaries, reflect the exceptional path of this nun who had been educated in the heart of a well-known Irish family, while other titles were obligatory readings for all nuns.[18] In my judgment, she entered with some of her books, for example, Luis Moreri's 1674 *Gran diccionario histórico*, a ten-volume work of considerable size and a common reference tool for Enlightenment thinkers. Moreri's dictionary covered topics of interest to students of secular and sacred history, geography, architecture, literary criticism, genealogy, modern and classical writers, and religious orders, among other subjects. It was an authentic treasure of wisdom. Despite her erudition, Sor María de la Cruz was never allowed to approach the *discretorio* (counsel board). She was barred, as were other "penitent" religious women, from officially making community decisions, as Moreri commented in his dictionary (154).

Hore never lost contact with the outside world. After becoming a nun, she began signing her secular poetry with the initials H. D. S. or D. M. G. H. She corresponded with Delio, Friar Diego Tadeo González (1734–93)—an outstanding member of the School of Salamanca—and was published several times in the *Semanario Erudito y Curioso de Salamanca*. All of her poems, of secular character, were praised by the "Monthly Censor" of the *Diario de Madrid*. By the end of her life, the woman who signed her poems as H. D. S. was recognized and praised for her erudition, although she continued to hide her identity behind the initials with which she shined in the secular world, as noted in the following passage from the *Diario de Madrid*, 8 June 1795: "The poems of the 11th and 21st signed with the initials H. D. S., seem to me to be by a woman from Cádiz, known by the name 'Daughter of the Sun'; her instruction in various languages, her select erudition, her good taste and intelligence, together with her personal attributes, have acquired for her the admiration of everyone who has dealt with her" (Serrano y Sanz 1:529n1). Not until decades later, still ignorant of her status as a nun, did readers discover the identity of H. D. S. She did not dare sign the following work, "Estaba Febo en el Parnaso,"[19] or any others unbecoming of a professed religious woman:

> Fenisa, que del Betis ascendía,
> osada llega entre otras concurrentes,
> y al ver de todas coronar las frentes,
> ¿Dónde está, dice, la corona mía?

> Fenisa, who was ascending from the Betis [Guadalquivir River],
> daringly arrived among other contestants,
> and on seeing the foreheads of the others adorned,
> she asked "Where is my crown?"

This nun of solemn vow expressed her desire for recognition as a poet. She ignored commentaries that disparaged educated women, especially vain women. She broke with the "common place of the modest woman writer" (Bolufer Peruga, *Mujeres e Ilustración* 318).

Her intellectual qualities were exposed to public contempt when, on 14 November 1787, she published in the *Correo de Madrid* an anonymous poem whose title revealed only the sex of its author: "Oda de una Poetisa a un Jilguero que cayó herido a sus pies" (Ode by a Poetess to a Goldfinch that fell injured at her feet). Another poem followed entitled, "Anacreóntica de la misma a la muerte de un hermoso Canario . . ." (Anacreontic by the same to the death of a handsome Canary . . .). Ten days later, on 24 November 1787, the *Correo de Madrid* published the following:

Un poeta, que no ha creído sea de mujer la bella anacreóntica, . . . dice su sentir en el siguiente.

>En mujer tanto primor
>No se encuentra tan aprisa;
>Y yo creo será, en rigor,
>De otro pájaro mayor,
>Que el pájaro y poetisa.
>—(Serrano y Sanz 1:527)

A poet who has not believed that the beautiful anacreontic was from a woman . . . expresses his opinions in the following.

>In a woman such charm
>Is not found so quickly;
>And I believe that it must be,
>Therefore, by another greater bird
>Than the bird and poetess.

María Gertrudis Hore experienced the multiple facets of the Enlightenment, including having her authorship called into question simply because her work was signed with a woman's name. Her poetry made it possible to assert that not all anonymous compositions or works written under a female pseudonym were actually male creations. By taking advantage of her family's position, the Enlightenment movement, and her geographical environment, Sor María de la Cruz enjoyed a solid education before and after taking the veil. However, her possibilities for personal development were strongly limited the moment she tried to stand up to the social mores concerning love in a society in which religious influences governed not only the citizenry's morals but also the very laws in force. Perhaps the false promises of freedom acquired by the citizens of Cádiz during the eighteenth century opened the doors of the "closed cloister" because, for women, not all the possibilities and promises of the Spanish Enlightenment were free of contradictions:

>Ella se impuso la pena
>del encierro que prefiere,
>cárcel donde el cuerpo muere,
>prisión donde el Alma reina:

....
y por su acción meritoria
puede alcanzar sin desgracia
perdón de culpas; ¿qué Gracia?
descanso eterno; ¡qué Gloria![20]

She imposed the penalty
of enclosure, which she prefers,
a jail where the body dies,
a prison where the Soul reigns:
....
and by her meritorious action
she can reach, without disgrace
pardon for her sins; Such Grace?
eternal rest; What Glory!

NOTES

1. See Morand, *Doña María Gertrudis Hore*.

2. See *Relación de los ejercicios literarios que la Sra. Doña María del Rosario Cepeda y Mayo*, esp. 33–36 and 38–41 for Hore's contributions.

3. Since most of these poems are not given individual titles, the first line of verse will be used to identify poems for which an alternate title was not given.

4. See Morand, *Una poetisa*.

5. *Bachillera* literally means "educated woman," but the term has been used pejoratively to diminish women's intelligence and abilities.

6. Margarita Hickey y Pellizoni published her collection of poetry and drama—*Poesías varias sagradas, morales, profanas o amorosas con dos poemas épicos*—in 1789. See María Salgado's discussion of Hickey in chapter 4 of this volume.

7. Inés Joyes y Blake published an introduction to her translation of Samuel Johnson's novel *Rasselas, Prince of Abyssinia*, which she addressed to her daughters, entitling it *La Apología de las mujeres*. See Bolufer Peruga, "Inés Joyes y Blake."

8. See Dalmiro de la Valgoma.

9. See Diderot et D'Alembert, s.v. "Cynosure" and "Ourse," for contemporary discussions of these constellations.

10. Either the poet's own self-censoring or censorship by the editors of the journals. Certainly Hore's poetry published after her death by Cueto, from Eustaquio Fernández de Navarrete's collection, shows numerous differences from manuscript versions, as these editors also executed a sort of censorship on her poetry.

11. Cueto did not publish the second line of this poem in his edition of the manuscripts contained in the Biblioteca Menéndez Pelayo de Santander, D 119.

12. See Sullivan.

13. See Lewis, *Women Writers,* esp. ch. 3, on the concept of happiness in the poetry of Hore.

14. See Bolufer Peruga, "Escritura," 219.

15. See Fernán Caballero; Cambiaso, fols. 177–78; Sebold; and Lewis, "Mythical Mystic."

16. See articles by Enrique Gacto, as well as the collection *Sexo barroco y otras transgresiones premodernas.* See also "Leyes de Toro"; and "Novísima Recopilación."

17. See Faus Esteve.

18. Her postmortem inventory details the following books: two sets of breviaries, one daily, and *Octavarios;* the Moreri dictionary, one *Diccionario de Lengua Castellana;* the *Christian Year* and *Madre Agreda,* both incomplete; *Padre Calino* and *The Educated Religious Woman; Introduction to the Devout Life,* by San Francisco de Sales; *Triumph of Religion;* and the *Foundation of the Sisters of Mula.* See "Inventario post mortem."

19. See Lewis, *Women Writers,* ch. 3, for a discussion of this sonnet and its daring implications for Hore as a poet.

20. The enigmatic title of this unpublished *décima* is: "La Pluma que tiene un corazón con Grillos de donde salen cadenas, una que tiene es al Mundo, y Rota" (The Pen that has a heart in Shackles from which extend chains, one that holds the World and the other Broken).

WORKS CITED

Aguilar Jiménez, Juan. *Procedimientos canónico-civiles respecto a las causas de divorcio y nulidad de matrimonio.* Madrid: Instituto Nacional de Sordomudos y de Ciegos, 1923.

Bernárdez Cantón, Alberto. *Las causas canónicas de separación conyugal.* Madrid: Tecnos, 1961.

Bolufer Peruga, Mónica. "Escritura femenina y publicación en el siglo XVIII: De la expresión personal a la *República de las letras.*" In *Género y ciudadanía: Revisiones desde el ámbito privado,* ed. Margarita Ortega, Cristina Sánchez, and Celia Valiente, 197–223. Madrid: Universidad Autónoma de Madrid, 1999.

———. "Galerías de *mujeres ilustres* o el sinuoso camino de la excepción a la norma cotidiana." *Hispania* 60–61.204 (2000): 181–224.

———. "Inés Joyes y Blake: Una Ilustrada, entre privado y público," In *Mujeres para la historia: Figuras destacadas del primer feminismo,* ed. Rosa Capel, 27–55. Madrid: Abada, 2004.

———. *Mujeres e Ilustración: La construcción de la feminidad en la Ilustración española.* Valencia: Diputació de Valencia, 1998.

Cambiaso, Nicolás María de. "Memorias para la biografía y para la bibliografía de la Isla de Cádiz." MS Biblioteca de Estudios y Temas Gaditanos, Cádiz.

Cernuda, Luis. *Pensamiento poético en la lírica inglesa del siglo XIX.* 2nd ed. Madrid: Alianza, 2002.

Cueto, Leopoldo Augusto de, ed. "Doña María de Hore." In *Poetas líricos del siglo XVIII,* Biblioteca de Autores Españoles, 3:553–59. 1869–75. Reprint, Madrid: Atlas, 1953.

Diderot, Denis, and Jean le Rond d'Alembert. *Encyclopédie ou dictionnaire raisonné des sciences, des arts et des métiers, par une societé de gens de lettres.* 17 vols. Paris: Briasson, David l'ainé, Le Breton and Durand, 1751–57.

Faus Esteve, Ramón. "La separación de hecho en el matrimonio." *Anales de la Academia Matritense del Notariado* 2 (1950): 295–365.

Fernán Caballero, "La Hija del Sol." *La Ilustración* 1.22 (1849): 174–75.

Gacto, Enrique. "El delito de bigamia y la inquisición española." In *Sexo barroco y otras transgresiones premodernas,* ed. Francisco Tomás y Valiente, 127–52. Madrid: Alianza, 1990.

———. "Entre la debilidad y la simpleza: La mujer ante la ley." *Historia 16* 145 (1988): 24–32.

Hore, María Gertrudis. "Anacreóntica de la misma a la muerte de un hermoso Canario que murió por el descuido de una criada que dejó caer su jaula." *Correo de Madrid,* 14 November 1787, 544–45.

———. "A vos padre amoroso." D 119, fol. 10a. Biblioteca Menéndez Pelayo de Santander.

———. "Bellísima Diana." D 119, fol. 5a. Biblioteca Menéndez Pelayo de Santander.

———. "Carta de M. G. H en 1780." Correspondencia particular del Magistral J. Martín y Guzmán, Director administrador del hospital (1776–80). sección 4, legajo 3196. Archivo Diocesano de Cádiz.

———. "Cuando huyendo las sombras." D 119, fol. 2a. Biblioteca Menéndez Pelayo de Santander.

———. "¿Donde Minerva, las Lechuzas tristes?" In *Relación de los ejercicios que la Sra. Doña María del Rosario Cepeda y Mayo,* 38–41.

———. "Estaba Febo en el Parnaso." *Correo de Madrid,* 19 December 1787, 624.

———. "Inventario post mortem de María Gertrudis de la Cruz Hore." Archivo Conventual de Santa María, Cádiz.

———. "La Pluma que tiene un corazón con Grillos de donde salen cadenas, una que tiene es al Mundo, y Rota." MS 4061, fol. 245. Biblioteca Nacional de Madrid.

———. "Los dulcísimos metros que tu pluma." D 119, fol. 6d. Biblioteca Menéndez Pelayo de Santander.

———. "Luego que de la corte." Idilio Anacreóntico. MS 3751, fols. 233–34. Biblioteca Nacional de Madrid.

———. "No me culpéis de ingrata." D 119, fol. 11a. Biblioteca Menéndez Pelayo de Santander.

———. "Oda de una Poetisa a un Jilguero que cayó herido a sus pies." *Correo de Madrid,* 14 November 1787.

———. "¿Quién dijera que una ave?" MS 3751, fol. 239. Biblioteca Nacional de Madrid.

———. "Sabia afrenta del hombre." In *Relación de los ejercicios que la Sra. Doña María del Rosario Cepeda y Mayo,* 33.

———. "Soberbio bruto que de instinto ajeno." MS 3751, fol. 236b. Biblioteca Nacional de Madrid.

———. "Zagal el más bello." Endechas. D 119, fol. 1b/c. Biblioteca Menéndez Pelayo de Santander.

———. *Poesías varias.* MS 3751, fols. 242–77; MS 4061, fols. 242–77. Biblioteca Nacional de Madrid.

Lewis, Elizabeth Franklin. "Mythical Mystic or *Monja Romántica*? The Poetry of María Gertrudis Hore." *Dieciocho* 16.1–2 (1993): 95–109.

———. *Women Writers in the Spanish Enlightenment: The Pursuit of Happiness.* Burlington, VT: Ashgate, 2004.

"Leyes de Toro." In *Los códigos españoles concordados y anotados,* 6:566–67. Madrid: La Publicidad, 1849.

Marchese, Angelo, and Joaquín Forradellas. *Diccionario de retórica, crítica y terminología literaria*. 4th ed. Barcelona: Ariel, 1994.

Morand, Frédérique. *Doña María Gertrudis Hore (1742–1801), vivencia de una poetisa gaditana entre el siglo y la clausura*. Alcalá de Henares: Ayuntamiento de Alcalá de Henares Concejalía de mujer, 2004.

———. *Una poetisa en busca de libertad, María Gertrudis Hore (1742–1801): Miscelánea y taraceas de versos, prosas y traducciones*. Cádiz: Servicio de Publicaciones de la Diputación de Cádiz, 2007.

Moreri, Luis. *El gran diccionario histórico o Miscelánea curiosa de la historia sagrada y profana*. Trans. Joseph de Miravel y Casadevante. 10 vols. Paris: Hermanos de Tournes, 1753.

"Novísima Recopilación." In *Los códigos españoles concordados y anotados*, 10:93. Madrid: La Publicidad, 1850.

Relación de los ejercicios literarios que la Sra. Doña María del Rosario Cepeda y Mayo, hija de (. . .) actuó los días 19, 22, y 24 de septiembre del presente año desde las nueve a doce de la mañana de cada día, teniendo solamente doce de edad, y poco menos de uno de instrucción en sus estudios. Cádiz: Manuel Espinosa de los Monteros, 1768.

Rivas Pérez, José María. *Aproximación a la música en Cádiz durante el siglo XVIII*. Cádiz: Fundación Municipal de Cultura, 1986.

Sebold, Russell P. "La pena de la Hija de Sol: Realidad, leyenda y romanticismo." In *Estudios en honor a Ricardo Gullón*, 295–308. Lincoln, NE: Society of Spanish and Spanish-American Studies, 1984.

Serrano y Sanz, Manuel. "Doña María Gertrudis Hore." In *Apuntes para una biblioteca de Escritoras Españolas desde el año 1401 al 1833*, 1, pt. 2: 523–33. Biblioteca de Autores Españoles, 268–71. 2 vols. in 4. 1903. Facsimile ed., Madrid: Atlas, 1975.

Sullivan, Constance A. "*Dinos, Dinos Quién Eres:* The Poetic Identity of María Gertrudis Hore (1742–1801)." In "Pen and Peruke: Spanish Literature of the Eighteenth Century," ed. Monroe Z. Hafter, special issue, *Michigan Romance Studies* 12 (1992): 153–83.

"Un poeta, que no ha creído sea de mujer la bella anacreóntica." *Correo de Madrid*, 24 November 1787, 565.

Valgoma, Dalmiro de la. *La Real Compañía de Guardia Marina (Catálogo de pruebas de Caballeros aspirantes)*. Madrid: Instituto Histórico de Marina, 1943.

3

Reasons for Education
New Echoes of the Polemic
ISABEL MORANT DEUSA

> The following essay is a translated excerpt from a longer article by Isabel Morant on women's education titled "Mujeres ilustradas en el debate de la educación" (Women and Education in the Enlightenment Debate). In the excerpt published here Morant discusses Josefa Amar y Borbón's book on education, *Discurso sobre la educación física y moral de las mujeres*, in the context of the European Enlightenment and its interest in women's education.
> —EDS.

With good reason, education has always been considered an issue of utmost importance and seriousness. Public and private happiness depend on it: if individuals were prudent, educated, wise, and moderate, and if every family were organized, united, and frugal, this would necessarily result in the general good of the state, which consists of the assembly, more or less numerous, of individuals and families. Thus, the better the education, the greater the number of happy individuals and the greater the advantages are for the republic.
—JOSEFA AMAR Y BORBÓN, *Discurso sobre la educación física y moral de las mujeres*

Josefa Amar y Borbón was a well-known and educated member of the Sociedad Económica de Amigos del País (Economic Society of the Friends of the Country) of Zaragoza and later of the same organization in Madrid. Her participation in the debate about admitting women to the Madrid society, which took place about 1786, would give her some public recognition. During the debate she wrote her famous piece in which she adamantly defended the talent and the intellectual and political capacity of women, as indicated in the title under which the work would be published in 1786: "Discurso en defensa del talento de

Translated by Diana Q. Burkhart

las mujeres y de su aptitud para el gobierno y otros cargos en que se emplean los hombres" (Discourse in Defense of the Talent of Women and Their Aptitude for Governing and Other Responsibilities Which Men Perform). Later, in 1790, she would publish her most significant educational work, *Discurso sobre la educación física y moral de las mujeres* (Discourse on the Physical and Moral Education of Women). The text was well received in its time and today can be considered one of the best collections of enlightened ideas concerning female education, comparable to works by François de Salignac de La Mothe-Fénelon and the marquise Anne Thérèse de Marguenat de Courcelles Lambert, both authors whom Josefa Amar knew and cited in her work (López-Cordón 32–38).

This latter work by Josefa Amar, like works by Mme de Lambert, reveals the polemic about women and female education. Amar's tone and arguments here are familiar to us from her earlier works, which point by point debunked the arguments that denied the intellectual capacity of women and pointed to the scant attention this issue received in society. In this new *Discurso*, nevertheless, she establishes a more positive tone, searching for an alliance with other educated individuals who, like herself, understand the value of, and social reasons for, supporting education. In a similar vein, she refers to many good authors who, according to her, have written in favor of education. She believes these texts should also include women authors, about whom, she points out, less has been written. The following passage justifies and gives credit to her endeavor to write about female education:

> The importance of the subject [of education] is dealt with in many books that have been written.... [However,] most of them only address how to teach boys, and the ones that deal with girls do so in such a passing manner that the issue seems unimportant. Furthermore, there is not a single work in our language that studies the two essential components of education: physical and moral education. For this reason, it does not seem inappropriate to publish this book. Even though it is far from perfect, it can at least serve to motivate other, more dignified authors. (59–60)

Josefa Amar, as we have seen in other cases, refers negatively to people who look down upon and neglect the education of women. Young women often abandon their natural inclinations and talent, grow up in houses where they receive little or no moral education, and become lazy women who dedicate their time to tending to their physical appearance. In the best of cases they learn to do domestic work from their mothers, who, ignorant themselves, are able to do little else for their daughters. The education that girls receive in convents is no better, because they are taught very little and they hardly study at all. Amar believes that finding a solution to the problem is the responsibility of everyone—the government, the family, and women themselves. However, these women are indifferent to their own education, nor is it valued by anyone else: "The education of women is an issue that is often considered of little importance. The state, parents, and even women themselves view learning this subject or that subject or even nothing at all in an indifferent manner. Who can point out the cause of this universal neglect?" (61).

Josefa Amar also alludes to the individuals who blame men for the total neglect of female education. They believe that men, in their effort to dominate women, would rather keep them in ignorance than enlighten them. Amar distances herself from this position, however, pointing out that not all of the opponents to women's education are men and that there are some individuals who are favorable toward it and who, like her, have written positively about it. Their names are cited throughout Amar's text as proof of the ideas Amar defends.

With regard to education itself, Amar affirms that there is an aspect of education that should be common to the education of both sexes: learning to fulfill one's moral obligations. This would apply to knowledge, religious practice, and observance of the civil laws of the country in which they live. However, there is also an aspect of education that should be specific to the female sex, for reasons that become explicit in the following text: "In private families women have a particular job, which is the direction and governing of the house, the care and raising of the children, and above all intimate and perfect harmony with the husband" (63).

We should observe, however, that it is the difference in social functions, not a difference in the basic nature of males and females, that for Amar justifies and makes imperative the idea of a separate and distinct education for women. The specific knowledge that education should provide women and not men concerns certain social tasks. However, this knowledge does not necessarily include everything education has to offer.

Josefa Amar also supports strict moral education, which should strengthen spiritual and rational values, over hedonism of the senses. She criticizes the custom of neglecting the cultivation of women's intellect and leaving them to the mercy of their so-called hedonistic impulses. These impulses are reflected in the negative image of women who seek to achieve and maintain beauty and live a life of leisure, free from intellectual pursuits. Amar, on the other hand, proposes that more effort be made to provide women with opportunities for the study of those sciences that are considered nobler, as well as more useful and more advantageous to them.

Amar recognizes, however, that this study is arduous for women. It is not really the difficulty of the material that poses a problem, but rather the indifferent if not disparaging attitude toward women's education. Studies are difficult to complete in general, but even more so for women who do not have the stimulus of a reward and cannot see on the horizon the possibility of being acknowledged for their merit in the same way that men are. Women, Amar insists, cannot make others recognize the value of their studies outside the confines of the home. Consequently, many of them abandon their studies because of a lack of motivation, and others do not even begin to study in the first place. However, Amar argues in favor of women's education, showing that some women have managed to stay afloat and that when there is a will, nothing can stop these women from dominating what are considered some of the most challenging subjects.

The women she cites with regard to this issue were well known. They were named repeatedly by both Spanish and foreign authors, particularly female ones, to demonstrate how the desire and the will to study have helped women achieve their maximum intellectual capacity. Amar, on the other hand, understands that she is dealing with a select group of women who are seen as exceptions to the rule, since women in general had low levels of education. Included in this group of exceptional women are female authors who, like Josefa Amar herself, write for other cultured and educated women with the intention of educating young women of their same social class.

Amar specifies that her book serves the purpose of educating women who share her moral and social condition. With regard to women of lower social classes, she states that they do not need the same education, because it would not be useful to them since the circumstances of their lives are different. She believes that for the majority of women "all they need to know is how to manage household chores" (73). A woman married to a common man does not need to know as much. Happiness in these marriages is achieved when the man applies himself to his job and the woman helps him as she is able.

According to Amar, it is certainly not believed that men and women could apply themselves with the same amount of intensity and have the same objectives in the study of certain subjects. In the same way, it is said that they should not be educated side by side in the same university or school, nor could they even study the same subjects. With respect to the differences between men and women, she believes that women should know how to do certain work that men would not be able to do, such as sewing or spinning. Similarly, governing the house is women's work, and the household would suffer if they did not tend to it:

> Let us not form an unrealistic plan, let us only try to rectify as much as possible what has already been established. In this case, women will cultivate their knowledge without any detriment to their obligations because, first, it can contribute to making the yoke of marriage smoother and more agreeable; second, it can help them perform their respectable duties as mothers of families; and third, it is knowledge that can be useful and advantageous at all stages in life. (72)

The formative plan that Josefa Amar proposed was certainly not an unrealistic one, as we shall see in the pages that follow. The plan was formulated according to known patterns that placed a special emphasis on moral education, customs, and women's domestic skills. Attention to physical education was, however, a noteworthy novelty. Above all, we should appreciate Amar's intention to expand women's education to the fullest degree. She proposes an expansive program that can adjust itself according to the range of possibilities of women's education. Lastly, it is important to point out that she believes that physical and moral education should also help women to achieve social prestige, moral autonomy, and personal happiness. In the following text, the author establishes a relationship between the development of the intellect, morality, and happiness: "The perfect education is composed of two parts—physical and moral. The first part is because of its relationship with the robustness of the body, necessary for the course of life and its functions. The latter organizes knowledge and customs, which is the only method of acquiring true and constant happiness" (75).

In the *Discurso sobre la educación física y moral de las mujeres* Amar dedicates several pages to the importance of moral development and the habits of women. She also talks about family and domestic responsibilities and the skills that all women should learn in order to fulfill these responsibilities. Lastly, she strongly recommends the study of literature according to women's ability and social stature. She also comments upon women's need to dedicate themselves to specific tasks, such as following determined paths of study. All of these ideas inform her recommendations for advanced studies for those girls who are capable:

> It is not intended that all women indiscriminately study and learn the subjects that will be discussed, first because it would not be convenient for all women to distract themselves so much from housework and second, and most importantly, [because] not all women are equal in their level of intelligence and application, which is also true with men. It is said, justifiably so, that one can find an equal amount of talent in both sexes, but that does not imply that all individuals have the same amount of talent. . . . Therefore, we are talking only about those women who, without neglecting the particular obligations of their sex, can and want to dedicate some time to their own enlightenment. (170–71)

Amar divides her book on education into two parts. The first part deals with physical education, whose declared objective is good health. It was already accepted that good health was necessary for working-class men and women who had to do physical labor; however, in her book Amar directs her attention to the good health of ladies, who needed to give birth to and raise robust children, helping to maintain their strength and health. The author laments that in Spanish culture physical strength is neither valued nor encouraged in women. Women, like children, are expected to be weak. It is accepted that women will become frightened for whatever reason or cry frequently, thus becoming cowardly and fearful, incapable of recognizing true dangers. According to Amar, weakness is particularly unsuitable for women, because children learn to make the same mistakes that their mothers made (81). Without physical education for women, society will lack strong and even-tempered mothers capable of giving birth and managing the care and health of the family.

Amar's interest in the health and physical and moral strength of women corresponds with the enlightened desire, held by the intellectual and political elite of the time, to increase and preserve the population. She was just as concerned about the care and improvement of public health, from which she wanted women to be able to benefit. Amar refers to the necessity that women, including older women, learn to take care of their bodies and their health, focusing on the particulars of their diet, hygiene, pregnancy, child rearing, and childhood illnesses. The topic of breastfeeding, which she supports, constitutes an important part of her section dedicated to children's health. As evidenced by her bibliography, which shows a great amount of erudition with regard to these issues, she appears to be cognizant of the new ideas that were circulating in progressive medical literature at the time.[1]

The second half of Amar's book is dedicated to moral education, which is understood first and foremost as a type of character building, as well as the development of traditional morality and of customs that are appropriate to young ladies. Amar refers to values and feelings that it is appropriate to develop in young girls. She refers to her pedagogy, showing the modes in which girls should be directed in order to develop the appropriate moral habits. She stresses the need to depend on the will of the students, who should receive instruction in self-awareness as well as in the rules of decorum that society demands of them. A young woman should know what is expected of her and be willing to accept the restrictions society places upon her. A special emphasis is placed on learning about religion, and she discusses how it should be taught and the readings that should support religious learning.

In all of her recommendations—from the study of home economics, to the study of languages, literature, philosophy, geography, and in some cases mathematics—Amar makes known her opinions about certain models of education. She distances herself from an education model that gives preference to sensibility and good taste, favoring instead a model based on cultivating the spirit and requiring meditation and domestic retreat. An example of this would be a well-educated father requiring his daughter to put forth a greater effort than would be expected of young women destined for a social life. Amar translates the contemporary French writer La Chapelle DuPuy as follows:

> Until now, I have not asked you to do anything but apply yourself to your reading, music, dance, and drawing: these things are good in themselves, but they are also important because of their relationship to education, like milk to the body; and even though I do not want you to neglect any of these areas, it would be regrettable for me to have taught you them if you would content yourself with this. It is reasonable that you have other, loftier considerations and other, more dignified work. (194–95)

For Josefa Amar, these considerations are none other than the study of languages and literature, which illustrate the understanding and belief in solid knowledge, which should continue and be useful throughout the life of each woman. Music, dance, and writing satisfy the youth, but they cannot be performed in old age, nor do they satisfy the spirit. To illustrate that, Amar quotes Mme de Lambert: "How fortunate it is to know how to live with oneself, to leave oneself behind violently, and then find oneself again with pleasure! Then one does not desire the hustle and bustle of others" (195). Amar concludes, "Thus spoke the celebrated Marquise Lambert, who knew the human heart completely" (195).

The influence of this celebrated Frenchwoman is evident elsewhere in Amar's book. In the last chapters, for example, Amar expresses the same concerns and moral demands that Lambert expresses. She reviews what are believed to be the vices and passions of women, among them being vanity (which leads them to exaggerate their finery and adornment), excessive curiosity, and the lack of modesty, among others. She also points out the inappropriateness of these behaviors and the need to repress them. Amar recognizes that beauty and good taste can be valued in women and that sex and class oblige women to adorn themselves. However, following her moral ideology, Amar recommends teaching girls moderation in their dress and use of cosmetics.[2]

Amar does not hold back when, like the moralists she cites, she points out the vices of women. She backs up her stance with quotes from well-known authors who are reputed to be strict moralists, such as Luis Vives and Fray Luis de León. She adds that women are no more evil than men and that vices can be found in men just as in women. Even so, Amar says, females seem to deserve the criticism they receive, because they enjoy flattery, they are excessive in their unnecessary talk, and they are interested in trivial topics. Vengeance, curiosity, and a tendency toward extreme love are thought to be passions most commonly associated with women. Nevertheless, Amar trusts that education will improve women's condition. She warns that in order for moral education to be effective and model good behavior, women should start when they are young, "when desires are more lively and hasty, when judgment is weaker, and the lessons of life are lacking, which can only be learned from the experience that adults have. Work and application will serve to occupy the spirit, and above all the beautiful painting of virtue and the disagreeable and ugly painting of vice" (211–12).

The same enlightened ideology that was circulating in other texts and authors from the end of the seventeenth through the eighteenth century is undoubtedly inscribed in Amar's writing. Far from denying women's education, these texts reclaim it to serve the purpose of preparing women to fulfill their obligations, which they assume are both natural and specific to them. Amar does not deny these points, but goes into them in great depth. She points out, as did the sources she cites, the importance that was conceded to the formation of female morality and habits. Along the same lines, Amar examines domestic issues, indicating the objectives of this type of education, which are to contribute to moral order and produce the well-being and happiness of families. Nevertheless, Amar, like Madame de Lambert before her, stands by her radical and politically charged argument in defense of women in literature and that literature can be taught and dominated by certain women. She does not deny the difference between the sexes, but she does not portray it as rigidly as other texts do. She insists that men and women are equally talented and that education plays an important role in the progress of women's morality. She does not want women to be constrained in their intellectual interests or in the areas of knowledge toward which they are disposed. They understand that education should provide women with greater moral autonomy, helping them to free themselves from the power and tyranny of men who attempt to assert themselves and feel superior. Education equalizes the sexes and contributes to a greater social and power equilibrium with men.

In her texts, Amar acknowledges the social issue that attributes to women a greater responsibility and obligation in the area of morality and customs. She admits the need for women to practice the norms of restraint and modesty, which are assumed to be supremely feminine virtues and obligations. In this sense, her proposals have an archaic and severely moralistic air, which might seem merely inherited from the past. Even so, there are many differences. Many of the male authors whom she cites distrust the will and moral action of women, insisting on the social obligation that binds women. The female authors, on the other hand, trust that women could, with the help of a good education, develop the necessary will and responsibility, as is manifested in the cases of the distinguished women whom Amar mentions. Certainly, in some passages Amar presents women as more morally secure and capable of morally governing themselves than certain men. Men do not feel the same type of social pressure, which often gravitates toward women. She complains about the *differences* between the sexes in this respect, pointing out that social norms excuse and release men from responsibility in regard to certain obligations that women have to fulfill. This often applies to sexual morality and to a commitment to strong feelings with respect to religion and family. Furthermore, this greater responsibility and moral demand that must fall on women is not perceived as it should be, as showing greater merit and as a way of distinguishing women who have particular qualities. Amar restates that women are obliged to practice virtue, as are men, but that men can display their merit and are recognized for it, while women's moral values will normally remain hidden between the walls of the home.

In their writings concerning the polemic about women's talent and education, both Josefa Amar and the earlier Madame de Lambert sought to produce the highest level of studies possible in that time period.[3] Both refer to women whom they value for being educated and cultured. However, Amar's defense of women in literature openly contradicts the new model embodied by Sophie in *Émile*, the educational work of Jean-Jacques Rousseau.[4] Rousseau's ideas were shared by many enlightened Spaniards of the time who publicly revealed their shock at women who attempted to achieve the same type of intellect as men, claiming that nature had designed them for other purposes. As the French pedagogue had written in his day, a woman should learn how to use a needle, not a pen. Rousseau's Sophie should receive a moral and domestic education. Literature, arts, and science are reserved for Émile, the man, whom Sophie should complement.[5]

In Spain, Rousseau was not cited directly, since his *Émile* was prohibited. However, his ideas were circulating and were shared by modern intellectuals who could view with a certain distance the educational goals of certain women, such as Josefa Amar, who wanted to achieve, if not equality between the sexes, then at least a similar level of knowledge, merit, and intellectual and governing ability as men. Amar certainly provides sufficient evidence to justify the studies that she proposes for women. For example, she provides the rhetorical proof that men and women are equally talented and that women with special abilities, such as herself, excel in their studies. She does not hide her unease with the negative effects caused by the new ideas that excessively emphasize the differences between the sexes, which might be inflicted on women who want to learn. Educated women such as herself either were not known about or were looked down upon intellectually by modern followers of Rousseau in Spain as well as in France. In this case her complaints and her radical demand for greater equality in the study of the arts and sciences are understandable.[6]

Many enlightened individuals in Amar's social environment, male and female alike, seemed to internalize a model that was closer to Sophie, the sentimental and moral woman, than to the cultured and educated woman. Cultured and educated women were looked down upon in the literature of their time and were considered, as the late Molière had described them, curious and nosey. Josefa Amar does not seem totally averse to the model that proclaims, if not the intellectual and moral difference between the sexes, then at least the inequality of the sexes when it comes to certain functions, and as a result she supports the idea of separating and differentiating women's education from men's education.

NOTES

1. See López-Cordón; and Bolufer Peruga.
2. These ideas are expressed throughout chs. 9–11 in pt. 2 of Amar's *Discurso sobre la educación*.
3. Anne-Thérèse de Marguenat de Courcelles, the Marquise de Lambert, wrote two influential works on education: *Avis d'une mere à son fils* (1726) and *Avis d'une mere à sa fille* (1728).
4. In her bibliography, Amar makes an indirect reference to Rousseau's *Émile* by recommending another French book on education, *Émile Chrétien, ou de l'education,* which Amar states is "the opposite of the *Émile* of Rousseau" (263).
5. See Morant Deusa, "Hombres."
6. See ibid.

WORKS CITED

Amar y Borbón, Josefa. "Discurso en defensa del talento de las mujeres . . ." (1786). In *La educación popular en España en la segunda mitad del siglo XVIII*, by Olegario Negrín Fajardo, 162–76. Madrid: Universidad Nacional de Educación a Distancia, 1984.

———. *Discurso sobre la educación física y moral de las mujeres*. Ed. María Victoria López-Cordón. Madrid: Cátedra, 1994.

Bolufer Peruga, Mónica. *Mujeres e Ilustración: La construcción de la feminidad en la España del siglo XVIII*. Valencia: Diputació de Valencia, 1998.

DuPuy La Chapelle, N. *Instruction d'un père à sa fille . . . sur les plus importants sujets concernant la religion, les moeurs, et la manière de se conduire dans le monde*. Basel: Jean Schweighauser, 1766.

Lambert, Mme de. *Oeuvres de Madame la Marquise de Lambert, rassamblées pour la première fois*. Amsterdam: Campagnie, 1747.

López-Cordón, María Victoria. Introduction to *Discurso sobre la educación física y moral de las mujeres*, by Josefa Amar y Borbón, 9–49. Madrid: Cátedra, 1994.

Morant Deusa, Isabel. "Hombres y mujeres en el espacio público: De la Ilustración al liberalismo." In *Orígenes del liberalismo: España, Europa, América Latina,* ed. Ricardo Robledo, Irene Castells, and María Cruz Mateo, 124–61. Salamanca: Universidad de Salamanca, 2003.

———. "Mujeres ilustradas en el debate de la educación: Francia y España." *Cuadernos de Historia Moderna* (Universidad Complutense de Madrid) 3 (2004): 59–84.

Rousseau, Jean-Jacques. *Oeuvres complètes*. Ed. Louis Barré. 12 vols. Paris, 1856–57.

4

Margarita Hickey's Guide to the Traps of Love

MARÍA A. SALGADO

Concerns about the overtly sexist codes of Spanish culture became part of Enlightenment Spain's public discourse after Padre Benito Feijoo (1676–1764) opened the debate in 1726 with his essay "Defensa de las mujeres" (Defense of Women).[1] Margarita Hickey y Pellizoni (1740?–1801?) came of age and composed her numerous poetic and dramatic writings during these "feminist" times. Not much is known about her life, though Constance A. Sullivan offers a general outline that places her birth in Palma de Mallorca. The date is imprecise, however; Manuel Serrano y Sanz sets it in 1753, but Sullivan dates it about 1740. Her father, Domingo Hickey, was a captain in the Edinburgh Dragoons, and her mother, Ana Pellizoni, belonged to an Italian family of singers. Margarita grew up with her two brothers and probably moved to Madrid in 1759 with her husband, an older man named Juan Antonio Aguirre (1703–mid-1770s) who was a well-to-do member of the lower nobility *(hidalgo)*. She bore a son who did not live long and adopted a girl, María Teresa. By 1779 Hickey was a widow, a still young, bright, and attractive woman. She belonged to the literary group known as the Montiano Circle, and Sullivan quotes sources that suggest that she was romantically involved with another member, the prestigious writer Vicente García de la Huerta (1734–87).

Hickey never remarried, choosing to spend her time in the pursuit of literature, writing, and publishing, sometimes under the name Antonia Hernanda de la Oliva, other times using her initials, M.H. After several unsuccessful petitions to get her work published, she published a book containing her poetry and a translation of Racine's *Andromaque* but disguised her authorship under the unassuming label "Una Dama de esta Corte" (A Lady of this Court).[2] Other works she wrote were unpublished, such as her ambitious poem "Descripción geográfica e histórica de todo el orbe conocido hasta ahora" (Geographic and historical description of all the world known until now), which was rejected by the Academy of History.³ Others, such as the manuscript of the second volume of her works, appear to be lost. The last year of her life that can be documented is 1801, when she wrote her last will and testament.

Hickey's writing was highly acclaimed in her day, but as has happened to most women writers, she was quickly forgotten. In fact, when Leopoldo de Cueto published his critical history of eighteenth-century poetry in 1893, he did not know her true identity, only her initials, M.H. Cueto praised her, nonetheless, explaining that during the reign of Fernando VI (1713–59) there was an important woman poet who in 1789 published some of her works under the name "A Lady of this Court." According to Cueto, the intellectuals of her time admired and applauded her, comparing her to Cristobalina, a woman poet celebrated by Lope de Vega. Cueto adds that since she was unknown outside literary circles, her name was forgotten; only her initials remained (2:272–73). Today, "M.H." has been identified as Margarita Hickey.

In the following pages I look at the poems of Margarita Hickey in her collection *Poesías varias sagradas, morales, profanas o amorosas con dos poemas épicos* (Various Sacred, Moral, Profane or Love Poems, with Two Epic Poems), published by the royal press in 1789, especially those that speak of women's experiences within the phallocentric codes of behavior that ruled relationships between men and women in eighteenth-century Spain. The book's title page serves as an index, providing information about its contents and those of the unpublished second volume. In this first volume we find her translation of *Andromaque*, a long poem to General Cevallos, and a collection of shorter poems titled "Poesías varias," which elaborate the general themes of love, amorous behavior, daily life, and human weaknesses and virtues. A reading of these poems reveals that they follow the didactic and direct approach favored by the Enlightenment aesthetics of *enseñar deleitando* (teaching while delighting). Their formal characteristics also reflect the variety of verse forms then in vogue. Despite this commonality, however, they are very dissimilar from most poems found in canonical texts in that the speaking voice is that of a female. The use of a feminine voice to express the love experiences of upper-class women and to deal with the complex patriarchal world in which they lived distinguishes these poems from the typical love poetry that dominated neoclassical verse. It is this feminine voice and her unique experiences that I examine, seeking to establish how an Enlightenment feminist viewed amorous relationships and the strategies she used to validate her voice.⁴

Love poetry is as old as literature, and its conventions are deeply entrenched and often male oriented. No one knew this better than Hickey. In a *romancillo* dedicating her book to a male friend and explaining her intent,[5] she admits as much by stating that her *poesías* are a direct answer to Ovid's art of love:

> Hallarás en ellas
> documentos finos
> de amar noblemente
> con afectos dignos:
> No de amar un arte
> como la de Ovidio,
> que más que de amor
> es arte de vicio.
> —(411)[6]

> You will find in them
> fine documents
> on how to love nobly
> with worthy affection:
>   Not an art of love
> like Ovid's
> which more than of love
> is an art of vice.

Hickey does not limit her feminist subversion to rejecting the Latin poet's highly erotic *Ars Amatoria*. She also convincingly subverts the discourse of the more modern and entrenched convention of courtly love by deconstructing its deceiving, highly elaborate baroque metaphors, effectively poetizing the straightforward everyday language of neoclassical aesthetics.[7] The most overt examples of this technique are her glosses of Luis de Góngora's (1561–1627) "Guarda corderos zagala" (Keep the Lambs Young Shepherdess) and Lope de Vega's (1562–1635) "Aprended flores de mí" (Flowers, Learn from Me). Hickey's rewriting of Ovid's male-centered art of love and her glosses of these two love poems make evident her strategy of validating her voice by placing her poems within a very canonical tradition. She was indeed conscious of the literary context within which she wrote and of the parameters her feminist discourse had to overcome.[8] Yet women's subversion took on new forms in eighteenth-century Spain, when questioning the status quo became the main aim of poetry and the aesthetics of *dulce et utile* provided feminists the ideal tools for carrying out their protest.

In discussing the theories of Spanish neoclassical poetry, Nigel Glendinning highlights the dual nature of the movement:

> Relevance, utility, and the pleasures of the senses are the major preoccupations of the eighteenth-century poetic theorists. "Aprovechar deleitando" is the aim of poetry in Luzán's terms. This is in part a reaffirmation of Horace's "Dulce et utile," although it also extends the classical ideal. The artist should ultimately subordinate art to politics, namely to the common good. Yet, strictly speaking political utility is rare in eighteenth-century Spanish poetry. (60)[9]

Poetry was shaped by this utilitarian desire to bring about a well-defined social and literary reform, and its verses were instrumental in the Enlightenment's project of modernizing Spain. Enrique Rull argues that the concept of *buen gusto* (good taste) inspired these authors to adopt topical disguises of exterior reality as well as of psychological and natural reality (17), turning the pastoral form into a social and literary convention that favored topics related to civic and human virtues as the Enlightenment understood them (23).

Hickey too wrote within the pastoral form on themes centered on civic and human virtues. It is also important to note that in addition to these elements, her poems introduce a very different and decidedly feminist political agenda. Unfortunately, nineteenth-century critics read her works as the writings of a woman scorned, a man-hater reminiscent of the *mujer esquiva* (aloof woman) common in Golden Age drama. Melveena McKendrick defines this stereotype as a woman who, "for some reason, is averse to the idea of love and marriage. As a natural outcome of this, she is usually, though not invariably, averse to men as well" (115). McKendrick attributes the construction of this character to man's inability to conceive that a woman could possibly dislike men (145).

Men's attitudes toward liberating women, or rather their representations on the stage, underwent some pragmatic changes during the Enlightenment, according to Kathleen Kish, but the basic sexist premises remained, since the concern of male dramatists such as Leandro Fernández de Moratín was not "to champion women's rights as a goal in itself but rather as a side effect of the advocacy of their real purpose: social stability" (186–87). The view that woman was determined by her nature to be attracted to man and marriage was the norm in Spanish culture.[10] It is thus not surprising that those critics who read Hickey's poetry viewed it as a product of her bitterness at having been rejected by men rather than as the conscious efforts of a feminist who wanted to reform the love customs of her day. Her decision not to remarry was similarly viewed as resulting from her rejection by men.[11] Serrano y Sanz's reasoning, including his suggestion that as the young widow of an old man Hickey could hardly wait to throw herself into the arms of any man who courted her, was typical of her male critics:

> [By 1779] D[oñ]a Margarita calls herself a widow. Young, beautiful, and with a rare imagination, she must have been courted and she must have responded with enthusiasm, as women do when they have only known the winter of love, represented by an old husband, in the flower of their youth. Her dreams were followed by disappointments, which she lamented in verses that were perhaps prosaic in their form but full of intense suffering, as one who translates to paper the bitter experiences of life. (506)

Although Serrano seems sympathetic to Hickey's plight as a woman and criticizes here the practice of forcing young women to marry old men (also a popular topic for many eighteenth-century male writers, such as Leandro Fernández de Moratín), his comments on Hickey's poetry are stereotypically chauvinistic. Notwithstanding Serrano's opinion, her lack of bitterness is obvious in the previously quoted *romancillo,* where she states that she writes of "how to love nobly / with worthy affection." Further evidence of her poetic intentions is found in the book's prologue, where Hickey comments that she publishes her translation of *Andromaque* to counter the negative influence of other translations, especially their misinterpretation of love. Other translations depict "loves that are sickly sweet, insipid and fastidious, in which the lovers and their beloved mutually melt with love without any result or benefit, because their loves are not directed toward any heroic goal with a good lesson" (xii). But she reveals her intention in the title of her translation of the seventeenth-century French work:

> Andromaque, / Tragedy by Mr. Racine, / Translated to / Castilian, to which

(in case it was represented) [and] according to the vogue in this country, / was given the following title: *No love is better / in noble and heroic souls, / than the love of glory and fame*. In contrast with that of the other very faulty *Andromaque* that is frequently represented in the Court, with the well-known title *There is no love that can equal / The love of a mother*. (xv)

Hickey also states that the examples of love in her poetry represent lessons she has learned in daily life. She emphasizes that her poems reflect personal experiences and suggests their exemplary nature: "I have not sought to hurt anyone with them, and only the variety of the cases and happenings that have made me see, know, and observe the dealings and relations of the world and of people [has] given me reason and occasion for the different subjects and topics with which I deal" (xiv). Her insistence on the importance of her experience as a means of knowledge—an integral aspect of the Enlightenment's epistemology—is central to the strategy she uses for legitimizing her feminist discourse through her poetry.

Examples of good love and indictments of worthless and dishonest love abound in Hickey's poems. In several instances these topics are suggested in the very title. Several extol the happiness and satisfaction brought about by love in an honest relationship, but many more give advice on how to recognize types of amorous behavior she condemns as reprehensible. In addition to poems on amorous subjects, she includes another category dealing with topics of human and civil interests. There are also poems written to celebrate the special festivities of Christmas and New Year's Day with "greater dignity," a eulogy to the death of a famous actress, and a brief pastoral novel in verse on the theme of man's inconstancy.

Margarita Hickey insists that daily experience has taught her about the traps of love, amorous misbehavior, and weaknesses of human nature that she reports. Some of these experiences were probably personal, but many others must have been lived through her relationships with friends and acquaintances. They indicate that she was a convinced feminist but never a man-hater, although some of her views on men's misbehavior and women's unhappy condition might lead readers to such a conclusion. The examples of reprehensible behavior and of the unequal relationship between the sexes that she describes in the two *décimas* presented below[12]—"Definiendo la infeliz constitución de las mugeres en general" (Defining the unhappy constitution of women in general), and "Definición de los hombres, en cuanto al género y manera de su querer quando aman, ó dicen que aman" (Definition of men, in regard to the kind and manner of their love when they love, or say that they love")—represent a summary of the list of male trespasses and female woes that she highlights in her poems:

"Definiendo la infeliz constitución de las mugeres en general"

> De bienes destituidas,
> Víctimas del pundonor,[13]
> Censuradas con amor,
> Y sin él desatendidas,
> Sin cariño pretendidas,
> Por apetito buscadas,
> Conseguidas ultrajadas,
> Sin aplausos la virtud,
> Sin lauros la juventud,
> Y a la vegez despreciadas.
> —(216–17)

> Destitute of goods,
> Victims of their sense of honor,
> Censored when in love,
> And neglected without it,
> Courted without being loved,
> Sought after by desire,
> Scorned after obtained,
> Without applause their virtue,
> Without laurels their youth,
> And despised in old age.

"Definición de los hombres, en cuanto al género y manera de su querer quando aman, ó dicen que aman"

> Son, monstruos inconseqüentes,
> Altaneros y abatidos,
> Humildes, si aborrecidos,
> Si amados, irreverentes;
> Con el favor insolentes;
> Desean pero no aman;
> En las tibiezas se inflaman;
> Sirven para dominar,

>   Se rinden para triunfar,
>   Y á la que les honra infaman.
>   —(217–18)
>
>   They are, inconsequential monsters,
>   Haughty and dispirited,
>   Humble, if rejected,
>   If loved, disrespectful,
>   If favored insolent;
>   They desire but do not love;
>   In indifference they become inflamed,
>   They are good for controlling;
>   They surrender to win,
>   And they defame the one who honors them.

Anyone reading only these two poems would certainly get an unbalanced impression of Hickey's ideas on amorous relationships and might tend to agree with Serrano about her bitterness and dislike of men. However, a deeper reading reveals that Hickey is describing from a feminist perspective the actors and the stage on which love relationships took place in her day. This reading is confirmed by poems that indicate that she sought an equal relationship between the sexes, such as the *seguidillas* explaining her criticism of men.[14] The principal reason for her position is men's insistence on being treated differently simply because they are men:

>   Pues que pretenden,
>   En amor diferencias
>   Que no se deben.
>   Que para eso son hombres,
>   Dicen muy necios,
>   Como si acaso el alma
>   Tuviera sexô.
>   —(190)
>
>   Since they pretend,
>   Differences in love
>   That have no place.

> That they are men,
> They say very foolishly,
> As if by chance the soul
> Had a sex.

Hickey's lack of bitterness is evident also in "Eulogy and praise of true love," where she makes clear her genuine appreciation of honest love, a highly spiritual and definitely married love. Married love is another theme on which once again Hickey departs from the male-centered view of canonical love poetry, as well as from the realities of daily life. Ovid's *Ars Amatoria*, courtly love, and the *cortejo* customs of her day clearly functioned outside the parameters of marriage.[15] Hickey's praise of married love may at first appear to make her poem part of the official Enlightenment campaign to promote social stability by reinstating the prestige of marriage. Nothing could be further from the truth, however, since it soon becomes obvious in this and other poems that Hickey is going against the official line. In fact, her feminist views were no doubt part of the problem the government was trying to control. Hickey begins her poem by placing love on a pedestal and quickly clarifies that she speaks of honest love, which she describes as a divinely inspired feeling—a "divine flame"—that unselfishly unites two souls in decent bonds from "the sacred hall / to the brilliant earth":

> ¡Oh amor, de las pasiones
> del hombre, la mas hidalga,
> la mas noble, la mas digna,
> la mas regia, la mas alta!
> . . . .
> Hablo del amor honesto,
> de aquella divina llama
> que del sacro consistorio
> a la tierra destellada,
> Uniendo en decentes lazos
> de un casto afecto las almas
> hermosea y vivifica
> la naturaleza humana.
> —(255)

> Oh love, of all man's passions
> the most illustrious,
> the most noble, the most worthy,
> the most regal, the highest!
> . . . .
>   I speak of honest love,
> of that divine flame,
> which from the sacred hall
> to the brilliant earth,
> Uniting the souls
> in the chaste affection of decent bonds,
> beautifies and comforts
> human nature.

Hickey's admiration for true love notwithstanding, other stanzas of this poem show that she was convinced that because of man's untrustworthiness this ideal love could not be attained. In a *romance* explaining whether loving and being loved produces the contentment most people proclaim, she affirms that this consensus is indeed true, but she hastens to add: "¿Pero dónde encontraremos / esa Fenis aplaudida? / ¿dónde esa feliz Arabia / está, que esas aves cria?" (273). [But where will we find / that applauded Fenix? Where is that happy Arabia / that produces such birds?"] She conjectures that perhaps such beings did exist in a past, mythical golden age; today, however, a woman only finds ungratefulness, perfidy, bad faith, infidelity, inconsistency, and lies. She suggests that one way of handling man's ungratefulness is to enjoy the flirting and never go beyond. Content yourself, she advises,

> Con la espuma solamente
> y solo la florecita,
> de los contentos y gustos
> con que el sagaz amor brinda:
>   Que consiste en ser amadas,
> deseadas, pretendidas,
> y sin querer a ninguno,
> verse de todos querida:
> —(271)

> With only the foam
> and only the little flower,
> of the contentment and pleasures
> that a shrewd love offers:
>   That consists in being loved,
> desired, pursued,
> and without loving anyone,
> see oneself loved by everyone:

Another, obviously more radical way in which she proposes to deal with the traps of dishonest lovers is to avoid men altogether: "Y en tan conocidos riesgos / la sola prudencia dicta / el evitarlos y huirlos . . ." (273–74). [And with such known risks / prudence dictates / to avoid them and run away from them. . . .] Hickey imparts her advice assertively, but she must have realized that avoiding men altogether, or not going beyond the flirting stage, was not practical in the real world. She therefore offers a third possibility in a *romance* extolling the "Ladies of Madrid" and women in general. She praises Madrid's women before going on to commiserate with them for the mistreatment they suffer when men take advantage of their good faith:

> Sexô hermoso, combatido
> sin piedad con furia tanta,
> á pesar y sin embargo
> de creer vuestras fuerzas flacas,
>   Por contínuos enemigos,
> que con soverbia arrogancia,
> . . . .
>   Continuamente os acechan,
> y suponiendoos incautas,
> de la Buena fe abusando
> os sitian, cercan y asaltan:
> —(228)

> Lovely sex, fought
> without pity, and with such fury,
> even though and despite

> believing your strength to be weak,
>   By constant enemies,
> that with proud arrogance,
> . . . .
>   Continuously lay in wait for you,
> and assuming that you are unwary,
> abuse your good faith
> besiege you, surround you, and assault you:

Hickey next assures women that she loves them and has written her poems to help them. She adds that her texts reflect her experiences and will teach them to deal with their lovers' treachery. The author, she says,

> hoy ofrece á vuestras plantas.
> Estos mal formados rasgos
> de sus poesias varias:
> . . . .
>   En las quales, al impulso
> de prolixas meditadas,
> continuas observaciones
> del hombre y de sus mudanzas,
>   Ha sacado las pinturas,
> que en ellas van dibuxadas
> con el buen fin y deseo
> de que al verlas, al mirarlas,
>   Precaviéndoos advertidas,
> en otras escarmentadas,
> contra enemigos tan fieros
> sepais defenderos cautas:
> —(229)

> puts at your feet today.
>   These ill-constructed verses
> of her various poems:
> . . . .
>   In which, moved

by meticulous thinking,
[and] continuous observation
of men and their inconstancy,
  [She] has drawn the pictures,
that are painted in them,
with the good goal and wishes
that upon seeing them, looking at them,
  Prudently warned,
learning from others,
against such fierce enemies
you will know how to cautiously defend yourselves:

Hickey concludes by suggesting her third option. If women enter a relationship, they must train men to become worthy of their love. That is, women must make men realize that they cannot be loved until they change:

Y el que quiera gloriarse
de que le estiman, le aman
. . . .
  Ha de saber adquirirse
discreto dichas tan altas,
y finalmente el que amado
ser quiera, amado se haga.
—(232)

And the one who wants to boast
that he is esteemed, loved
. . . .
  Must know how to acquire
discreet such high happiness,
and finally the one who loved
wants to be, must make himself be loved.

Hickey's insistence that man needs to become trustworthy before he can be loved indicates her deep-rooted conviction that love relationships are doomed because of man's arrogance. Most of her examples of man's selfishness highlight topics from the courtly-love tradition, especially those that refer to men's behavior while seeking women's favor. These poems unveil in a direct language the dangers hidden behind the gifts, the amorous language, and the obsequiousness of would-be lovers. There are also examples of the abhorrent behavior men exhibit after securing their dominance. The *endechas* in which she advises a nun against leaving the convent to get married are exemplary.[16] Hickey contrasts the unselfish, devoted love of a husband like Christ with the untrustworthy love of a human in order to underline the most salient faults of marriage. She begins with a series of rhetorical questions highlighting the speaker's reluctance to understand the nun's behavior:

>¿Qué aprehension? ¿qué desdicha?
>¿qué locura? ¿qué engaño?
>¿qué necia fantasia?
>¿qué ansia? ¿qué error? ¿qué encanto
> Te fuerza á que te apartes,
>tan fiel Pastor dexando,
>de aprisco tan seguro,
>de tan constante amparo?
>—(299)

>What apprehension? what wretchedness?
>what madness? what deception?
>what foolish fancy?
>what longing? what error? what enchantment
> Forces you to leave,
>abandoning such a faithful Shepherd,
>such a secure sheepfold,
>such steady shelter?

She next asks whether the nun, Filotea, has considered the good things she is rejecting in favor of the deceits and bitterness found in worldly relationships. How can she compare, Hickey asks, the calm, repose, peace, stillness, tranquility, pleasure, and gifts of her loving heavenly Husband with the risks of entering the tempestuous, stormy, changeable sea of marriage? She offers as proof of her arguments in favor of convent life two witnesses, Rita and Teresa of Ávila. Rita's wish to become a nun was opposed by her parents, who preferred that she marry;

she acquiesced and found only "hardships, sorrows, / unpleasantness, bitterness / and grief" (303). Her misery was such that her husband agreed to her entering a convent. Mystical experiences made Teresa realize the profound unworthiness of this world, where all is "misery, slime, and revulsion" (305). In case these saintly experiences fail to make Filotea realize the peace and contentment of her life, Hickey offers examples of bad human marriages. She first reminds Filotea of her Husband's perfection:

>Tu esposo, Filotea,
>Es hermoso, es bizarro,
>Es noble, es rico, es cuerdo,
>Es poderoso, es sabio:
> Es constante, seguro,
>Valiente y esforzado;
>—(907)

>Your husband, Filotea,
>Is handsome, is dashing,
>Is noble, is rich, is prudent,
>Is powerful, is wise:
> Is constant, certain,
>Brave and courageous;

Hickey follows the lengthy description of the Husband's divine attributes with a question that cleverly introduces the answer through an even lengthier list of weaknesses associated with human husbands:

>¿Sabes por quien le dexa
>tu necio y ciego engaño,
>por quien todo es miseria,
>pobreza, tierra, barro,
> Inconstancia, locura,
>inconseqüencia, enfado,
>beleidad, ignorancia,
>sobervia, desacatos;
> Falacia, alevosia,

> perversidad, engaño,
> mentiras, asechanzas,
> traicion y doble trato?
> —(309)

> Do you know for whom
> your foolish and blind deceit leaves him,
> for whom all is misery,
> baseness, mud,
>   Inconstancy, madness,
> inconsistency, annoyance,
> fickleness, ignorance,
> arrogance, disrespect;
>   Fallacy, malice,
> perversity, fraud,
> lies, tricks,
> treason and double dealings?

Fearing that this abstract list may not be persuasive enough, Hickey describes specific cases of abuse at the hands of husbands as she attempts to show Filotea that she may be leaving Christ for a man whose insane jealousy may lead him to kill her based on a suspicion of infidelity:

> . . . fiero,
> desconocido, ingrato,
> en pago de los gustos
> que en gozarte ha logrado;
> . . . .
>   A la menor ofensa,
> Al mas ligero agravio
> Que los zelos le finjan,
> Furibundos é insanos,
>   A una leve sospecha
> De ofendido, vengarlo
> á costa de tu fama
> y vida quiera ayrado:
> —(310)

> . . . haughty,
> changed, ungrateful,
> to repay you for the pleasures
> that he has enjoyed by possessing you;
> . . . .
>   At the least offense,
> At the slightest insult
> That jealousy feigns,
> Raging and insane
>   At a trifling suspicion
> Of having been offended, he will avenge it
> at the cost of your fame
> and your life:

Another example warns Filotea against allowing any man to own her. Men abuse their power, forgetting that marriage is an equal partnership:

>   Evita de los hombres
> El dominio tirano, . . .
> Avasallar pretenden
> Á la que el cielo santo,
> Por noble compañera,
> No por esclava ha dado
>   Advierte que son muchas
> Las que gimen debaxo
> De las iniquas leyes
> Del hombre y de su mando:
> —(311–12)

>   Avoid men's
> Tyrannical rule, . . .
> They seek to subdue
> The one that heaven,
> Has given him as a noble partner,
> Not as a slave:
>   Notice that many are the ones

That moan under
The unjust laws
Of man and his rule:

The poet concludes by asking Filotea to excuse her lengthy advice, which was needed to help her understand that only God is good and only he deserves to be faithfully loved.

Hickey's defense of women and her feminist advice are eloquent, but her praise of women is not absolute. She recognizes that women too can benefit from lessons in civility and unselfish behavior. She criticizes some of these faults in a satirical *romance* condemning human weaknesses. She specifically attacks the vain efforts with which ugly women attempt to look pretty and the affected aloofness and disdainful attitudes of beautiful women. More condemning is her criticism of women whose lack of education and moral values makes them place material possessions above all else:

> La Dama poco instruida,
> Mal impuesta en los deberes,
> Y en las heróicas virtudes
> Que al bello sexô competen;
>   Locamente enamorada,
> Y atraida futilmente
> De los que llamó un discreto
> Embustes resplandecientes,
> Cree, que donde no hay presentes,
> Donde no hay gala, no hay trenes,
> Coche, libreas, equipages,
> . . . .
> el mérito y la hermosura,
> ni parece ni merece:
> —(401–2)

The ill brought up Lady,
Badly informed of the duties,
And of the heroic virtues
That are incumbent upon the fair sex;

> Foolishly in love,
> Uselessly attracted
> By what a wise person called
> Shimmering lies
> Believes that if there are no presents,
> No displays, no lavishness,
> Carriages, liveries, baggage,
> . . . .
> worthiness and beauty
> have no prestige and no merit:

After criticizing this ignorance, Hickey offers her model of correct behavior, embodied in the Roman lady Cornelia, whose children were her greatest treasure:

> Estos son, pues, mis tesoros,
> Mis galas, mis ricos muebles,
> Mis diamantes, esmeraldas
> Y mis preciosos haberes:
>   Con cuya heróica respuesta
> Cornelia discretamente
> Á su huespeda enseñada
> Dexó, á distinguir de bienes:
>   Y á saber en adelante
> Diferenciar sabiamente
> Los reales y verdaderos,
> De los que son aparentes:
> —(407)

> These are, then, my treasures,
> My ornaments, my rich furnishings,
> My diamonds, emeralds
> And my precious holdings:
>   With this heroic answer
> Cornelia discretely
> Taught her guest

> To distinguish between possessions:
>   And to know from then on
>   How to wisely differentiate
>   The real and true ones,
>   From those that are apparent:

My reading of Margarita Hickey's *Poesías varias* underlines that they can be used as a guide to woman's behavior and to man-woman relationships. The traps of love she unmasks aptly summarize her experiences in the arena of love and human relations in late eighteenth-century Spain. She criticized stereotypical weaknesses legitimized by the rituals of courtly love. She also aimed to expose the underside, the real-life experiences behind canonical amorous discourse. This inversion allowed her to highlight the plight of real people who suffered some of the most salient abuses and inequalities identified with amorous relationships. The abused and neglected wife, the deceived young girl, the abandoned woman, the jealous lover or husband, the philanderer, the arrogant seducer, the fortune hunter, the avaricious old man, the bragging Don Juan—these are the real-life characters that hide behind the elaborate metaphors with which male amorous discourse has traditionally seduced women. By exposing the human misery masked under male patriarchal discourse, Hickey's poems teach of human experiences that are valid across time and space. The fact that her verses still can be read today with as much delight and benefit as they provided when she first wrote them says much about the artistry and eloquence of her expression and the passion with which she conveyed her feelings. It is thus valid to conclude that Margarita Hickey's neoclassical strategy of replacing the deceitful, baroque language of courtly love with the pragmatic discourse of an Enlightenment woman was doubly successful. On the political level, it spread her feminist message criticizing the inequalities of men and women in love, while on the literary level it poeticized her life experiences in the straightforward language of everyday speech.

NOTES

1. While others before him, such as Teresa of Ávila, Sor Juana Inés de la Cruz, and María de Zayas, had called attention to men's unfair treatment of women and defended (often their own) feminine intellectual abilities, Feijoo was the first in Spain's Enlightenment period to argue for women's equality and to speak to the importance of women's experience. See Coughlin.

2. The title page of *Poesías varias* repeats that the author of the poems is "Una Dama de esta Corte," adding that they are published by "M.H." Her initials also appear on the official documents granting her permission to publish her poem to Cevallos. This coy strategy of placing her initials in key sections of the book allows her to remain anonymous while offering a clue to her authorship.

3. Women's difficulties in dealing with the Spanish academies have been well documented. One of Hickey's contemporaries noted in the *Literary Report* that the gentlemen of the academy "are convinced that the talents of women are inferior to those of men" (Flores and Flores 77).

4. I read Hickey's voice keeping in mind the context Susan Snider Lanser sets up for women's narrative: "I maintain that both narrative structures and women's writing are determined not by essential properties or isolated aesthetic imperatives but by complex and changing conventions that are themselves produced in and by the relations of power that implicate writer, reader, and text. In modern Western societies during the centuries of 'print culture' with which I am concerned, these constituents of power must include, at the very least, race, gender, class, nationality, education, sexuality and marital status, interacting with and within a given social formation" (5–6).

5. The *romancillo* derives from the *romance*, a poem structured in an indeterminate number of eight-syllable lines with vocalic rhyme in the even numbers.

6. In quotations I reproduce the original orthography. All translations are my own.

7. In her dedication Hickey, like her neoclassical male colleagues, emphasizes favoring a direct, clear, simple language (422).

8. Hickey joined an impressive line of women writers who treated the problems of love and male-female relationships. Among the writers from Spain and Spanish America, one of the most outstanding examples is María de Zayas (1590–1661/69), who in her *Novelas amorosas y ejemplares* (Amorous and Exemplary Novels), of 1637, warns women about men's treachery and denounces the abuses and injustices they suffer. Equally subversive were the "feminist" poems by the Mexican Sor Juana Inés de la Cruz (1651–95). Outside of the Spanish world, Hickey might have known also the highly influential *Carte du Tendre* (Map of Tenderness), contained in Mme de Scudéry's (1607–67) novel *Clélie* (1654–60), which expresses a variety of love feelings and charts the way to a woman's heart.

9. *Aprovechar deleitando*, "to take advantage while delighting," is another formula for *enseñar deleitando*. Despite Glendinning's assertion to the contrary, the numerous political works in defense of women written by Hickey and other contemporary feminist poets question his conclusion.

10. McKendrick finds that men of the seventeenth century believed in natural law: "[W]oman was created of man in the Garden of Eden to be his helpmate; on the temporal level he is therefore her first cause and the final end; love and marriage are her birthright; toward them her entire nature is directed, and in them she finds her fulfillment. To this natural law no woman, unless she has a religious vocation, is an exception, and the foolish, misguided woman who considers herself immune to love, who claims to dislike men, or who prefers to avoid matrimony, must therefore be led, or driven, back into the path of sanity and reason—and true happiness" (116–17). These ideas, she adds, were not "mere dramatic platitudes; they were seriously held by the men of the age" (117).

11. Hickey stresses the importance of a woman's freedom while giving advice against marriage: "Never place your faith in anyone, / Maintain your hand free, / Flee the inhuman bond, / That the most obsequious lover / Is, when transformed into a husband, / An insufferable tyrant" (216).

12. A *décima* is a poem of ten eight-syllable lines.

13. An exacerbated code of honor strongly associated with Golden Age theater.

14. A *seguidilla* is a poem of either four- or seven-line stanzas, popular and frequently humorous, sung or used as an accompaniment for dancing.

15. Martín Gaite loosely defines the *cortejo* as a custom in which an upper-class husband allowed his wife, more or less tacitly, to establish a relationship with a particular man, who had free entrance into the lady's home supposedly to help the lady in her dressing room, advise her in matters of style, accompany her to church and the theater, bring her gifts, and entertain her with his conversation (xiv). See López-Cordón's discussion of this custom in chapter 6 of this volume.

16. *Endechas* commonly express feelings of sadness. They use a repeated metric combination arranged in six- or seven-syllable lines, often assonant. In Hickey's poem, the pastoral setting follows neoclassical conventions as well as those of mystic poetry, particularly Juan de la Cruz's (1541–91) and Teresa de Ávila's (1515–82).

WORKS CITED

Coughlin, Edward V. "The Polemics of Feijoo's *Defensa de las mujeres.*" *Dieciocho* 6 (1986): 74–85.

Cueto, Leopoldo Augusto de. *Historia crítica de la poesía castellana en el siglo XVIII.* 3 vols. 3rd ed. Madrid: Sucesores de Rivadeneyra, 1893.

Flores, Ángel, and Kate Flores, eds. *Poesía feminista en el mundo hispánico (desde la Edad Media hasta la actualidad): Antología crítica.* Mexico City: Siglo XXI, 1984.

Glendinning, Nigel. *A Literary History of Spain: The Eighteenth Century.* London: Ernest Benn, 1972.

Hickey, Margarita. *Poesías varias sagradas, morales y profanas o amorosas: con dos poemas épicos en elogio del Capitán General D. Pedro Cevallos: Obras todas de una dama de esta Corte.* Madrid: Imprenta Real, 1789.

Kish, Kathleen. "A School for Wives: Women in Eighteenth-Century Spanish Theater." In *Women in Hispanic Literature: Icons and Fallen Idols,* ed. Martha Miller, 184–200. Berkeley and Los Angeles: University of California Press, 1983.

Lanser, Susan Snider. *Fictions of Authority: Women Writers and Narrative Voice.* Ithaca, NY: Cornell University Press, 1992.

Martín Gaite, Carmen. *Usos amorosos del dieciocho en España.* Madrid: Anagrama, 1994.

McKendrick, Melveena. "Women against Wedlock: The Reluctant Brides of Golden Age Drama." In *Women in Hispanic Literature: Icons and Fallen Idols,* ed. Martha Miller, 115–46. Berkeley and Los Angeles: University of California Press, 1983.

Rull, Enrique. *La poesía y el teatro en el siglo XVIII: Neoclasicismo.* Madrid: Altea, Taurus, Alfaguara, 1987.

Serrano y Sanz, Manuel. *Apuntes para una biblioteca de autoras españolas desde el año 1401 al 1833.* Biblioteca de Autores Españoles, 268–71. 1903. 2 vols. in 4. Facsimile ed., Madrid: Atlas, 1975.

Sullivan, Constance A. "A Biographical Note on Margarita Hickey." *Dieciocho* 20.2 (1997): 219–29.

5

Illustrating Sainthood
The Construction of Eighteenth-Century Spanish American Hagiography

ELISA SAMPSON VERA TUDELA

Where does one see that profound ennui, those pale and wasted bodies, all those symptoms of Nature languishing and eating away at itself?
—DENIS DIDEROT, *La religieuse*

Beauty, grace and spirit are jewels which are not valued; all admiration is kept for experience, maturity and wisdom.
—FRAY BENITO JERÓNIMO FEIJOO, "Carta de un religioso a una hermana suya," 1726

The difficulty of thinking about convents and nuns in the context of the Enlightenment is easily illustrated by invoking Diderot's 1760 novel *La religieuse*. Enclosed against her will, the heroine is subjected to the degradations and perversions that Diderot believes are the consequence of removing women from the world and placing them in the cloister. Though perhaps not as vivid in their representations of convents, most French and English Enlightenment thinkers agreed that as institutions they lay somewhere between prisons and madhouses and that the nuns themselves were active perpetuators of ignorance in society (Hufton 12; Choudhury). Thus it is rather surprising to find that in Spain the situation was somewhat different. The epigraph from Feijoo, in which it is clear that the cloistered woman possesses a number of qualities precisely because of her lack of experience of the world, would seem to contradict Diderot. Moreover, apart from Feijoo, two other important exponents of Enlightenment thought in Spain, the author and statesman Gaspar Melchor de Jovellanos (1744–1811) and the social and educational reformer Pablo de Olavide (1725–1803), were also positive about the role that nuns and convents could play in the society of *luces* (Bolufer Peruga).

This essay focuses on religious women during the Spanish American Enlightenment, a movement that has traditionally been disregarded, considered "colonial" in the most derogatory sense. By studying the apparently insignificant subjects of nuns and convents in the Spanish American colonies as exemplified in the confessional letters of an eighteenth-century Mexican nun, Sor Sebastiana Josefa de la Santísima Trinidad (ca. 1700–1757), I seek to reevaluate their significance and formulate an interpretation of the Spanish American Enlightenment that takes them fully into account. Through a study of these texts and their context, I seek to recover the precise language of an eighteenth-century debate about religion, subjectivity, and gender in colonial Spanish America rather than imposing a largely alien critical vocabulary on it.

Over the last thirty years there has been a push to think of the Enlightenment not only as an intellectual construct or an ideology but also as a culture or a project in which modernity took shape.[1] This change of focus has brought positive results for the study of women and the Enlightenment in particular, allowing them to be seen as playing an important part in it.[2] The groundbreaking work that has emerged as a result usually draws a fascinating picture of, among other developments, the flowering of women-run salons and the growth of a female press and of female literacy more generally. All this would seem naturally to exclude nuns as subjects for study, and even the philosophes excluded them for being aristocratic, archaic, and removed from the world. However, the two principal reasons for this exclusion of nuns—the Enlightenment's perceived secularizing character and its supposed privileging of experience as a category of knowledge—do not adequately describe the character of the Enlightenment in Spain and its colonies.[3]

In terms of secularization, descriptions of the milieu have often been very culturally specific, referring almost exclusively to a French context. According to this interpretation, the Enlightenment was a time bomb set to go off in France in 1789 (Haakonssen 1). In the Hispanic world—and, one would assume, in other contexts also—developments could have been somewhat different, and indeed in recent years research has called into question most aspects of this interpretation of the Enlightenment, leading to a proliferation of enlightenments geographically and culturally and to a profound questioning of the role of secularization in eighteenth-century thought.[4]

The relevance for the Hispanic Enlightenment of these new interpretations of the role of religion is elegantly alluded to in Eduardo Subirat's discussion of the etymology of the Spanish word meaning "to enlighten": "*Ilustrar* is equivalent, then, to interior inspiration and illumination, to a divine dawning of light, and it thus designates the process of a mystical experience" (16). Subirats underlines that these meanings are almost entirely absent from the word in English, German, or French, and he uses this fact to construct a comparison between the eighteenth century in Spain and in the rest of Europe. For Subirats, in the Hispanic context, the "new" Enlightenment is inescapably caught in the "ancient" *iluminismo.* By focusing on his linking of *ilustración* and *iluminismo,* and by establishing the historical fact that some of the great exponents of *iluminismo* in the Hispanic world were women (many of them nuns), I argue that the discourse of religious women must necessarily be part of any investigation into *ilustración.*

With regard to the second reason for excluding nuns from a study of the Enlightenment—its privileging of experience—the invocation of mystical experience as central to *iluminismo* and thus to *ilustración* is a good starting point for contesting the exclusion. In the classic interpretation of the Enlightenment as overwhelmingly secular, convents and nuns were clearly unwelcome reminders of the *ancien régime:* institutions and people that failed to fit into the increasingly narrowly defined (and gendered) spheres of public and private and the realms of experience that were licit in each. If we question this characterization of the Enlightenment in the Hispanic context, however, then we are also obliged to reassess categories of experience and to include religious experience. For Theresa Ann Smith, the dichotomy between faith (private) and reason (public) needs to be challenged in the Hispanic context. Smith calls for a new language in which to describe the Hispanic Enlightenment, one that avoids loaded terminology formulated to describe the Enlightenment in France, England, and the United States (6).

Scholars have concentrated on the role of eighteenth-century convents mainly as educational institutions or as havens where intellectual women could produce enlightened writings.[5] But as we shall see in the case of Sor Sebastiana, it is in the most traditional of conventual spiritual writing—the confessional letter and the hagiography—that we can learn about the Enlightenment in the periphery of the Hispanic world.

The eighteenth century was the time of Bourbon reforms in Mexico, and in July 1770 the crown ordered a complete report on the church in America.[6] The new Bourbon administration made it clear that it considered convents in the New

World, and in Mexico in particular, to be sinking ever deeper into a mire of impious customs, corrupt administration, and luxurious indolence. From keeping too many servants, to wearing ornamental habits, including bracelets and silk veils, to allowing men (workers, boys, etc.) unrestricted access to the cloister, the criticisms laid at the door of American nuns were damning (Lavrin, "Ecclesiastical Reform"). As a result, convents were ordered to reform. The principal form this took was the imposition of what was known as the *vida común*. This meant in effect the enforcement of vows of poverty, and in Mexico strict Capuchine rule was imposed on all convents. The tremendous upheaval in terms of religious observance embodied in the *vida común* reform was made more complex by the fact that in strict economic terms the eighteenth century was a period of expansion and success for many convents, in stark opposition to the situation of many male religious orders and their institutions (Brading, *Church and State* 82–102).[7]

Thus, Sor Sebastiana was writing at a time of tumult and change, as well as achievement for female religious orders and institutions.[8] She herself was a successful heroine who seems to have had something of a cult already attached to her persona before her death. Two years after Sor Sebastiana's death her brother, Miguel de Maya, a Franciscan friar, donated sixty of her letters to the abbess of the convent of San Juan de la Penitencia, where Sor Sebastiana had professed and lived. He then commissioned Father José Eugenio Valdés to write a hagiography of his sister, and it is these letters Valdés uses as his primary source. His text was published as a magnificent hagiography of the nun in 1765, financed in part by Sor Sebastiana's devotees.[9] Sor Sebastiana was promoted by Valdés as a particularly virtuous *criolla* nun, an exemplar of piety with which to vindicate the orthodoxy—spiritual, cultural, and political—of this sector of colonial society.[10]

The sixty letters Sor Sebastiana wrote to Valdés, which run to three hundred closely written folios, show that although the normal condition of being a woman in this period prohibited or at the very least circumscribed access to writing, being a nun seems to have *enforced* writing upon certain women.[11] The extant letters are very coherent in structure and fairly repetitive, and they contain transcriptions of verse written by the nun. Although Sor Sebastiana used a thematic template provided by her confessor and her poetry is derivative of devotional forms, the individuality of the language and tone of the writing rules out any mechanical copying, and it is this voice and its possible relation to enlightened discourse that I explore here.

Sor Sebastiana's writing belongs to a tradition of works carried out by women in order to fulfill a vow of obedience and are intimately related to the sacrament of penance and the practice of confession. The audience for this kind of writing was very particular, however, and most nuns certainly never saw their manuscripts go into print.[12] The circumstances of Valdés's reworking of the letters were very different. His intention was clearly to publicize Sor Sebastiana's saintliness and to give impetus to her request for beatification. The economic, social, and even spiritual advancement that a successful "local" saintly cult could effect has been well documented (Vauchez; Christian). The New World was no exception in this and in some ways could be said to be more needful than anywhere in the Old World of indigenous saintly cults in order to supplement its imported relics and devotions and more broadly to prove the success of the evangelical mission.

Valdés's annotations and addenda serve to place Sor Sebastiana in a tradition both of writing and of saintly predecessors. He is precise about the spiritual methods she follows, reproducing the sections of St. Ignatius of Loyola's *Spiritual Exercises* (1541) that she found most useful. Sor Sebastiana's devotion to this kind of *oración metódica*, as it is called by Andrés Martín, is counterpointed by her reading of Pedro de Alcántara, one of the main exponents of a more contemplative style of prayer, whose works were censored in the Index of 1558.[13] In fact, Valdés links Sor Sebastiana not only to Alcántara but also to Catherine of Bologna, Saint Teresa of Ávila, Madre Ágreda, Marina Escobar, and Madre María la Antigua, each of whom had come under censure from sections of the ecclesiastical hierarchy which wanted to eradicate any traces of *iluminismo* in the saints carried to the altars. The fact that in her letters Sor Sebastiana also describes her devotion to the more reputable spiritual methods of Loyola (which were championed by the Counter Reformation church) saves her from the charge of exhibiting a contemplative style "para mujeres de carpinteros" (for the wives of carpenters), as Fernando de Valdés, the composer of the 1558 Index, contemptuously characterized this kind of spirituality (Bataillon 702).

Thus it seems clear that there was some attempt, mostly by her confessor, to prove that Sor Sebastiana's spirituality was "modern"—the term *ancient* was used for a discredited mystical tradition. It bears mentioning that it is unclear whether modern was any more "enlightened" in this context, but perhaps the point here is the juxtaposition of the two models and their gendering: the orthodox Counter Reformation spirituality, embodied by Loyola, and the discredited mystical tradition, embodied by a catalog of women.

However much Valdés is at pains to point out the canonical and orthodox base of Sor Sebastiana's spiritual and literary genealogy, it is apparent that the Mexican nun also belongs to a tradition, if not of *mujeres de carpinteros* specifically, then certainly of *mujeres* in general. More and more critical work has been devoted to tracing this predominantly female literary and devotional tradition, which, if not officially indicted as heterodox, certainly remained marginal to the main tradition (McKnight, Myers). The narratives of these writing women reveal a "community of mutual readership among nun writers that spans centuries and oceans" (McKnight 2). One of the most influential books in relation to the female tradition in the Hispanic world continues to be Arenal and Schlau's *Untold Sisters*.[14] This work was among the first to investigate the notion of a female literary community sharing a common language. The authors coined the expression *mother tongue* to refer to the work of influential women—"mothers"—in a literary and religious tradition that they argued grew "largely separated, although partly parallel to the culture of men" (2).

This tracing of women's texts across geographical and cultural boundaries offers a significant and valuable critical option, allowing women's writing to be located within a female textual lineage. In relation to convent writing, however, we must be wary of thinking of writing nuns as an isolated community. The *vida* in particular, when written by women, is distinguished as a literary genre by its *mediated* nature, and there was little sense in which the nun's cell could be considered "a room of her own." This is especially true of the writings directed toward such a public end as canonization. Moreover, the majority of the "mothers" available as models for writing nuns were women whose own work had been authorized by men as worthy of emulation. This mediation, even with regard to models, in a tradition that could be argued to be partially parallel confirms that convent writing, like the convent itself, might be a woman's space but it was inserted into a largely man-made world.

The motif of reform, which we have already touched on in relation to the *vida común* controversy, illustrates this imbrication of the "female" sphere of the convent with the "male" sphere of the public world and the resulting mediation, at both real and rhetorical levels. It has become something of a commonplace to claim that the convent in this period was like a "microcosm through which all the unavoidable tiny details of everyday life throbbed, as well as the most exalted moments of desire for divine union with God" (Lavrin, "Cotidianidad" 204; Vigil). In the hagiography of an individual nun like Sor Sebastiana, living in a community of nuns, the narrative of the quotidian was necessarily one of division and conflict.

Quite apart from the historical motives for representing reform so evident in eighteenth-century Mexico, there were also formal, rhetorical imperatives pushing our would-be saint Sor Sebastiana to represent reform in her life story. The would-be saint had to stand out from her community. Thus, Sor Sebastiana declares that during her short sojourn in the convent of Bethlehem while waiting for a more suitable patron and dowry she was deaf and blind to all manner of ceremonies, music, and plays:

> When I was in Bethlehem there were great ceremonies, visits by archbishops and the viceroy, and the convent was adorned with elaborate decorations, music and gracious masques, dances and many entertainments. All this was done with such good taste that most noble people, who appreciated such graciousness, came to the convent. Of all this I neither heard nor saw a thing. The disturbances that were caused by such things upset me, but I said nothing, knowing that I was there as if I did not exist; useless, not serving any purpose amidst these ladies. Little notice was paid me, and this was a great comfort. (Santísima Trinidad, legajo 22, fol. 117)[15]

What is striking here is Sor Sebastiana's use of the stereotype of enclosed femininity and experience. As a "good" nun, Sor Sebastiana finds the convent too open to experience and proceeds to construct her own cloister from her body (denying the power of her senses) and her mind (escaping reality into contemplation). Moreover, the description of the "bad" nuns and convent is an intensely clever piece of rhetoric, with Sor Sebastiana showing herself to be fully in control of the artifice she deploys. Her declarations of complete humility before the other nuns serve instead to set her above them in her glorious and saintly desire for abjection.

This frank account of the cloister as fragmented by conflicting emotions and desires is a representational strategy that strikingly reveals the great passions and dislikes awakened by Sor Sebastiana's individual approach to spirituality and by her confessed desire for sainthood. Sor Sebastiana reports that one of the nuns dislikes her so much that she insults her with a torrent of abuses, claiming that she is an "argumentative manly woman" who misleads people so that they will take her to be a saint. Sor Sebastiana adds dryly that while this nun "called me so many things she very rarely called me by my name" (legajo 55, fol. 339).

These strategies of marking difference in the cloister are not at all unusual for this type of literature (Certeau 25). What is remarkable about Sor Sebastiana is the emotional charge, the passion inherent in the saintly voice being individuated.

For example, in her description of the process of writing itself, she tells us that it involves a kind of attention to past experience that obviously places a strain on her.[16] In a striking image, her thoughts seem to her a labyrinth in which she loses all hope and explodes with impatience: "Sometimes I don't see how to understand my own labyrinth of thoughts where all hope is lost . . . it's impossible to understand how so much can fit into my thoughts, so that my head is bursting and I feel I will lose my equanimity" (legajo 42, fols. 263–64).

These moving descriptions of the grim reality of confessional writing practices provide significant insights into the cloistered environment, which encouraged self-reflection and constrained women to narrate their "selves" by ordering them to write down their experiences. General confession had been instituted as an annual sacrament by the Council of Trent, thereby making it, along with the practices associated with it, a privileged method of religious acculturation. Confession involved the priest, and more generally the ecclesiastical authorities, in a dialogue with an individual, whose boundaries came to be redefined precisely by this process of constructing and narrating the passing of time and the actions that occurred in such temporal space.[17]

The minuteness of these *exámenes de consciencia* that Sor Sebastiana put herself through in order to write her confessional letters and their status as "evidence" in the trial of her spiritual authenticity and candidacy for sainthood are clear.[18] The trope of writing as suffering was clearly intended to secure belief in the writer's words by invoking the Christian tradition associating martyrdom with spiritual enlightenment. In this context, Sor Sebastiana's pain is the guarantee of her truth. Her emotional exclamations are often of despair or inadequacy, and in one particularly dramatic instance a self-condemnation and accusation of heresy. Sor Sebastiana could not have been unaware of the resonance of such vocabulary in this context, and her use of it reveals a confidence in her own ability to manage the codes governing the representation of spiritual experience. Emotion certainly enjoyed a privileged position among these codes, but Sor Sebastiana's expression of it remained problematic. Holy women in particular were in danger of being accused of feigning or simulating, and the invocation of strong emotion as the touchstone of feminine truth constituted something of a paradox. Nevertheless, it remained a convincing argument and the preferred way of expressing the truth of feminine spirituality—much more telling (and without a doubt more likely to capture a reader's attention) than a defense of the nun's pious reading and her knowledge of religious practice would have been.[19]

The radical impetus that such displays of emotion could embody, however much they were harnessed toward orthodox ends, is most vividly apparent in Sor Sebastiana's assertion of her desire for sainthood—"Oh, How I wish I were a saint!" (legajo 10, fol. 74)—though it is certainly not confined to this wish. Sainthood was conferred by the ecclesiastical authorities and was certainly not something a humble nun ought to desire. She could desire saintliness—*ser santa*—but not to be a saint—*ser una santa*. Behind what might seem a dry semantic point lay the threat posed to ecclesiastical authority by a nun's candid self-expression and the dangers she exposed herself to in expressing this desire. Sor Sebastiana not only wanted to be a saint, she also wanted an evangelical mission for herself, imagining that she possessed a knowledge that should be communicated: "With what yearning my soul desires to preach this truth to everyone and especially to all nuns, for I am pained to see them so concerned with possessing temporal things" (legajo 31, fol. 173). Although Sor Sebastiana modified her wish from wanting to preach to all people to wanting to evangelize nuns in particular, her assertion remained impossible to reconcile with the Pauline injunction that women should remain silent in church.

For Sor Sebastiana, the necessary accompaniment to such masterful desires and will was an equally strong sense of self-doubt. This was not as paradoxical as it first appears, for both positions required a defined sense of self to begin with. Thus, Sor Sebastiana's repeated wish for self-destruction can be interpreted as a tribute to the existence of such a self in the first place. It is certainly often formulated in the language of personal desire and will: "and that I do not carry out the wish that I have to throw and smash myself down the stairs . . . in the choir and during the Holy Office, I want to throw my prayer book I am so strongly taken by guilt" (legajo 4, fol. 32). A similarly positive reading can be given to her yearning for solitude and a hermit's life: "I am tormented at not being able to be in a deserted place, among animals, where my complaints could fly and breathe in the fields without fear" (legajo 5, fol. 38).

Once more, it is their emotional power that rescues these declarations from pure destructiveness. In the following letter, for example, the disgust and anger toward her own failings is such that Sor Sebastiana describes herself as reduced to rabid bestiality and idiocy. Nevertheless, the strong and shocking rhetoric of this description works to provide exemplary proof of the opposite, of the power of her desire for perfection: "I am at points ready to lose patience and speak nonsense and let myself be lost, for nothing is of any good to me. I am so furious in my rebellion and wickedness that I give out snorts like the most rabid beast, all the while suffering such dreadful anxiety it leaves me mindless" (legajo 37, fol. 221). A similar rhetorical move is to be found in what is perhaps her most climactic expression of despair, in which she excommunicates herself and defines herself as unchristian: "Remaining in this idiocy as if I were not a Christian, being certain that I could not be saved in this extreme state" (legajo 60, fol. 358).

I would argue that Sor Sebastiana's use of such extreme vocabulary reveals an extraordinary mastery of spiritual politics and, paradoxically, of her own orthodoxy. Her confidence in her spiritual self is often most visible in her relation to evil and the devil, where she can display her strength without any need for restraint. Sor Sebastiana's challenge to evil is based on the protection God affords her as a pious subject, and so she issues a defiant order to the devil, addressing him in the familiar second person, something she would probably usually reserve for children and servants: "I know you, so go [*Ya te conozco, anda vete*], you'll get nothing from me, for my Lord, who raised me and is my master, will defend me with his divine power and I should not fear, and I am subject to his divine will" (legajo 53, fol. 329).

In the narrative of her spiritual experiences, with God on her side, Sor Sebastiana is free to indulge in such assertions of her power over evil. What is so extraordinary is that, as we have seen, she also hazards such statements outside this safe narrative realm, not only in moments of self-reflection but also in the narration of her relationships with her confessors.[20]

Like the majority of her contemporaries, Sor Sebastiana repeatedly acknowledges the confessor's superiority, indulging him with phrases of formulaic modesty and humility in her writing. Simultaneously, however, in the particularly small and insignificant matter (as she ironically puts it) of the progress of her own soul to salvation, she declares that she, and only she, is privy to the truth (legajo 3, fol. 25). These kinds of comments in her letters, stating her unhesitating autonomy from her confessors, constitute perhaps her most surprising assertions of selfhood, understood as a sense of an individualized desire or emotion, mounting a challenge not only to ecclesiastical but also to sexual hierarchies. The men who oblige Sor Sebastiana to write must subsequently deal with the real consequences of her "self": her individuality and freedom in spiritual matters:

> This peace and calm lasted only a few days, my soul entering such a storm of regrets that I could not understand my desolation. I felt so much anger against you my Venerable Father, as if you were responsible for all my

pains, though unaware of all that was happening to me. I cannot describe the bitterness that my soul suffered; my heart was pierced by pain, so much so that I could do nothing because of the anxiety. I was so suspended that I could not say a word or pray, having such a wound in my heart that I cried out. I knew it would be better not to confess to you, Father, for I was sorry that in my foolishness I had told you these sins and everything else when there was no need if I was not to proceed. So I was ashamed, and also of the fact that my things seemed wicked to your grace, and if I were to go back to you I would not get any consolation, for I would say only what was necessary, the rest being dangerous. Suddenly I felt such disgust for the father of my soul that I wanted to insult him with bad words. I was like a gentile. (legajo 26, fol. 146)

In this instance there is almost a sense of the carnivalesque in her writing, a world where a woman gives her opinion of learned men and feels disgust for their opinions and finally even perhaps for God, since the last "father of my soul" invoked by the nun could be either her confessor or God himself. Moreover, according to her own words the strength of the emotion is such that it can make a gentile out of her.

The interest in studying this extraordinary and apparently transgressive voice, with its assertions of myriad emotional states, from need, to anger, to distress and exultation, is more than simply documentary, though this of course is a legitimate and valuable aim in itself. In Joan W. Scott's terms, Sor Sebastiana's voice and its inflection by emotion demonstrate the role of gender as a useful category for the historical analysis of the Enlightenment in colonial Spanish America. If we consider Sor Sebastiana's letters and the voice they represent, it would appear that cloistered women were permitted a surprising degree of liberty and autonomy.[21] The key idea here is that writing actually empowered nuns, despite the various limits it simultaneously imposed.[22] We should resist the temptation to idealize the cloister as a parallel or separate feminine sphere, however. There is, particularly in the case of some interpretations of the Enlightenment that see it as overregulating other feminine spheres such as the home and family, a strong scholarly desire to find in the convent a haven from such interference.[23] However, as has been argued previously, there is overwhelming contextual and historical evidence to show how "permeable" cloisters in Mexico were to the outside world in the eighteenth century.[24] Everything, including the representation of self, is negotiated in the convent.

From the very first hagiographies of women to eighteenth-century ones, spiritual women negotiated a difficult road, often leading to their being designated a heretic or hysteric. It was this perilous narrative path that Sor Sebastiana chose to follow in her writings. The emphasis on emotion and feeling that has emerged as a trademark of her figuration of herself becomes then even more significant, for it was around this theme that she built her defense of her spiritual practice, and consequently it is around emotion and feeling that the normally rigid form of hagiography can be seen to bend and adapt. While the changes are minor in scale, and the piety expressed in her writings remains very much a Tridentine legacy, the emphasis on subjective reaction and emotional memory could be construed as linked to changes in the notion of sensibility and experience that are at the heart of a gendered understanding of the Enlightenment project in the Hispanic world.

Spiritual discourse resumes the constellation of sensibility and experience that was a central preoccupation of the Enlightenment. At its heart is an attempt to think through the opposition between mind or spirit and body that was also central to the eighteenth-century intellectual debate, and both discourses certainly share a strikingly similar conceptual vocabulary. Mystics (real and imagined) were never really far from the thoughts of many philosophers, and Diderot in *Sur les femmes* (1774) invokes Pythia and the priestess at Dodona to remind us that "religious and poetic enthusiasm had long been part of the same family" (Sherriff 55). He also flags the dangers posed by these inspired women, women whose spiritual discourse "carries them away" and culminates in their challenging authority and transgressing sexual boundaries. In the eighteenth century, suspicion and fear of mystics did not so much demonize as medicalize them, but the essence of the exclusionary logic remained the same: feminine sensibility predisposed women to these delusions.[25] For this reason, we would do well to read Sor Sebastiana's transgressive voice with caution, for although her invocation of emotion may indeed seem enlightened, it remains fundamentally tied to her biological femininity in her own and, more significantly perhaps, Valdés's representation of it:

> And in many of her letters, though she may be dealing with many different points, she comes out with this kind of exclamation, for her zeal is all fire and catches light everywhere, not containing itself in her breast.... [I]t comes out of the margins of her eyes, lips and hands—the latter crossed and gesturing like [those of] one who humbly begs; cheeks streaming tears and mouth spilling tender words. (229–31)

The powerful excess of emotion is transmuted by Valdés from voice to fluids and other matter (tears and fire). These overflow the margins not only of Sor Sebastiana's letters but also, significantly, of her body, which is figured as the medium that expresses this passion. It would appear that ultimately emphasis on emotion or passion for women returns them to a notion of femininity overwhelmingly defined by biology.[26]

The Enlightenment was a time of tremendous intellectual and cultural ferment, and as Mónica Bolufer Peruga's work on sensibility demonstrates, notions of gender were also subject to flux. Therefore, even the very small variations registered by Sor Sebastiana's transformation of hagiography are tremendously significant. Though perhaps it is premature to define this Mexican nun's "vida" as an "Enlightened hagiography" it is only by exploring the forced pairing of such unlikely terms in these kinds of writing that we may be able to think more precisely and more creatively about what Subirats describes as "this religious and mystical dimension [which] cannot be separated from the philosophical understanding of the Enlightenment" (16).

NOTES

1. See Darnton.

2. Among those who have argued for the importance of women to the Enlightenment are Dena Goodman and Ruth Graham. See also Kerber for the American context; and Bolufer Peruga and Smith for Spain.

3. Peter Gay studies the Enlightenment's aggressively secular character—"the rise of modern paganism"—and its promotion of experience as the only viable source of knowledge.

4. See Pocock's *Barbarism and Religion*, with its central suggestion that the Enlightenment was first and foremost a movement to protect civilized society from the resurgence of religious extremism, along with David Sorkin's work on Reform Catholicism in the Holy Roman Empire as a genuinely independent movement with significant social and political impact.

5. See Morand's discussion of Hore in chapter 2 of this volume for an example of the convent as a liberating space. For an overview of teaching orders, see Hufton.

6. For a general introduction to the "enlightened" nature of these reforms, see Rodríguez Garza and Gutiérrez Herrera.

7. For more on convent life and the controversies over convent reform in eighteenth-century Mexico, see Muriel; and Sampson Vera Tudela.

8. For Lavrin ("Ecclesiastical Reform"), the period was one of incredible economic and political expansion. Anthony Wright considers eighteenth-century Mexican convents to be the most extreme example of the "integration of religious and civil life" in the Catholic world, with nuns retaining their personal income and convents making loans at interest and employing lay agents (142).

9. In *Colonial Angels*, 35–54, I examine the interplay between Valdés's and Sor Sebastiana's writing on the same subject (her life) in order to explore the nun's relation to broader colonial writing practices. See also the appendix for excerpts from Sor Sebastiana's letters and translations of them.

10. A *criollo* is someone of Spanish blood born in the Americas. See Alberro for a concise introduction. For general background on the relationship between different racially determined groups in eighteenth-century New Spain, see Brading, *Church and State*, *Classical Republicanism*, and *First America*. For *criollo*'s use and significance in a convent setting in the New World, see Sampson Vera Tudela, 14–34.

11. The original manuscripts are in the Biblioteca Nacional, Mexico City, and are numbered. They are cited by letter number and folio.

12. The most obvious exception to this generalization in New Spain is of course Sor Juana Inés de la Cruz.

13. The first hagiographies of Loyola, by Pedro de Ribadeneira (1526–1611) and Giovanni Pietro Maffei (1536?–1603), respectively, are now generally considered to have exaggerated the militant side of Loyola's character and work.

14. For the strength of the Hispanic tradition, see also Surtz. On Saint Teresa in particular, see Bilinkoff; and Weber.

15. All translations are mine.

16. Sor Sebastiana often expresses the pain and depression she suffers (legajo 41, fol. 253; legajo 5, fol. 38).

17. For McKnight, "[a] study of the *vida espiritual* demands a specific engagement with the emergence in early modern Europe of the phenomenon of human subjecthood: the human capacity and responsibility for naming and determining self" (19). Although clearly nuns wrote themselves into what McKnight describes nicely as idealized and ideologized models, she argues that there was still room for maneuver and individuation.

18. See Vauchez for the growing importance of forensic categories in the narration of saints' lives by this period.

19. This whole argument can be viewed as a variation on the theme of *docta ignorantia*, according to which the nun's discourse is emptied of agency and authority: she is simply the mouthpiece of the divine.

20. The archetypal relationship is that between Catherine of Siena and her confessors. Interestingly, the mutability of and uncertainty about sexual authority is integral to the archetype.

21. This insight has been at the heart of scholarship on nuns and convents in both the European and American contexts by, among others, Jacobsen Shutte, McKnight, Lavrin, Myers, Arenal and Schlau, Burns, and Medina.

22. Weber calls this the "rhetoric of femininity" in her study on Saint Teresa.

23. See Mack on the negative impact of the Enlightenment.

24. For the most recent account of relations between the cloister and the outside world in the period, see Lehfeldt.

25. The classic reference is Certeau, but see also Beatriz Quintanilla-Madero's discussion of hysteria in chapter 9 of this volume.

26. As Smith shows eloquently in her study of Spanish women translators, playing the emotional

card alongside the rational one in the eighteenth century ultimately "undermined the attempt to make women equal citizens of a liberal state based on rational, public debate" (14).

WORKS CITED

Alberro, Solange. *Del gachupín al criollo o de cómo los Españoles de México dejaron de serlo.* Mexico City: Colegio de Mexico, 1992.
Arenal, Electa, and Stacey Schlau. *Untold Sisters: Hispanic Nuns in Their Own Works.* Albuquerque: University of New Mexico Press, 1989.
Bataillon, Marcel. *Erasmo y España: Estudios sobre la historia espiritual del siglo XVI.* México City: Fondo de Cultura Económica, 1966.
Bilinkoff, Jody. *The Avila of St. Teresa: Religious Reform in a Sixteenth Century Convent.* Ithaca, NY: Cornell University Press, 1989.
Bolufer Peruga, Mónica. *Mujeres e Ilustración: La construcción de la feminidad en la Ilustración española.* Valencia: Institució Alfons el Magnànim, 1998.
Brading, David. *Church and State in Bourbon Mexico: The Diocese of Michoacán, 1749–1810.* Cambridge: Cambridge University Press, 1994.
———. *Classical Republicanism and Creole Patriotism: Simon Bolivar (1783–1830) and the Spanish American Revolution.* Cambridge: Centre of Latin American Studies, University of Cambridge, 1983.
———. *The First America: The Spanish Monarchy, Creole Patriots and the Liberal State, 1492–1866.* Cambridge: Cambridge University Press, 1991.
Burns, Kathryn. *Colonial Habits: Convents and the Spiritual Economy of Cuzco, Peru.* Durham, NC: Duke University Press, 1999.
Certeau, Michel de. *La fable mystique: XVième–XVIIième siècle.* Paris: Gallimard, 1982.
Choudhury, Mita. *Convents and Nuns in Eighteenth-Century French Politics and Culture.* Ithaca, NY: Cornell University Press, 2004.
Christian, William, Jr. *Apparitions in Late Medieval and Renaissance Spain.* Princeton, NJ: Princeton University Press, 1981.
Darnton, Robert. "In Search of the Enlightenment." *Journal of Modern History* 43 (1971): 113–32.
Diderot, Denis. *La religieuse.* Ed. Robert Mauzi. Paris: Armand Colin, 1961.
Gay, Peter. *The Enlightenment: An Interpretation.* 2 vols. New York: Knopf, 1966–69.
Goodman, Dena. "Women and the Enlightenment" In *Becoming Visible: Women in European History,* ed. Renate Bridenthal, Susan Mosher Stuard, and Merry E. Weisener, 233–62. Boston: Houghton Mifflin, 1997.
Graham, Ruth. Foreword to *Women and the Enlightenment,* ed. Margaret Hunt, Margaret Jacob, Phyllis Mack, and Ruth Perry, i–vii. New York: Haworth, 1984.
Haakonssen, Knud. *Enlightenment and Religion: Rational Dissent in Eighteenth-Century Britain.* Cambridge: Cambridge University Press, 1996.
Hufton, Olwen. Introduction to *Women in the Religious Life: Year Book of the Department of History and Civilization,* 11–26. Florence: European University Institute, 1996.
Jacobsen Schutte, Anne. "Inquisition and Female Autobiography: The Case of Maria Cecilia Ferrazzi."

In *The Crannied Wall: Women, Religion and Arts in Early Modern Europe*, ed. Craig A. Monson, 105–18. Ann Arbor: University of Michigan Press, 1992.

Kerber, Linda. *Women of the Republic: Intellect and Ideology in Revolutionary America*. Chapel Hill: University of North Carolina Press, 1980.

Lavrin, Asunción. "Cotidianidad y espiritualidad en la vida conventual novohispana." In *Memoria del Coloquio Internacional Sor Juana Inés de la Cruz y El Pensamiento Novohispano 1995*, ed. Instituto Mexiquense de Cultura Toluca, Estado de México, 203–19. Toluca: Universidad Autónoma del Estado de México, Instituto mexiquense de Cultura, 1995.

———. "Ecclesiastical Reform of Nunneries in New Spain in the Eighteenth Century." *Americas* 22.2 (1965): 182–203.

Lehfeldt, Elizabeth. *Religious Women in Golden Age Spain: The Permeable Cloister*. Aldershot, Hants: Ashgate, 2006.

Mack, Phyllis. Introduction to *Women and the Enlightenment*, ed. Margaret Hunt, Margaret Jacob, Phyllis Mack, and Ruth Perry, 9–15. New York: Haworth, 1984.

Martín, Andrés. *Los recogidos: Nueva visión de la mística española, 1500–1700*. Madrid: Fundación Universitaria, 1975.

McKnight, Kathryn Joy. *The Mystic of Tunja: The Writings of Madre Castillo, 1671–1742*. Amherst: University of Massachusetts Press, 1997.

Medina, Manuel Ramos. *Conventos de monjas: Fundaciones en el México virreinal*. Mexico City: Condumex, 1995.

Muriel, Josefina. "La vida conventual femenina de la segunda mitad del siglo XVII y la primera del XVIII." In *Memoria del Coloquio Internacional Sor Juana Inés de la Cruz y El Pensamiento Novohispano 1995*, ed. Instituto Mexiquense de Cultura Toluca, Estado de México, 285–93. Mexico City, 1995.

Myers, Kathleen. *Word from New Spain: The Spiritual Autobiography of Madre María de San José (1656–1719)*. Liverpool: Liverpool University Press, 1993.

Pocock, J. G. A. *Barbarism and Religion*. 4 vols. Cambridge: Cambridge University Press, 1999–2005.

Rodríguez Garza, Francisco Javier, and Lucino Gutiérrez Herrera, eds. *Ilustración Española, reformas Borbónicas y liberalismo temprano en México*. Mexico City: Casa Abierta al Tiempo, 1992.

Sampson Vera Tudela, Elisa. *Colonial Angels: Narratives of Gender and Spirituality in Mexico, 1580–1750*. Austin: University of Texas Press, 2000.

Santísima Trinidad, Sor Sebastiana Josefa de la. "Cartas." Biblioteca Nacional, Mexico City.

Scott, Joan W. "Gender: A Useful Category of Historical Analysis." *American Historical Review* 91.5 (1986): 1053–75.

Sherriff, Mary D. *Moved by Love: Inspired Artists and Deviant Women in Eighteenth Century France*. Chicago: University of Chicago Press, 2004.

Smith, Theresa Ann. *The Emerging Female Citizen: Gender and Enlightenment in Spain*. Berkeley and Los Angeles: University of California Press, 2006.

Sorkin, David. *The Berlin Haskalah and German Religious Thought: Orphans of Knowledge*. London: Valentine Mitchell, 2000.

Subirats, Eduardo. *La Ilustración insuficiente*. Madrid: Taurus, 1981.

Surtz, Ronald E. *Writing Women in Late Medieval and Early Modern Spain: The Mothers of Saint Teresa*. Philadelphia: University of Pennsylvania Press, 1995.

Valdés, José Eugenio. *Vida admirable y penitente de la V. M. Sor Sebastiana Josepha de la SS. Trinidad*. Mexico City: Biblioteca Mexicana, 1765.

Vauchez, André. *La sainteté en occident aux dernières siècles du Moyen Âge: D'après les process de canonisation et les documents hagiographiques*. Rome: École Française de Rome, 1981.

Vigil, Mariló. "Conformismo y rebeldía en los conventos femeninos de los siglos XVI y XVII." In *Religiosidad femenina: Expectativas y realidades siglos XVII–XVIII*, ed. Angela Muñoz and María del Mar Graña, 165–85. Madrid: Al Mudayna, 1991.

Weber, Alison. *Teresa of Ávila and the Rhetoric of Femininity*. Princeton, NJ: Princeton University Press, 1989.

Wright, Anthony D. *The Counter Reformation: Catholic Europe and the Non-Christian World*. London: Weidenfeld & Nicolson, 1982.

PART II

WOMEN'S LIVES

Material and Social Practices

This second group of essays explores how historical women's lives were affected by new customs, manners, and practices directly related to Enlightenment values. María Victoria López-Cordón Cortezo demonstrates how the transformation of social manners was effected from the top down: aristocratic and upper-class women played a significant role in the later eighteenth-century transformation of gender roles, and their behavior in turn influenced that of women of lower social rank. Rebecca Haidt examines how women's activities, decisions, and choices concerning certain classes of household items, textiles and clothing in particular, transcend the limitations of conceptual structures such as the "public" versus the "private" sphere and provide fresh evidence of eighteenth-century women's experience and activities in their society. María José de la Pascua Sánchez's study of legal documents reveals the life practices and survival strategies of women living alone at a time when women's roles were largely defined by their relations to men as daughters, wives, or mothers. She finds that women increasingly asserted their rights within the marriage contract, but she also notes the longevity of traditions such as the honor code, since women living alone were subject to the policing of their morality. De la Pascua's study connects poignantly with Morand's analysis in chapter 2 of the strained marriage of María Gertrudis de Hore and its effect on her intellectual and creative experiences. Beatriz Quintanilla-Madero analyzes José Ignacio Bartolache's medical discourse about female hysterics in an early Mexican periodical, the *Mercurio Volante* (1772–73), and contends that it is an index to women's lives at that time—what they wore, what they ate, where they lived, their daily routines—as well as to physicians' attitudes about them and their lives. Bartolache's periodical is evidence of a transition during the Enlightenment from traditional moral and religious interpretations of women's illness to a natural and empirical assessment tempered with sympathy for their difficult position in society. Quintanilla-Madero's study of Bartolache's essay complements Sampson Vera Tudela's analysis of Sor Sebastiana's impassioned discourse in chapter 5 by providing a glimpse into women's lives and experiences in eighteenth-century Mexico.

6

Women in Society in Eighteenth-Century Spain
Models of Sociability

MARÍA VICTORIA LÓPEZ-CORDÓN CORTEZO

*I*n the eighteenth century, the number of meeting places for people of the same social class and similar concerns seems to have multiplied. In these places individuals shared news, exchanged opinions, or simply passed time playing cards, listening to music, or drinking coffee. What was novel was not the academies, the discussions, or the meetings in the noble halls themselves but the institutionalization of some of these gatherings either by the king or by some generous host in the form of a regulated activity, as well as the opening of the spaces that sheltered these activities to a greater number of people, though always within the limits constituted by the urban elite or, in many cases, by the more restricted republic of letters. Thus, a historical period that has often been identified with the triumph of privacy presents the paradox of being at the same time one that decisively propelled public life, amplifying the social space in which it developed. To the extent that the boundary between the two is, in our time, much less rigid than initial studies seemed to indicate, it may be appropriate to depart from certain stereotypes, such as the one that reduces the presence of women to the domestic arena, considering their presence outside of it a rarity. This was never the case, no matter whether we understand the term *society* in its original and broadest sense, as a natural or agreed-upon group of people, or in its more restrictive sense, as a well-defined and therefore more limited group of men and women who share a common culture and regulate their relationships through courtesy. This latter definition is the one that will be used here.

A useful realm for studying the processes of change and understanding the relationships between persons of different sex, age, and category, this diffuse and

Translated by Eunice Anne Rojas

regulated society, to which only the most privileged people belonged, whether by origin, fortune, or intellectual capacity, developed new norms during the eighteenth century that were destined to take hold in the rest of society. Just as the private sphere was originally created by an act of rebellion on the part of individuals attempting to find an intimate space for relaxation and reflection away from promiscuity or from community life, the public sphere was for many a difficult conquest, arrived at by force of will, by merits that were not easily recognized, and by a tedious acquisition of the language and the conventions considered essential for participating in certain activities. This was the case not only in palace festivities but also in literary or scholarly gatherings, and the requirements of public life were also present when one wanted to participate in a celebration or gain admittance to any one of the forms of social entertainment that were in fashion.

Moreover, even when the activities linked to introspection and silence, such as studying or reading, took place in a reading circle or in a library that was not strictly private, the formal conventions were no less strict. It is true that everyone expressed and extolled the intimate pleasure of satisfying the desire for knowledge in solitude and silence, but it is no less true that they also hoped to receive certain compensations in the form of recognition or praise for the results achieved through this pastime. This included women, as Josefa Amar y Borbón noted, who not only longed "anxiously for attention in return for their graces" but desired "praise for their cleverness in addition." Not content with the self-satisfaction that knowledge gave them, they wished for their "merit" to carry with it "fame and immortal glory" (Amar y Borbón 66, 61, 67). Of course, this was no easy task, and it required them to act with special prudence, showing themselves little by little in those places where the norms and conventions of each activity were learned and letting their presence be known discreetly in the forums where reputations were forged. For all these reasons, it is interesting to examine this process from several different perspectives, indicating which ambits proved to be most permeable and served as examples or through which means of insertion into these public spaces women's presence was increasingly evident, without forgetting those circumstances that, as woman's status and role in the family changed, favored an enhanced adjustment to the norms of the century.

A Model of Sociability: The Court

The court, always a strategic place in which to exchange favors and services and an essential point of reference from a cultural point of view, was also a sexually differentiated space that began to lose the rigid compartmentalization that had characterized it from the beginning. The presence of the queen, along with the numerous female personnel in her service, was a dynamic element enabled by the imposition of the hereditary principle and the growing power of the monarchies. The queen's role in the ceremonial that surrounded the manifestation of the royal majesty and in court life in general began to increase, so that every day there were fewer official or commemorative activities in which she did not participate.[1] The importance of this process can be measured by the marked institutional character of the events at which she was present, demonstrating that at the beginning of the eighteenth century the wife of the king was already an essential part of the impersonal and abstract monarchy to which homage was paid.

It is true that the authority and grandeur surrounding the royal women emanated, not from them, but rather from their intimacy with the sovereign, yet this very fact explains that they could represent him better than anyone else during his absences, as Luisa Gabriela de Saboya represented Felipe V, or that they could substitute for him in order to avoid an alteration in the operation of the State, as in the case of Isabel Farnesio. The queen, therefore, at times as ruler and at times with no specific title, developed a clear political role and became a subsidiary wielder of power. Even though circumstances did not always warrant direct intervention of this type, by the eighteenth century the queen's role already had such powers associated with it that no queen in the century, whether Isabel Farnesio, Bárbara de Braganza, or María Luisa de Parma, failed to take initiative or to gather services and loyalties around her, multiplying the public presence of her image not only through the events that surrounded her life, such as marriage, births, anniversaries, or funerals, but also through other events that shaped the reign, especially in its artistic and cultural aspects.

As a consequence of this increase in the activities of the queen, there rose around her a group of people specifically dedicated to her service, namely, her court, structured as such in the time of Felipe II (López-Cordón Cortezo, "Entre damas"). Included in this court were the chief lady-in-waiting *(camarera mayor)*, the ladies of honor *(dueñas de honor)*, the ladies-in-waiting *(damas)*, the escorts *(guardas menores)*, the handmaidens *(azafatas)*, the chambermaids *(camaristas)*, the bath maids *(dueñas de retrete)*, and numerous governesses *(ayas)*, laundry-women *(lavanderas)*, seamstresses *(labradoras)*, and other girls of all sorts who were paid by the royal treasury and who, like the masculine personnel, received promotions, raises, and bonuses.

With the establishment of the Bourbon monarchy and the changes it produced in etiquette and in court life, there appeared new customs propagated by a queen who was bored to tears by the company of young girls and old maids (Martín Gaite 33). For this reason, starting in 1714 the unmarried daughters of families linked to the nobility and the administration of the state were no longer designated as ladies-in-waiting. In their place were appointed married women who were closely linked to high-ranking palace officials, because they could participate with less inhibition in the official celebrations and events (Martín Gaite). Although the chief lady-in-waiting had always held a position of great importance because of the duties she performed and her direct relationship with the sovereign, when her designation was made subject to all sorts of political intrigues, as in the case of the princess of the Ursines, elected by Louis XIV to serve María Luisa Gabriela de Saboya, the prominence of this position reached new heights. This princess's personality was emphasized with admiration by Saint-Simon, evidence that she was an exceptional person at that time and that her role, both personal and political, was an example of the blurring of the lines between public and private spaces that took place even in the highest social circles. Nevertheless, she had no successors, since neither Isabel Farnesio nor Bárbara de Braganza had "favorites," preferring instead, to the surprise of many, the company of their royal consorts and their ministers to the exclusive companionship of ladies.

The queens' great influence over their respective husbands and their intervention in public affairs did not go unnoticed by their contemporaries, who witnessed an increase in the activities shared by both sexes in the palace. When María Amalia de Sajonia died in 1761 and Carlos III eliminated the Queen's Household, integrating its personnel into the sole Royal Household, which existed from then on, the tendency intensified. Although her daughter-in-law, María Luisa de Parma, maintained her maids and ladies-in-waiting, she did not strictly follow protocol; she regularly attended meetings in the prince's quarters and later organized her own, more open circle, which was of course mixed.

That the queens not only played an important role in the dynastic politics but also intervened in the highly restricted areas of the affairs of the state or the concession of honors is evident from the propaganda of the time, which, with few exceptions, legitimized this role. In this way María Luisa Gabriela de Saboya, the first wife of Felipe V, was praised for her talent as a ruler and for her decisions, which were "not characteristic of her age or of her sex" (Pérez Samper 86). Although her actions were more polemic, it was noted that Isabel de Farnesio kept watch with similar zeal "over her own royal progeny, over the Palace and her family, and over the State and the people" (Arias Somoza 12). Bárbara de Braganza was considered to have "great understanding and remarkable memory," which justified her participation with the king in carrying out the affairs of the kingdom: "Whoever might see our queen not only take care of the administration of the palace but also administer the public affairs of the kingdom would not judge her a woman, but would more accurately call her a man" (García Caro).

On the other hand, we know that María Amalia de Sajonia had participated in business together with the future Carlos III in Naples, but in Spain she was only praised for her role as exemplary wife and mother since she apparently had no time for anything else. Although history was not benevolent to María Luisa de Parma's reputation, of all the queens of Spain she was the one who best organized her own propaganda centered on the events of her life, from her wedding[2] to the births of her children,[3] institutionalizing the works of praise *(elogios)* that, starting in 1794, were given to her in celebrations in her honor. These celebrations, held by the members of the Association of Ladies of the Economic Society of Madrid (Junta de Damas), were important events in court life. They emphasized both her "domestic virtues" and her "heroic actions" of great "public utility," such as her shrewd suggestion that worthy men be incorporated into the government or her surrendering of her jewels to the "urgent needs of the nation" (Fuerte-Híjar 3, 12).

All of these sovereign women were credited with attributes inherent to their roles, as well as their prudence, decisiveness, and wisdom, which allowed them to emerge legitimately into the area of public activity and even in the more restricted affairs of state. Nevertheless, this manifestation of power was not without risk when women's behavior, whether real or fictitious, no longer adhered to the model or when their actions were interpreted through different norms than those of court society.

Induction from Above

The prominence of the queens and the increase in the presence of women in court life, with their progressive incorporation into regulated or informal activities from which they had previously been excluded, were not the only novelties with respect to women of the eighteenth century. If, from their privileged position, the queens modeled patterns of conduct and introduced styles sometimes at the periphery and other times at the very center of the royal family, the women of the court multiplied the effect, both within and outside the court, and effected changes that little by little were introduced into palace life, from the disposition of the rooms to the palace menu, to be adopted by other social groups who, in turn, served as examples.[4] Some of these changes were minor but no less significant. For example, the king and queen's dining together constituted a small revolution that soon was imitated. Also not without consequences was the close bond between the queens and their children, whom they educated and for whom they publicly showed their affection. Following in this pattern, it also became common to go out for a walk and to open one's home to people who were not close family members. The obligations that court etiquette demanded began to apply on a different scale to the wives of important dignitaries, who were required to attend certain functions, to receive in their homes those same people they called on, or to ask favors of their powerful husbands. The decorum and modesty of earlier times were no longer sufficient; it became necessary to display those "political manners" that corresponded to one's position and birth (Durán de la Rocha), which allowed people "to present themselves at gatherings with the necessary formalities" (Amar y Borbón 216).

We know from many different sources that this new behavior was not easy to learn. Thus, during the first third of the century some ladies of noble birth who were not a part of court life and the majority of those who belonged to the ascending nobility scarcely moved except in the company of other women, and when circumstances required them to have contact with members of the opposite sex, their behavior was distant and bound by conventions. They did not know how to participate in mixed company, nor were they comfortable in it, since their excessive shyness caused them to remain in the corner, quiet and somber, while the men played cards or amused themselves with other pastimes. As one astute spectator observed, they made a bad impression, because they "never stopped changing places and looking for each other, and, holding hands, they would walk from balcony to balcony talking like parrots" (Martín Gaite 33, 148).

This behavior affected even the highest classes. For example, when Saint-Simon went to pay his respects to the Marquise of Grimaldo, the wife of Felipe V's prime minister, he was surprised by her way of receiving him, which was so different from the manner in which of woman of her class would have received him in Paris: "I found her at the far end of the room in front of the door with the company of men and women on both sides. She rose when she saw me enter but did not take a step, and when I approached her she bowed as nuns do in a sort of curtsy. When I went to leave she did it again, without advancing a step nor with any excuse for what she was doing . . . , as is the custom of the country" (333).

Nevertheless, the politeness that prevented most women from speaking with men if they were alone or that produced awkwardness did not prevent some of them from acting in a more relaxed manner if there was sufficient pretext to justify it, such as at a concert, a dance, or a fireworks show, or from sitting in the company of men at a dinner as if the strict rules had been suspended (Saint-Simon 334).

During the first half of the century many other visitors bore witness to the fact that the *estrado*, an elevated platform where women sat together, often on cushions or low seats, which was still relatively commonly used, helped to accentuate women's embarrassment and affectedness, since they were never on the same plane with their visitors, whether they were seated or standing (Martín Gaite 33). In addition, in the important homes, where the *estrado* had been replaced by richly furnished parlors, the longstanding traditions of bowing and curtsying were being replaced by traditions that encouraged physical contact between the sexes, not only because of the new fashion of sofas but also because the new etiquette rehabilitated the courtly tradition of offering one's arm to a woman (Muñoz 20–21, 144).

After the turn of the century the changes were more perceptible. Not only did men and women no longer need a pretext in order to meet but women were the focus of these encounters. To this effect the Englishman Joseph Townsend, during his stay in Madrid, noticed that "the women were the ones who received all the visitors of the family" and that the visitors, "instead of knocking on the door or asking the doorman," walked straight into the parlor, where their hostess was "surrounded by her friends," who were "generally men." He also describes in detail an evening at the home of the Duchess of Berwick:

> The enchanting manners of the duchess and her sister, the Princess of Stolberg, the unaffectedness and freedom that we all enjoyed made time go by most agreeably. The duchess and three of her friends occupied a whist table, some of them stepped away to converse, others listened to the piano, and the duchess entertained herself for a while almost every afternoon drawing under the direction of the Prussian ambassador, whose good taste and skill made him one of the best artists. I also tended to pick up the pencil to take advantage of the lessons. At eleven we would sit down to enjoy an elegant dinner, and around one in the morning I would retire to walk almost two miles back to my rooms in the palace. The duke generally arrived in time for dinner but would immediately go to bed. (209–10)

If the queens, first in the Alcázar and later in the palace, protected musicians and artists and imposed their taste in areas from fashion to interior design,[5] the female members of the nobility were not to be outdone and in fact rivaled their male relatives in the importation of luxury objects and in paying attention to their favorites. These noblewomen were also beginning to partake in new types of entertainments, participating enthusiastically in theatrical events and in masked balls such as the one organized by the Count of Aranda in 1775 (Martín Moreno 354). Demonstrating some sort of talent in public, whether it was playing an instrument, singing, or dancing, came to be expected, regardless of reputation or social standing (Cadalso 101).

Noblewomen also adopted with enthusiasm a new custom, undoubtedly Italian in origin, that would eventually put an end to the former rigors of etiquette between the sexes. This was the famous *chichisveo*, intimate and personal conversation between a man and a woman,[6] which later became the custom of the *cortejo*, or gallant male escort, without which no married woman of any reputation would dare to present herself in public. Townsend describes the custom in this way:

> If the lady is at home, he is at her side; when she goes out, she does so on his arm; and if she participates in a dance, she does so with him. In the first of two minuets in which a woman participates during a dance she has as a partner her *cortejo*, and in the second one a stranger. While she dances with the first partner she tries to show her vivacity and grace, but when she dances with the second partner she does so with indifference, if not disgust, and seems to gaze at him with disdain. (211)

Just as characteristic of feminine Spanish customs as the *basquiña*, a type of overskirt, or the *mantilla*, the practice of the *cortejo* was frequently noted by foreign observers, who did not know whether to be more surprised by the freedom of behavior that it indicated or by the tolerance displayed by the husbands. Not until the queen herself adopted the custom, as in the case of María Luisa de Parma and her escort, Manuel Godoy, did it have political consequences and did the privileged class begin to put on parade a morality that they themselves had considered to belong more to the bourgeoisie than to aristocrats.

If traditions were changing and women were learning to act naturally in their own right in drawing rooms and at social celebrations, it is no surprise that some of them, less frivolous or better prepared, would open their homes to academic gatherings and that others would insist on participating in some of the literary and erudite societies that were flourishing at the time. In the case of the first group, their status as hostess assured their prominence, as was the case with Josefa Zúñiga y Castro, the widowed Countess of Lemos and Marquise of Sarriá, who directed La Academia del Buen Gusto (Academy of Good Taste) and was one of the queen's ladies, as well as sister-in-law to the powerful minister Carvajal. Many other distinguished ladies participated in this academy, which was open from the year 1749 to 1751, some actively and others as mere "onlookers" (qtd. in Luzán 43).[7]

Those who presided over Madrid's social life at the end of the reign of Carlos III and the beginning of that of Carlos IV enjoyed greater continuity. The most important protagonists, namely, the Countess-Duchess of Benavente, the Duchess of Osuna, who gathered the most significant people of the time in her country palace, La Alameda;[8] the Countess of Montijo, who had a more exclusive circle from an intellectual point of view; the Duchess of Alba, who liked to rival Queen María Luisa herself; or even the more discreet Marquise of Fuerte-Híjar, combined these activities with their participation in the Junta de Damas. These ladies had no cause to envy the most distinguished men of the rest of Europe, since their gatherings were also fluid, their members interchangeable, and the spatial metaphor of the "open house" that was generally applied to the Parisians was also perfectly fitting for them, with their rooms organized according to the French system of *enfilade* (Tovar 59; Navascués Palacio 11), in which the aristocrats, politicians, and men of letters mingled in animated conversation (Hellegouarc'h xvi–xx). None of those attending felt the slightest hesitation about presenting their works, reading their poetry or essays, or even performing plays, in all of which the ladies participated actively not only as members of the audience but also, occasionally, as actresses, translators, or even painters with the blessing of the Academy of San Fernando. Social status was undoubtedly the ticket to freedom for these women whom no one, much less their protected artists, would dare to disparage, even though they were not exempt from reticence and censure for what was truly considered a novelty: their emergence in the public and cultural life of the moment.

Those women of more modest status who followed their lead experienced more difficulties. The fact is that even though the new sociability opened the doors of communication, it did not impede strong misgivings about women whose only recommendation was their own talent. For example, at the *tertulia* organized at the home of Augustín de Montiano y Luyando, his wife, Josefa Manrique, who had been in the service of Queen Isabel Farnesio, as well as his niece Margarita, along with other ladies, were usually in attendance. Among these ladies was the young Margarita Hickey, who must have begun there her amorous relationship with the playwright Vicente García de la Huerta (Palacios Fernández 99) and who was beginning to become known as a poet. The experience served both to teach her "how to deal with and to communicate with the world and its people" and to propel her literary vocation (Hickey xiv), but her difficulties in publishing her works did not diminish. Her early withdrawal from public life demonstrates the weakness of her position and the manner in which social communication did not impede the continued existence of certain barriers. She writes in the 1789 edition of her *Poesías:* "I know, I have dealings with, and I communicate with some people whose intelligence and good sense could and possibly should have guided me. However, since I held some of them in too great esteem, some in too little, and the majority I assumed to be full of prejudice against the works of women, I have distrusted the critics and have chosen the public as my only judge" (140). She was not unaware that this public to which she subjected herself comprised those very people whom she distrusted, but she was confident that the silent judgment of the reader would be more benevolent.[9]

Another notable female writer of the time, María Rosa Gálvez, frequented the literary gatherings and moved freely in court environments, perhaps aided by her family name. Her writings, which in many cases made reference to contemporary events or described royal sites, demonstrate well her full integration in this milieu, which permitted her to undertake writing for the theater and to make a name for herself among the writers of the moment (Andioc 100). Her life was so brief, however, and she was forgotten so quickly that it is difficult to evaluate the effect her work had on her contemporaries.[10]

Since eighteenth-century women had a place in society and were subject to its rules, in order to understand their situation, we must consider them active subjects. Because they were not limited to the private and domestic sphere and their protagonism was not limited to familial relationships, women made their presence felt in all aspects of social life, from the material to the symbolic. It is true that the institution of the family was the space reserved for most women and that it formed their horizon, but it is no less the case that from the highest places models were promoted that extended beyond it and that a more shared sociability introduced changes in behavior and customs. I am speaking, of course, of privileged sectors, but it should not be forgotten that a majority of women would never conquer the street because they were always present in it.

NOTES

1. For this and other aspects of the queen's changing role, see Cosandey.
2. See *Sonoros regocijos*.
3. The press of that time published some of these works, such as the poems *Soneto en elogio de la fecundidad de la Reina* . . . and *Décimas*, which appeared in the *Diario de Madrid* on 22 February 1791.
4. On the effects of an increase in female personnel on palace etiquette, see López-Cordón Cortezo, "Mujer, poder y apariencia," 55ff.
5. See Callejo Delgado; and Martín Moreno, 42, 222ff., and 343ff.
6. See Martín Gaite's *Usos amorosos del dieciocho en España*, which reproduces various statements regarding the moral disapproval of this practice and also of its extent.
7. Some of the participants in the academy were the Duchess of Arcos, Ana María Masones de Lima, Countess of Ablitas, Leonor de Velasco y Ayala, Marquise of Estepa, and Catalina Maldonado y Ormaza, Marquise of Castrillo (Serrano y Sanz 2:572; Tortosa Linde 68; Palacios Fernández 98–102).
8. See Janis Tomlinson's discussion of the Duchess of Osuna in chapter 13 of this volume.
9. See María A. Salgado's discussion of Margarita Hickey in chapter 4 of this volume.
10. See Mónica Bolufer Peruga's discussion of Gálvez in chapter 1 of this volume.

WORKS CITED

Amar y Borbón, Josefa. *Discurso sobre la educación física y moral de las mujeres*. Ed. María Victoria López-Cordón. Madrid: Cátedra, 1994.

Andioc, René. Introduction to *La familia a la moda: Comedia en tres actos y en verso*, by María Rosa Gálvez. Ed. René Andioc. Salamanca: Universidad de Salamanca, 2001.

Arias Somoza, Antonio. *Oración fúnebre en las reales exequias de la Reyna Madre Nuestra Señora Doña Isabel Farnesio*. . . . Santiago: Ignacio Aguayo i Aldesmunde, 1768.

Cadalso, José. "Carta 56." In *Cartas marruecas*. Madrid: Espasa-Calpe, 1982.

Callejo Delgado, María Jesús. *El Real Sitio de la Granja de San Ildefonso*. Barcelona: Lunwerg, 1996.

Cosandey, Fanny. *La reine de France: Symbole et pouvoir, XVe–XVIIe siècles*. Paris: Gallimard, 2000.

Durán de la Rocha, Andrés. Prologue to *Idea para la educación de un joven*. . . . Madrid, 1743.

Fuerte-Híjar, Marquesa de [María Lorenza de los Ríos y Loyo]. *Elogio de la Reina Nuestra Señora*. . . . Madrid, 1798.

García Caro, A. *Sermón fúnebre predicado en las honras por nuestra Católica reyna Doña Bárbara de Portugal*. . . . Madrid, 1758.

Hellegouarc'h, Jacqueline. *L'esprit de société: Cercles et salons parisiens au XVIIIe siècle*. Paris: Garnier, 2000.

Hickey, Margarita. *Poesías varias, sagradas, morales y profanas*. Madrid: Imprenta Real, 1789.

López-Cordón Cortezo, María Victoria. "Entre damas anda el juego: Las camareras mayores de Palacio en la edad moderna." *Cuadernos de Historia Moderna: Anejos* 2 (2003): 123–52.

———. "Mujer, poder y apariencia o las vicisitudes de una regencia." *Studia Historica: Historia Moderna* 19 (1998): 49–66.

Luzán, Ignacio de. *La poética o reglas de la poesía en general y de sus principales especies (Ediciones de 1737 y 1789)*. Ed. Isabel M. Cid de Sirgado. Madrid: Cátedra, 1974.

Martín Gaite, Carmen. *Usos amorosos del dieciocho en España*. Madrid: Siglo XXI, 1972.

Martín Moreno, Antonio. *El siglo XVIII*. Vol. 4 of *Historia de la música española*, ed. Pablo López de Osaba. Madrid: Alianza, 1985.

Muñoz, Antonio. *Aventuras en verso y en prosa del insigne poeta y su discreto compañero, escritas por.* . . . Madrid, 1739.

Navascués Palacio, Pedro. *Palacios madrileños del siglo XVIII*. Madrid: Ayuntamiento, Delegación de Cultura, 1978.

Palacios Fernández, Emilio. *La mujer y las letras en el siglo XVIII*. Madrid: Laberinto, 2002.

Pérez Samper, María de los Ángeles. *Poder y seducción: Grandes damas de 1700*. Madrid: Temas de Hoy, 2003.

Saint-Simon, duc de [Louis de Rouvroy]. "Viaje por España (1721–1722)." In *Viajes de extranjeros por España y Portugal desde los tiempos más remotos hasta comienzos del siglo XX*, ed. José García Mercadal, 3:324–50. Madrid: Aguilar, 1962.

Serrano y Sanz, Manuel. *Apuntes para una biblioteca de escritoras españolas desde el año 1401 al 1833*. 2 vols. Biblioteca de Autores Españoles, 268–69. Madrid: Rivadeneyra, 1903.

Sonoros regocijos, octavas jacoserías . . . con el motivo de las felices bodas de los Serenísimos Príncipes de Asturias. 1765. Archivo Histórico Nacional, Madrid, Consejos, legajo 50819, lib. 428.

Tortosa Linde, María Dolores. *La Academia del Buen Gusto (1749–1751)*. Granada: University of Granada, 1988.

Tovar, V. "La renovación de la arquitectura palacial de Madrid y los Goyeneche." In *Juan de Goyeneche y su tiempo: Los navarros en Madrid; Ciclo de conferencias celebrado del 10 al 24 de marzo de 1999 en la Real Academia de Bellas Artes de San Fernando*, ed. María Concepción García Gainza. Pamplona: Gobierno de Navarra, Departamento de Educación y Cultura, 1999.

Townsend, Joseph. *Viaje por España en la época de Carlos III (1786–1787)*. Trans. Javier Portus. Madrid: Turner, 1988.

7

The Wife, the Maid, and the Woman in the Street

REBECCA HAIDT

A woman is walking in a modestly furnished room. The heels of her embroidered shoes clack softly on the wood floorboards. Her silk dress rustles as she crosses to a chair near the windowlight. As she sits down, she takes her free hand to raise the back gathers of her skirt out of the way; the shimmering fabric balloons for a moment by her hip as she settles herself. She hears her husband coming down the hallway with the visitors, and she takes this moment to look around her. The brass candlestick on the table is polished, and its gleaming metal reflects the shine of her yellow silk, which (she notes to her satisfaction) looks more expensive than it was.

Outside, a few feet away, a woman is walking near the edge of the unpaved, narrow street. She is carrying a cloth bundle containing a pair of shoe buckles that her mistress is sending to pawn. She pulls her worn wool petticoat away from the dirt kicked up by the hooves of horses passing close to her, anxious to protect it. It was passed to her by her employer as a part of her wages, with no promise of another one until next year. Picking her way through the filth, she traces in her mind the work she must do after returning from the errand on which she has been sent.

Ahead of her, she catches sight of a woman trudging toward the plaza. This woman carries a heavy basket filled with lengths of fabric, and the maid quickens her steps to approach her: she has just remembered that her mistress also asked her to bring back some muslin. The vendor, bent under the weight of her wares, walks looking down toward her own patched and dirty skirt. Carrying this load is less noxious than the work she used to do as a ragpicker, but it is more tiring, and she faces another day of straining her arms from the continual motion of raising them against the binding basket straps, spreading fabric swatches fluttering into the air, and shouting as she hawks them to the passerby.

Of course, these three fictional women left no records of their own experience, but then most eighteenth-century women did not record their ambitions or document how they filled their days. Indeed, it is difficult for scholars to determine what the *actual* experience of such women might have been. We wonder, how did a middle-class wife *feel* about the concerted moralizing of ecclesiastical and civil authorities concerning a woman's obligation to stay in the home? Were there happinesses and satisfactions for the domestic servant in her daily work? Did the itinerant vendor fear for her safety on the street? Without information drawn through the vision of the individual's own experience, it would seem that we will not know.

In fact, most people's impressions and feelings have always been inaccessible to others. But in the effort toward reconstruction of lives lived, scholars privilege certain kinds of recorded information as representative of social phenomena and accord to other types of information a lesser status within the category of evidence. Students of Spanish history accept the notion, for example, that during the eighteenth century there were clearly "masculine" and "feminine" spheres of experience, relying on public-evidence representations of women's lives, such as tracts advocating that women dedicate themselves to domestic duties or speeches delivered in the course of the debates over the admission of women to the Sociedad Económica Matritense in the 1770s and 1780s.[1] Lacking texts in which individuals speak of their own, private understandings of such supposed spheres of difference, what other recourse do we have?

I argue here that the attempt to investigate eighteenth-century Spanish women's experience should go beyond archival sources and official recordkeeping to take into account material evidence of women's work and lives. Dependence on written records can prove an obstacle to the tracking of eighteenth-century women's experience, for the majority of women who could write did not write as much as men who could write did; what records and texts women produced may not have been collected through official channels; and women may not have contributed to authorship of the wide range of extant period texts—from legal documents to satirical theatrical skits—depicting women. Yet it is indisputable that most women worked with objects (e.g., textiles) whose uses are well documented. Women used their hands and their creativity to buy, sell, craft, mend, care for, and rework items such as linens, ceramics, needles, clothing, and decorative household objects. Middle- and upper-class women were responsible for managing the household space and the textiles that entered and left that space, whether it was a tiny one-room dwelling or a large house; domestic working women and women who were itinerant vendors or performed other street labor were also managers of cloth things in their multiple interfaces between what traditionally have been conceived of as separate, "public" and "private" spaces. In San Fernando, a Madrid workhouse/prison for prostitutes, female inmates carded wool that would be sent outside to workshops and factories for spinning and weaving. Attention to women's uses of one particular class of things—in the case of the present essay, textiles—across these multiple spaces can provide a fuller picture of women's experiences and serve to fill some of the gaps left by reliance on official records.

Border Crossing: Women's beyond "Public" versus "Private"

In 1775 Pedro Rodríguez, Conde de Campomanes, reminded his cohorts in the Sociedad Económica Matritense that the home was women's sphere, and "laws have little influence concerning the internal government of families" (Negrín Fajardo 144). What might Campomanes have meant by this? He made his statement as part of a lively debate concerning the potential admission of women to the Sociedad Económica, and he was arguing in favor of their admission precisely because women were charged with "the internal government of families." Though Campomanes conceived of the home as a private, as opposed to a public, sphere, he nonetheless exhorted his colleagues to acknowledge the applicability of public-sector theorizing to private management of households, focusing particularly on the concepts of *utilidad* (usefulness) and *industria* (industry). He hoped that women could come to understand the advisability and advantages (the usefulness) of dedication to certain manual labors (the industry) intrinsic to the well-ordered running of a household: "a general persuasion of the usefulness of industry, systematically imparted by mothers, will reveal the most secure path toward the spread among us of womanly industriousness" (144). Many Spanish eighteenth-century economic theorists held that reform of women's domestic conduct was essential to "accompany legislative measures and political actions" and crucial for meeting the goal of placing Spain "on the level of the other European nations" (Bolufer Peruga and Morant Deusa 184). Women's application to domestic tasks would lead to better household management, which in turn would benefit local and state economic prospects.

Some eighteenth-century theorists posited, with Francisco de Cabarrús, that women's most important domestic work was "distributing every hour of the day between religion and nature's obligations" (Negrín Fajardo 153). Others, such as Campomanes and Luis de Imbille, acknowledged that women's household work required *aplicación*, or dedication to specific tasks, and noted that women's *aplicación* included manual labors such as the preparation of primary materials for further elaboration by artisans (e.g., preparation of wool for eventual weaving), embroidery, and lacemaking (Negrín Fajardo 144, 149). The theorist Josefa Amar y Borbón stipulated that women of all classes should learn to sew and embroider as a characteristic component of womanhood: "A lady with a spinning wheel or sewing project . . . looks just as appropriate as the man of letters in his study, the artisan in his workshop, or the laborer in his field" (160). Middle-class women's household work included following a budget, crafting household items in order to save money, and practicing "the science of household management and labors": "knowing how to run a house, perform manual labors, and direct the work of domestic servants" (Bolufer Peruga and Morant Deusa 208). Domestics were called on to perform a wide range of tasks, from hair styling to mending to cleaning. And the wives and daughters of artisans were expected to contribute to, as well as to supplement, the labors of their husbands, brothers, and fathers. As Joan Sherwood points out, "[W]orking wives were essential to the support of a family on the poverty line" during the eighteenth century (65). The wives of artisans, *jornaleros* (day laborers), and laborers might earn money working as domestic servants, as wet nurses (in private households or at foundling homes such as the Inclusa in Madrid), by taking in washing, and so on.

Indeed, women's work was never confined exclusively to the home. The middle-class housewife who knew how to follow a budget and direct the errands of a *criada* (maid) had knowledge of a range of sites and contacts outside the home from which to purchase goods and food for the family and to which to send items to be repaired, bartered, or sold. The artisan-class woman would find her work taking her to any number of sites outside the home in which her family lived. Sherwood has documented the high number of working-class women who regularly left their homes to travel to the Inclusa to offer their services as wet nurses.[2] The Conde de Campomanes's comment about the separation between "laws" and the "internal management of the home" addresses the fact that the home was a place of liminality, of traffic between inside and outside, public and private, with women's work, activities, and decisions impossible to confine solely to the interior.

The house, after all, was one of the prime sites of interface with and reproduction of society. Society and its various dimensions—economic, commercial, moral—circulated through the household. As Serrana Rial García points out, it is a great error to suppose that domestic activities had only a private dimension: "in fact, all women, even those who did not do paid work outside the home, participated actively in production and in urban economic relations" (37). The sourcing of goods from market or vendor, their disposition within the rooms of a home, their care, replacement, bartering—such activities serve as markers of women's economic agency, discretion, and power with regard to a variety of social spheres. Nonetheless, until recently scholars of eighteenth-century Spanish culture have paid little attention to the household, to its things, their provenance, their materiality, as a site for knowledge of women´s experience outside of public-evidence representations of confined domesticity.

The Limitations of Records

Although most women were expected to make their major contribution to society within their own or relatives' homes or within their husbands' or fathers' workplaces, the officially recorded occupations of, and economic opportunities open to, women do not necessarily reflect the actual ways in which women actively participated in society during the period. As Mónica Bolufer Peruga and Isabel Morant Deusa point out, "[T]he hidden contribution made by women in the form of domestic work, contacts, and capital [such as dowries and inheritances] was fundamental to the functioning of family, commercial, and manufacturing enterprises" (184). Attempting to trace such contributions solely through corporate or municipal records will yield little fruit, for household tasks and the innumerable errands that brought into play networking among households and wider communities were both extremely laborious and unaccounted for in official documentation.

For example, one source of documentation is that kept by manufactories (with regard to orders or sales of raw or finished goods to other factories) within a chain of production and distribution. Yet during the mid- to late eighteenth century there were no established networks of factory-fed production and distribution for some of the most time- and labor-intensive work performed largely by women in support of the household: the preparation of raw materials such as wool, the confection of cloth and clothing, and the preparation of food for domestic consumption as meals. Domestic tasks also were not supplied (as they would be toward the end of the nineteenth century) by utilities within a large-scale production and distribution network. Lighting, heat, the bringing of combustible materials and water into the home, and the taking away of waste products and dirty water from the home were unavoidable tasks in women's daily lives through to the middle of the nineteenth century, in the absence of extensive and easily affordable services from municipal or private gas companies, electric companies, and sewage systems. Further, Carmen Sarasúa notes that crucial home-based tasks such as health care, child care, and the education of children remained largely undocumented due to the lack of institutional providers of medical care and public education (197–98). Thus, countless things that women of many classes did to create home lives, to manage things in the home, and to run the home as a functioning interface among various spheres and members of society are largely unrecorded in official discourses. The care of the young and the elderly, the cooking of meals, and the gathering and bringing home of fuel are activities that seem to belong to the "private" sphere, in large part because existing institutions (courts, guild corporations, shops, municipal and royal governments, etc.) did not document such activities through the paper trails typical of public-sphere forms of evidence—legislation, account ledgers, municipal zoning codes, urban maps, newspaper articles, legal documentation such as probate inventories or wills, and so on.

Yet I would argue that women's activities in the home become accessible upon consideration of some of the material goods that women managed, made, sold, and traded. One class of household items that transcends the limitations of conceptual structures such as "public" and "private" spheres, "domestic" and "outside" work, and "home" as distinct from "institutional" or "business" sites is that of textiles. An integral part of eighteenth-century women's work in the home in all social classes was the "conversion of household linens and old clothes into other garments and linens" (Walker 90). Women purchased household linens from street vendors, such as the female seller of "musulina y cortes de chalecos" (muslin and piece cloth for shawls) depicted in the 1798 collection *Los gritos de Madrid*, no. 22 (fig. 1); from owners of textile stores; and through friends or family traveling abroad or to well-known centers of textile production. They bought old linens and garments from secondhand dealers and supplied both secondhand dealers and ragpickers with textiles no longer of use in the home. The records of the Inclusa show that the institution received monthly donations from the customs house in the form of bales of "*talegas y quiebras*—literally odds and ends—from the royal textile factory" (Sherwood 16); these scraps were used for multiple purposes by the women who worked in the Inclusa, from dipping in milk so that a hungry infant might suckle it for nourishment, to diapering, to forming into crib bedding. Women were more

FIG. 1. *Musulina y cortes de chalecos, Grito de Madrid*, no. 22, 1798. Reproduced with permission from *Los gritos de Madrid* (Madrid: Ediciones Guillermo Blázquez, 1982).

likely than men to steal clothing and household linens. They were conscripted for home work as adjuncts in textile production, performing basic tasks such as carding, spinning, cleaning, and stretching of animal fibers (Haidt, "Well-Dressed Woman" 152).

While historians traditionally have linked women's roles as the takers and receivers of textile goods to their obligations within the household, such a connection develops from notions of female *dependence* rather than with regard to the interactive *agency* of women's involvement with household goods such as textiles (Walker 92). The conceptual model of female dependence on males within households is integral to "a type of historiographic production that perpetuates the marginality of women . . . analytically subordinating to a pre-established discourse the spaces of women, their options, their actions, their survival strategies" (Carbonell Esteller 129). Alternative approaches to the study of women's roles in diverse social spheres with regard to the culture of textiles posit the centrality of women in early modern urban labor and material-goods markets. "It was women," argues Montserrat Carbonell Esteller, ". . . who were the chief protagonists in the mobility of the early modern labor market and who . . . lent domestic/family economy its profile of labor diversity, characterized by fragility and the constant need to reorient strategies" (127). Family and domestic economy depended on multiple factors for the maintenance of a household, requiring of all household members (and especially women) versatility in skills and the ability to strategically perform multiple and rapidly changing tasks.

Those strategic tasks included participation, at a variety of levels, in the trade in new and secondhand clothing and textiles, in the cycle of textiles from raw production through manufacturing and into rags and waste, and in the black-market transferal of stolen linens. The handling, distribution, and management of textiles, whether in the form of purchases, pawning, or sales of secondhand clothing; the determination of which textiles were to be cast off as rags and which could be reused within the home; the purchase of lengths of manufactured cloth; the cleaning of garments; the repair of damaged possessions crafted from textiles; and so on—these were key forms of distribution of merchandise through various spheres we have tended to theorize as separate, from home to warehouse to open-air market. Women were major actors in these cross-sphere transactions and distributions, participating in various ways that defy traditional categorizations of "work." Yet women's experience as such is not registered in standard historical sources such as guild membership lists or shopkeepers' tax rolls.

Certainly much of women's experience with textiles derived from the connotations of fabrics and their contextualized cultural meanings. For example, the cost of clothing, new or used, lay almost entirely in the materials from which it was made (Blum 9); textiles were prohibitively expensive for women of the working, artisan, and even middle classes, and those of the upper class and the aristocracy relied on the costliness of sumptuous or fine textiles to communicate privilege. Women (and men) of several classes knew the names of many distinct textile types and were aware of the relative values of a range of linens, wools, and silks.[3] Antonio Matilla Tascón lists scores of eighteenth-century *pragmáticas, cédulas,* and other government documents conveying precise stipulations concerning commerce in textiles, goods distinguished for legislative purposes by a vast vocabulary of precise terminology (Haidt, "Well-Dressed Woman" 145).[4]

And women's experience of work with regard to institutions of textile production or distribution varied over time, depending on their age, legal status, and class. For example, a widow's right to assume the trade in secondhand textiles following her husband's death was stipulated in the mid-eighteenth-century *Ordenanzas* of the Madrid Secondhand Dealers' Guild; yet there is no mention in the

Ordenanzas of women's actual work as assistants prior to their husbands' death. Nor, for that matter, is there mention of single women, such as daughters, working as secondhand dealers. Guild records and legal codes from the seventeenth and eighteenth centuries tell us nothing, for example, about the rights or obligations of Spain's single women; legislation and stipulations concerning women focus on women's entry into the legal and institutional spheres through the marriage contract (Friedman 52). And yet unmarried women of all types—daughters, single women—were, during their own lifetimes, agents in the functions of diverse businesses. We know that eighteenth-century women of all ages were crucial to the expansion of, and moved in multiple ways through, spheres of economic activity, those pertaining to textiles being among the most important. In early modern Europe, urban women spent their days in tasks and occupations that crossed boundaries of walls, streets, parishes, and neighborhoods; as Monica Chojnacka points out, streets described as full of women "were streets full of female work" (55). Yet where is their experience of that work *recorded?*

Redefining Production: The Case of the Circulation of Textiles

So much depends on how records function—or do not function—to reflect real-world data. The purposes and intended uses of documentation are inseparable from their eventual content. One of the most important types of sources for information concerning eighteenth-century demographic, social, and economic issues was the *catastros* and *censos* commissioned by various ministers throughout the second half of the century. The midcentury Catastro de Ensenada, for example, aimed, not to collect specifics concerning the populace, but rather to gauge the extent of national riches and resources; thus it "conveys better data about lands, herds, and occupations than about workers themselves" (Durán 23). There is no information concerning the gender of those employed in commerce or industry; thus, despite the *catastro*'s minutely configured overview of employment, it does not tell us whether any of the documented tailors, weavers, cloth sellers, launderers, and so on, were women (25).[5] The *censo* of Floridablanca, conducted in 1787, was a model of period demographics with regard to social categories, but although it provides vast quantities of data concerning groups and classes of occupations, it lacks precision as to how many laborers, weavers, artisans, or domestic workers were women, even though "a good part of them . . . were women" (31).

Such official surveys shared in a set of assumptions that acquired increasing valence in eighteenth-century economic thought. They posited, for example, that formations of work, labor, and production were documentable within a geography of public spaces. Pedro Rodríguez, Adam Smith, and other late Enlightenment economic thinkers theorized public spaces—the shop, the factory, the warehouse, the shipping office—as those through which the creation of durable goods on the scale of mass production would contribute to economic prosperity. And they theorized *men* as the workers who would produce the public-sector wealth of the prosperous nation. Credit, a growing and powerful instrument of growth, was also theorized as a male-specific public-sphere tool: as one late eighteenth-century economist put it, credit to businesses and owners would "keep up the circulation in trade . . . by men's duly performing their contracts, agreements, and promises" (Rosen 53). Eighteenth-century notions of "productivity" and interest in promoting credit were focused, not on the kind of purchasing and production for which women were largely responsible—that directed toward daily consumption or toward the traffic in household goods—but on investment and the growth of private capital in public spaces and institutional relationships. Thus, period theorizing and official documentation of credit, trade, and economics provide only scant evidence of women's activities. They make little mention, for example, of the legions of women and girls employed in homes as subcontractees for essential textile-industry activities such as spinning and embroidery or as piecework laborers in lacemaking. Nor do they record the labors of the women who worked in cramped conditions as *calceteras* (stocking makers), *costureras* (tailors of garments such as cuffs and shirts), *planchadoras* (ironers and pressers), and *lavanderas* (laundresses). In fact, barred from access to guild apprenticeships, with limited opportunities for going into business for themselves if they were not widowed, such working women in Europe and its colonies were not understood to be permissible agents or recipients of the kind of credit that economic thinkers increasingly saw as essential to circulation and trade, even though their undocumented, domestic labor fed public-sector, credit-worthy industries.

Yet many married women did have financial instruments of credit available, through pawn and black-market routes. Clothing and household linens were costly and desirable and thus particularly easy for women to dispose of for money purposes, owing in part to "the ubiquity of both pawnbroking, which provided a credit system for a great part of the population, and a thriving market in used clothes" (Walker 91). At the Inclusa in Madrid, the blankets and ragged clothing sent along with the babies serviced by wet nurses often were not returned with the children; it "was assumed that the missing clothing had been sold" by the nurses to scrape together some money for the support of their families (Sherwood 16). The pawning of household linens and clothing, the passing of used goods from one woman to another, and the selling of such goods to dealers were operations by which women moved household items into circulation, apart from the kind of production economists theorized would benefit the national economy. The trade in secondhand goods and the market for stolen household items were enormous economic sectors across Europe during the period.[6] But they did not promote "production" in the classical economic sense, and thus they did not receive the textual documentation that students of the period, in attempting to reconstruct past experience, tend to privilege as evidence.

We know that the circulation of linens and the care, working, and repair of textiles were important components of most women's daily experience during the eighteenth century. We would have to draw on a wide variety of sources, both written and nonverbal, to better understand their complexities. For example, from probate inventories (performed, admittedly, for a small number of individuals relative to the size of the population) we can extract certain sorts of information concerning the number of garments possessed, the general type of cloth of which they were made, and in some cases their condition. Nonetheless, as Daniel Roche points out, "since the clothing of the inventories is neither wholly that of daily life nor wholly that of the collective imagination, it offers a mixed and tenuous indication of lost realities" (141). Some paintings indicate details of how clothing items, such as pockets, were used by women of various classes as an element of their autonomy in daily routines.[7] We can study eighteenth-century textiles and garments in costume collections to observe the numerous workings of seams, patchings of holes, and conversions of items—a skirt becomes a pair of pockets, lace cuffs become decoration on a collar. And everything was handmade, everything is the product of somebody's—some wife's, some maid's, some woman's—time and labor: unrecorded labor that we think of as "private" or "domestic" but that was entwined intimately with that performed in what we think of as "public-sector" industries such as papermaking or textile importing.

Women's work with textiles conditioned the viewpoint of the individual; it linked, that is, to a lost world of perceived nuances and cultural cues. For example, we do not know with certainty just how worn and mended a cloth item became before it was acceptably understood to be a rag, disposable. We do not know which sorts of fabrics women advised one another to prefer or avoid with regard to factors such as stain resistance, texture, or ease in stitching and reworking. Which kinds of textiles did women prefer for functions such as carrying bundled items on errands? What personal credit arrangements did secondhand vendors make with female clients? None of this has been recorded, but all of it was part of actual daily experience related to eighteenth-century household material culture.

The wife is wearing a dress made of imported silk, but she has pawned some shoe buckles to scrape up the last bit of money for it. On that errand she has sent her maid, whose used petticoat is partial compensation for the hard work that makes possible a daily routine in her mistress's household—though she would never be represented as a "producer" by theorists of national economy. In the street, the maid hurries toward the itinerant vendor, who, having once been a collector of cloth scraps and refuse, well understands women's transferal of household textiles to the paper-producing sector—though such work was not theorized (in the way that needlework was) as pertaining to a culture of "aplicación mujeril." The wife, the maid, and the woman in the street all were contributors to the local economy, creators of a complex series of interfaces between home and market, public and domestic spheres. They were not writing, but they were working and walking, and on their backs, in the bundles they carried, in their textile transactions and transformations, are aspects of women's agency ready to expand our understanding of Enlightenment experience.

NOTES

1. See Negrín Fajardo.
2. See Sherwood, chs. 3 and 4, for more on the multiple, public-sphere survival strategies of the wet nurses of the Inclusa.
3. See Haidt, "Name."
4. For example, "que se sellen todos los . . . lienzos pintados" (Matilla Tascón 55) [let all the painted cloths . . . be stamped]; "se permite la entrada y uso en Cataluña de tejidos de hilo y algodón blancos y azules que llaman 'blahuetes'" (70) [the entry and use in Catalonia of woven linens and white and blue cottons called "blahuetes" is permitted].
5. See María José de la Pascua Sánchez's discussion of the *catastro* in chapter 8 of this volume.
6. See Roche, esp. ch. 12.
7. See Van de Krol.

WORKS CITED

Amar y Borbón, Josefa. *Discurso sobre la educación física y moral de las mujeres*. Ed. María Victoria López-Cordón. Madrid: Cátedra, 1994.
Blum, Stella. "The Eighteenth-Century Woman." In *The Eighteenth-Century Woman*, 6–18. New York: Metropolitan Museum of Art, 1981. An exhibition catalog.
Bolufer Peruga, Mónica, and Isabel Morant Deusa. *Amor, matrimonio y familia: La construcción histórica de la familia moderna*. Madrid: Síntesis, 1998.
Carbonell Esteller, Montserrat. "Las mujeres pobres en el setecientos." *Historia Social* 8 (1990): 123–34.
Chojnacka, Monica. *Working Women of Early Modern Venice*. Baltimore: Johns Hopkins University Press, 2001.
Durán, María Ángeles. "Notas para el estudio de la estructura social de España en el siglo XVIII." In *Mujer y sociedad en España 1700–1975*, ed. María Ángeles Durán and Rosa María Capel Martínez, 15–45. Madrid: Ministerio de Cultura, Dirección General de Juventud y Promoción Socio-Cultural, 1982.
Friedman, Ellen G. "El estatus jurídico de la mujer castellana durante el antiguo regimen." In *Ordenamiento jurídico y realidad social de las mujeres: Siglos XVI a XX*, ed. María Carmen García-Nieto París, 41–53. Madrid: UNAM, Seminario de Estudios de la Mujer, 1986.
Haidt, Rebecca. "The Name of the Clothes: 'Petimetras' and the Problem of Luxury's Refinements." *Dieciocho: Hispanic Enlightenment* 23.1 (2000): 71–75.
———. "A Well-Dressed Woman Who Will Not Work: *Petimetras*, Economics, and Eighteenth-Century Fashion Plates." *Revista Canadiense de Estudios Hispánicos* 28.1 (2003): 137–57.
Los gritos de Madrid: Colección de setenta y dos grabados. 1798. Madrid: Ediciones Guillermo Blázquez, 1982.
Negrín Fajardo, Olegario. *Ilustración y educación: La Sociedad Económica Matritense*. Madrid: Editora Nacional, 1984.
Ordenanzas del gremio de tratantes en ropas usadas, y todo menage de casa. Madrid: Josef Franganillo, 1799.
Rial García, Serrana M. *Las mujeres en la economía urbana del antiguo régimen: Santiago durante el siglo XVIII*. A Coruña: Edicios Do Castro, 1995.
Roche, Daniel. *The Culture of Clothing: Dress and Fashion in the Ancien Regime*. Trans. Jean Birrell. Cambridge: Cambridge University Press, 1996.
Rosen, Deborah A. *Courts and Commerce: Gender, Law, and the Market Economy in Colonial New York*. Columbus: Ohio State University Press, 1997.
Sarasúa, Carmen. *Criados, nodrizas y amos: El servicio doméstico en la formación del mercado de trabajo madrileño, 1758–1868*. Madrid: Siglo Veintiuno, 1994.
Sherwood, Joan. *Poverty in Eighteenth-Century Spain: The Women and Children of the Inclusa*. Toronto: University of Toronto Press, 1988.
Van de Krol, Yolanda. "'Ty'ed about My Middle, Next to My Smock': Women's Eighteenth-Century Pockets." In *Eighteenth-Century Women's Working Dress*. Tidy Symposium Papers. N.P., 1997.
Walker, Garthine. "Women, Theft, and the World of Goods." In *Women, Crime, and the Courts in Early Modern England*, ed. Jennifer Kermode and Garthine Walker, 81–105. Chapel Hill: University of North Carolina Press, 1994.

8

Women Alone in Enlightenment Spain

MARÍA JOSÉ DE LA PASCUA SÁNCHEZ

Women Alone?

What do I mean by *women alone*? In Olwen Hufton's pioneering work "Women without Men" this kind of interrogation seems habitual as she expresses doubt about an appropriate title: "Women without the Family"? "Women Alone"? The final decision, "Women without Men," was successful because it referred back to the real meaning of the circumstances that surrounded this type of women. The expression *women alone* comes to mean the same thing, although in the current essay it refers to a qualification used in the period as often by women themselves to explain their situation as by the authorities to designate them. Nevertheless, I am aware that its application can give way to debate, a debate encouraged largely by the difficulty of translating all the varied experiences of these women to a concrete form.

Even so, and because language constructs the world in which we move, I have decided upon a formula that, on the one hand, can populate itself with victimist meanings owing to an association with common words of the *ancien régime* (*woman alone = poor = destitute*) and, on the other hand, suggests further associations that were present in the mentality of the ruling classes of the time period I hope to highlight (*woman alone = woman who is not dependent = free woman*).

The problem of how to categorize and study women alone was left unexplored for a long time because it was considered a marginal topic (Palazzi), and historically its most obvious use, denoting single women, has been in demographics. Following eighteenth- and nineteenth-century planners' and moralists' preoccupation with the negative consequences of the abundant number of single women in western Europe, this analytic perspective was privileged. In this way, beginning in the

Translated by Catherine Osborne

1960s, historians have quantified and analyzed female "singlehood" and its impact on fertility rates, relating female celibacy (transitory or definitive) to the sphere of birthrate and its problems. Over the last few years, research on poverty and welfare (in which the presence of women, widows, and the unhappily married is noteworthy) has increasingly brought the study of women who are alone into the field of social history. This research transcends analytical perspective that focuses excessively on single women and extends the analysis to insist that solitude is not a state but rather an experience that implicates single women, widows, unhappily married women, or separated women. Nevertheless, this lack of precise definition has resulted in a certain lack of historiographic attention to a large group of women who played a significant role in *ancien-régime* societies. Let us keep in mind that they were women with limited autonomy in a society that considered their situation inconvenient.

The expression *women alone* can, I think, be used to designate women socially signified as alone, that is, not dependent upon any man. This meaning reflects another fear that the thinkers of the eighteenth and nineteenth centuries expressed, although not with such frequency as that regarding the relationship between female celibacy and declining population: the fear related to the social and cultural consequences of the presence of women having an uncertain civil—that is, social—status.

Thus, a situation recurrent throughout history can be analyzed on the basis of a concept destined to provoke a change in the traditional point of view on the subject. If formerly the focus was on the social problem posed by these women, the concept of women alone introduces a theoretical correction by emphasizing that the category includes, above all, women who for one reason or another act with a certain degree of autonomy. The analysis of women's life experiences in a symbolic context wherein woman is socially defined through her dependent relationship with a man reveals the common perception that women alone occupy an unnatural and potentially subversive position. It is necessary to categorize this situation with precision in order to avoid falling into an empiricism that would reduce analysis to mere anecdote. The analysis goes beyond breaking with stereotypes and does not exclude the different autonomous experiences covered in the concept of women alone. It includes the experiences of women alone who are "widows," "single," "unhappily married," experiences colored by age, class differences, or family situation.

Women alone have been visible through their overrepresentation in declared and assisted poverty, an initial variable whose analysis reveals a process of impoverishment that is associated especially with the experience of feminine solitude that advances with age, when these women cease to be useful in the activities to which they have dedicated themselves (in general, those derived from an improvised economy). Regardless of these conclusions about the poverty of women alone, which seem to reaffirm themselves in both classical and recent research (Carbonell; Hufton, *The Poor;* Sarti), we must not forget that class differences contribute to the diversification of the group. Being a woman alone with economic possibilities is not the same as being a woman alone without them. Having a recognized professional activity or a business is not the same as working in domestic service or surviving by begging, by living off the charity of relatives, or by prostituting oneself. Testimonials from diverse sources and records of documents confirm that the experiences of women alone differ not only as a function of these circumstances but also according to their recognized authority, their social contexts, and their own perception of themselves. If the link between poverty and a bad reputation was established rapidly in the symbolic culture of the eighteenth century, introducing a hierarchy among the women themselves in addition to an ideologized interpretation of feminine poverty and social treatment, then life experience itself contributed to the modification of attitudes along with habits.

I discuss this last aspect more fully later, based on the results of my research on women alone, but first I am interested in taking up the theoretical approaches to this subject. In order to understand the reality of women alone, we must distinguish between times and spaces. We are familiar with the situation of women alone, especially in an urban milieu—in the Protestant as well as the Catholic world—in imperial cities of the early modern age such as Rothenburg (Rowlands), in seventeenth-century Piamonte (Cavallo and Cerrutti), in eighteenth-century Rome (D'Amelia). Nevertheless, we are poorly informed about their situation in a rural environment. Moreover, the variable of time must be introduced: historical time and, more specifically, individual time, through the notion of the life cycle. Being alone is not a destiny; nor does widowhood, singlehood, or the absence of a husband mean being alone for the rest of one's life.

It is thus especially important to articulate the concept of women alone in connection with the notion of the life cycle, which allows the consideration of a larger number of women than could be considered using more restrictive criteria. Additionally, the articulation of both makes possible the contrast of diverse experiences of solitude, including those in the life of one single person. If we consider the complexity of the processes of constructing identities—that is, of the negotiation among individuals and regulating norms—and of the role of reflection on one's own experience in these processes, we comprehend that a woman can go through different life situations, which might translate to different ways of interpreting gender roles. In this sense, it is possible to correct a certain essentialist tendency in the history of women and to more effectively interpret the role of female agency.

For example, in sixteenth-century Seville, considered by M. E. Perry to be a city "in the control of women," unmarried women and widows, women not dependent on any man, and married women with absent husbands, who had to face the absence of the men in the family, many of whom had emigrated to the New World, took advantage of the circumstantially open interstices of a gender system that excluded them from many realms of experience. Their growing presence in the world of work and their greater visibility in the public space were not reflected proportionately in the symbolic realm, for there was increasing interest on the part of the authorities, especially in the second half of the sixteenth century, to silence this process. This is not to say that the experiences of these women were of no use in affirming their authority and extending their influence (Perry 23–41).

A different line of research has shown the special relevance of certain factors for women: the status of the family the woman is born into; the structure of the domestic aggregate and hereditary practices; the emigration of the men of the family; work; and so on. Around these revolves the life of a collective that frequently faces numerous social risks, but also a life that leads to other experiences. In Spain, some women already had occupied the place that corresponded to them as singular women who distinguished themselves in such related fields as culture and religion or in activities considered masculine, such as power, war, or conquest. There were women who chose the religious path, avoiding the state of matrimony and, therefore, direct dependence on a man, such as Teresa de Jesús (1515–82), the reformer of the Carmelites; Isabel de la Cruz, the teacher of the *alumbrados* (enlightened ones), a heretical group that sprang up in sixteenth-century Castile; or Magdalena de la Cruz, a nun in the convent of Santa Isabel de Córdoba who was condemned by the Inquisition in 1554 for being deceitful and possessed. There were women devoted to arts and letters, such as Antonia Luisa de Carvajal y Mendoza (1566–1614), a poet and missionary, or Catalina de Mendoza (1542–1602), a painter, both from the aristocratic Mendoza family, which desired to give its daughters the means to acquire knowledge (Nader). There were women who discovered new worlds, such as Isabel Barreto, born in Galicia in the last quarter of the sixteenth century, who was committed to the conquest of the Solomon Islands, or those who contributed to the Spanish conquest of America, such as Catalina de Erauso. Nevertheless, our encounter with women whose agency was undoubtedly less notorious yet also configured itself as an alternative that subverted the roles imposed by the discourses of power and the stereotypes of gender has taken somewhat longer. Here I will attempt to analyze some experiences of women in eighteenth-century Spain, especially those who left their testimony in the city of Cádiz.

As contradictory as it may seem, the most abundant investigations locate these solitary women in the home, and more specifically, as the heads of families. One place where the leadership of the female home is documented is in the censuses or population counts. Widows especially are mentioned as responsible for their families. So are single women who lived alone or with other women and married women who became heads of households after their husbands' emigration or desertion. Classic studies have already emphasized the demographic weight of these homes headed by women in western Europe (Fauve-Chamoux; Hufton, "Women without Men"; Palazzi; Wall). In reference to Spain, the Catastro de Ensenada allows an order of magnitude of the phenomenon based on zoning analyses dating from the middle of the century.[1] For Galicia, in northwest Spain, a region from which there was a major emigration by men during the eighteenth century, homes headed by widows and single women constituted more than 25 percent of the registered homes; in some urban locales they constituted nearly 30 percent (Rial). At about the same time, in Burgos, on the northern plateau of Castile, women ran 10 percent of homes (Sanz), while the highest figures for the entire peninsula, at least according to what can be deduced from current research, were recorded in the south, in Granada. In 1752, widows, single women, and women married to absent husbands headed 26.78 percent of homes in Granada (Birriel Salcedo). In reference to Cádiz, my analysis of the Padrón of 1773 reveals a reduced number of feminine heads of households, about 10 percent of all heads of households (De la Pascua Sánchez, "Social Reproduction").[2]

Beyond a Prosopography of Women Alone

Because the experience that forges women's identities derives from their material situation in society and from their interpretation of that situation, in order to understand these women we must consult sources that include life stories. Censuses and registries make these women visible, offering us the order of magnitude of the social phenomenon of feminine solitude, but widowhood, singlehood, or a bad marriage are situations lived in the first person. The individual recounting of some of these situations comes to us through diverse documents, of which judicial records are possibly the most familiar.

The employment of judicial records has a long historiographic trajectory, and its condition as the basic resource in representative works of recent social history—such as *The Cheese and the Worms*, by Carlo Ginzburg, and *The Return of Martin Guerre*, by Natalie Zemon Davis—excuses it from an exhaustive evaluation. The argument over its character as a "hostile chronicle" or regarding its condition as "just one witness" has had sufficient resonance. I therefore dwell on only one of the aspects that these judicial sources offer and that, beyond the concrete facts regarding a conflict in which the protagonists are women, invite multiple social readings of feminine agency. Sentences, when they exist, declarations of witnesses, documental proofs, and above all the discourses given by these women before the judge, whether directly or through an attorney, provide us examples of first-person narrative practices. In the sense in which the historian Rudolf Dekker defines them—those texts in which the author writes about his or her acts, thoughts, and feelings (12)—we can classify these texts as *egodocuments*. In these documents of petitions made before a judge, we may read a story in the succession of events on which a claim is based or in a supposedly exculpatory justification. Life experience appears integrated in the accepted social values, from whose key life itself can be interpreted. But these stories do not merely contain a dialogue between the subject and the social and cultural world in which he or she finds him- or herself immersed; they also offer distinct arbitrated formulas for confronting some restrictive social norms.

Women alone faced very powerful social pressure regarding their sexual behavior. The need to respond to a social maxim that measured honor by the absence of relations with men turned family members and neighbors into judges and prosecutors who executed accusatory zeal without hesitation if the case arose. The capacity of denunciation that the law bestowed upon relatives and neighbors supposed a problem for women alone, who were made uncomfortable or were persecuted with judgments regarding their honor. The testimony of some of these women allows us to comprehend not only their personal circumstances but also the way in which these values originated in the practices of a determined social context. There were instances of exile because of bad conduct, although they do not seem to have been frequent at this point in the modern age. The legal brief of María Lucena, a resident of Medina Sidonia, in Cádiz, whose husband was missing in the Indies, contains a petition for remission of the penalty of exile;[3] it permits an analysis of the play of social possibilities that a woman's supposedly dishonest conduct provoked.

Before soliciting the suspension of the penalty, which had been imposed because of her neighbor's denunciation, María would have to request the permission of the ecclesiastical judge to go to the courts. Once this was obtained, she would have to request permission through her attorney to return to her domicile. This was not so much to defend María's honor as it was to defend what was more socially relevant, namely, her husband's honor. Thus, the attorney informed the judge that she was married to "an honorable person of good reputation" and that her banishment could cause "public scandal" prejudicial to the good name of her husband. The argumentation of the petition likewise reveals the professed social mentality. The attorney stated that not only had the denunciation not provided proof of her guilt, although it might exist, but "there is no law that requires that the transgression of married women be published; rather, we see the practice of all the ecclesiastical and secular tribunes to hide and cover these transgressions to avoid greater evils." It was necessary, the attorney concluded, that when her husband returned from the Indies he find her in his house and in his good graces. The attorney asked clemency of the court because "she is alone and unprotected."

The desired social good was the public honor that fundamentally affected the husband, and the request for the lifting of the sentence for this purpose seems to have been supported more by her state of being "alone and unprotected" than by her innocent behavior. This case seems to show us two rival interpretations: one that makes neighbors and the wider social circle "guardians" of women's conduct and one that is looser (and possibly more real?), which the attorney refers to when he alludes to a jurisprudence based on a conception of honor as *publica vox et fama*, which attempts to diminish conflicts with prudence and without scandal.

Although this case takes us back to the second half of the 1600s, there is proof that problems of reputation constituted another of the constants for women alone during the modern age—married women, single women, and widows. Many single women who became engaged and had intimate relations with their fiancés before marriage suffered similar difficulties. When the marriage did not take place, they appealed to a judge as victims of a betrayal, demanding the restoration of lost honor through marriage or, in its absence, reparation in the form of a dowry. These spousal demands, which appear frequently in the ecclesiastical tribunals of the Catholic world during the modern age (see Brucker; Cavallo and Cerrutti; Claverie and Lamaison; Farge; and Ruggiero), open the door to a space to which the historian rarely has access: that of the early relationships between young couples. The reconstruction of the guidelines of behavior between these young people shows honor to be the dominant value; it also shows, at least for the eighteenth century (De la Pascua Sánchez, *Mujeres solas*; Demerson and Demerson; Dubert; Poska),[4] the openings through which apparently prohibited practices were able to enter. In these lawsuits it is made clear that young lovers found spaces and moments for love and that under the protection of dreams and projects, real or fictitious, they found the acquiescence of their familial and social circles—an acquiescence likely expectant and vigilant but also permissive.

Petitions for certificates of widowhood conserved in the same documental archives continue to shed light on these aspects of women's experience. In August 1772 Josepha Solis, the widow of Francisco Calavesani, who had died in Mexico about 1760, requested a document acknowledging her widowhood. She repeated the petition a year later and again in October 1775. On this last occasion she expressed the inconveniences of not possessing such a certification, for she had struck up a friendship with a young bachelor and contracted, soon after, a future engagement. Her fiancé's frequent visits were producing "much attention and scandal in the neighborhood" and "offense to [her] esteem," and since she wanted to marry legally, she required a certificate showing her to be a widow.[5]

The series of proceedings for certification of widowhood from the bishop of Cádiz, on which I am currently working and which elucidate, obviously, the most problematic cases—husbands absent for a long time, husbands who had died in tragic circumstances or in far-off places—reveal more than problems of honor. Those women that the censuses seemed to leave in a state of permanent widowhood continued their lives upon the death of their husbands and established new relationships. On occasion, the declaration of widowhood seems to have put an end to the solitude of women whose husbands had spent many years away from their company.

Sebastiana Marchante, a resident of the Isla de León, very close to Cádiz, lost her husband, who had been absent for twelve years. His death, according to the testimony witnesses gave, occurred while he was living among other deserters in a mountainous and unpopulated region close to La Habana. In 1795 Sebastiana

Marchante presented various witnesses to declare her "a widow and free to choose a new [married] state."[6] Isabel Pacheco was in a similar situation, in that when the appropriate commission for information about her widowhood was opened (1794), she had already spent eight months in negotiations to obtain testimony regarding the death of her husband in Orán, where he had been incarcerated for his "continual crimes." The circumstances of his death in a prison battered by an earthquake and by the war against African tribes justified, according to her, the loss of the death certificate and her long pilgrimage in search of creditable witnesses. The license of the vicar-general put an end to a long period in which she had been "held back in her choice of the married state."[7]

The objective of the opening of these commissions of information was so clear that some proceedings process the justification regarding widowhood at the same time that they processed the justification of liberty to celebrate new nuptials. This was the case of Josepha Roldán. Her husband had died in 1809, in a battle against French troops during the War of Independence; nevertheless it would be nine years, and after having celebrated her engagement, before she solicited both justifications.[8]

The proceedings did not always turn out fairly. The legal briefs about bigamy conserved in the archives of the Inquisition signal other outcomes. Fiscal declarations, which include the results of lawsuits, summaries, and legal briefs of all kinds, show the activity of various tribunals in Spain and Latin America from 1710 to the early nineteenth century (De la Pascua Sánchez, *Mujeres solas*, ch. 3). Although the critical period of persecution of bigamy in Hispanic realms was 1550–1650, coinciding with the effort to impose the Catholic model of marriage, the 330 cases documented in this series for the eighteenth century make possible an analysis of certain behaviors related to this crime. Moreover, here we concentrate on women's bigamy, evidence for which was found in 25 percent of the documents. These women's circumstances, their words, their life stories, extracted from summaries written by the administrative personnel of the Inquisition, are mediated, but even so they conserve a certain pulse of life that enables us to better understand these women. The nuances that emerge from the various cases reveal very diverse situations and derive from will, opportunity, or necessity. But overall, bigamy appears to have been a way to escape solitude or a frustrated marriage, constituting for our protagonists in general an escape forward.

The case of María López belonged to a group of cases in which women decided against all obstacles to remarry.[9] The principal impediment was that although she was separated from her husband, he was alive, and then came the other obstacles: the denunciation of her husband's family upon learning of her intentions; the scandal among her neighbors, witnesses to María's three-year cohabitation with her new partner; and the investigation opened by the Inquisition regarding her situation. In this case, as in others, absence seemed to play an important role, although it is impossible to determine whether it was merely a strategy to deal with an unhappy marriage or the cause of the unhappiness. The fact is that when she decided to remarry, María's husband had been absent for almost a year, and when a relative warned her about the impossibility of entering into a new marriage while her spouse was still alive, María responded: "[I]t doesn't matter, the worst they can do to me is oblige me to live with Crespo." Next came the falsification of proofs and the Inquisition tribunal's sentence, which condemned her to the loss of her goods and to prison.

In another case, Beatriz de Mena, a native of Lisbon, married in Madrid very young and lived with her husband barely two months.[10] After this brief period her husband left for Valencia to study medicine. When his letters stopped arriving after four or five months, she left for Lisbon to live with her mother. Upon the death of her mother, in 1755, she joined a company of actors who were returning to Spain, passing herself off as the wife of one of the actors so that she could travel with the company. Upon the death of her supposed husband, all of the other actors considered her a widow, and one asked for her hand in marriage. She accepted and lived with him until she was denounced. A long time had passed, almost twenty-five years, since she left Madrid, but the zeal of her parish priest in Cádiz, where the couple was living at the time, uncovered the infidelity upon learning that her husband was living and working as a surgeon in Cifuentes, near Guadalajara. The court condemned her to perform some spiritual exercises and to abandon the cohabitation with her current partner; she declared herself repentant and decided to correct her life.

It seems clear that mobility and the absence of a partner contribute to bigamy. But women with absent husbands have other reasons. Complaints about their husbands, denunciations of them for their failure to fulfill their obligations as the head of the family, and demands for the goods to which they and their children have a right are expressed repeatedly in the *Requisitorias a Indias* (Warrants to the Indies), a series from the Diocesan Archive of Cádiz comprising 336 proceedings undertaken between 1695 and 1804 with the objective of reuniting married couples. This documentation has as indisputable protagonists women with absent husbands, the majority of whom had emigrated to Hispanic America in search of fortune. Their wives and children had stayed in the peninsula, frequently without sufficient economic means to get ahead; among 170 women of whose economic situations we are aware, 169 lived in poverty. The long absence of many of these husbands, their failure to communicate and their lack of interest regarding the situation of their families, and the difficulties of daily life compelled these women to demand their rights by employing a legal process of forced repatriation.

Beginning in 1544, under Carlos I, laws continued to appear prohibiting the presence of married men in America without their wives' permission. These same laws foresaw the collaboration between civil and ecclesiastical justice to effect the forced embarkation and return home of those men who were demanded by their wives, as well as their property. But these women did more than initiate the process of their spouses' repatriation: they appeared before judges to tell their stories, stories of both denunciation—of their husbands for failing to comply with the terms of a matrimonial contract—and affirmation—of themselves and their social function as heads of real and true families. The requisite proceedings and the pleas that initiate them with an abbreviated story of what has occurred allow the historian to analyze what Norbert Elias calls the "elasticity of social position" (Elias), that is, the varied forms of relationships between the positional dynamic and the individual dynamic. In the history of these women, this play between social position and individual dynamic not only allows the departure from a victimist discourse, which it is easy to fall into when confronted with stories like these, but also facilitates the perception of these women as a sum of individualities, distancing us from an essentialist vision that condemns them to be "one" in a social universe that in western Europe since the Renaissance has been oriented toward understanding the subject as an autonomous being.

Why do the *Requisitorias a Indias* offer these possibilities? For our purposes, their adaptation derives from their goal of reuniting married couples and finds justification in men's failure to comply with a marriage contract formulated in the patriarchal code. It is husbands' failure to comply with the contract that gives meaning to the written lawsuits that these women present before the ecclesiastical judges; it is precisely the breaking of the terms of this contract by the absent head of the family that obliges a woman to replace him in basic family functions—feeding and educating the children, caring for themselves, and, fundamentally, representing themselves before the law and society without masculine mediation. But this assumption of functions implies a break with the model of dependence in which they have been socialized and, as compensation, an assumption of the paradigm of autonomy.

In these lawsuits, moreover, the women speak. Even though they speak through an attorney, even though their words are wrapped in the language of a secretary of the Curia, even though they might express themselves by means of a discourse that is fundamentally flawed (they use the arguments that they know to be socially convenient), there are in their words an appraisal of their experience and an assessment of their word. Even more, there is a story of life itself, and it is precisely in this subjective ordering of their experiences that they become aware of the meaning of what they do on a daily basis and how they might embark upon a process of alternative identification. This process has both material and symbolic aspects, from the perceived need to administer their own properties and those of their children to the need to represent themselves before the law as the only ones responsible for themselves and their descendents. We cannot expect this process to lead to the construction of a new identity without fissures or contradictions. At the moment of assessing their circumstances, these women question the values in which they have been socialized at the same time that they use them as arguments to prove the dysfunctionality of the family model that was in force. The materials for the construction of this alternative identity are not all new; among them survive the remains of the paradigm of dependence in which these women were socialized. Nevertheless, my quantitative analysis of many of the proceedings and the numerous life stories that they contain make clear the close relationship between life practices and autonomy (De la Pascua Sánchez, *Mujeres solas*).

Here I shall limit myself to the commentary of only one case, that of Juana Pérez, a woman who after years of waiting and deceptions, shows, in her declaration before the judge, great expository clarity both in analyzing her life and in signaling, based on the possibilities that she perceives, her objectives. Before Juana Pérez gave notice of her appeal in 1790, she had been married to Benito Quijano, who was missing in Veracruz, for thirteen years. Her husband had left with her consent two years after their marriage, making her promises that she believed. When he returned five years later, "seemingly exceedingly impoverished and unhappy," she believed in him again and lived with him for fourteen months, during which time their daughter was born. Then Benito left again, this second time it seemed definitively, since he not only failed to send any help whatsoever but acted as if he did not know of Juana whenever someone approached him to deliver her letters. Realizing that her husband had property—according to her, worth more than 10,000 pesos—while she and their daughter had to maintain themselves through personal work, "which, as women's work, barely provided enough to eat miserably, and they were always naked," she requested that "they immediately seize from her aforementioned husband all of his goods, from which they would make a balance sheet, and half of these and the existing money that they found with him be delivered with all security to her in this place for deposit, reducing half of his goods to cash to facilitate delivery" (De la Pascua Sánchez, *Mujeres solas* 262).

Juana does not request the return of her husband or an allowance, to which she has a right; she knows that he would only pay it to her in the first months and then flee or change his name. She demands half of the wealth that is due to her according to the regime governing the domestic Castilian community. And by demanding that right she declares herself capable of assuming legal responsibility for administering the wealth alone, without masculine mediation.

There were other situations of solitude, involving other experiences. Those I have analyzed were less the result of willful choice than consequences of different circumstances. But this real solitude, neither sought nor chosen, forges tactics that led women to accept their solitude and draw from it new life projects.

NOTES

1. The Catastro de Ensenada was an important counting of the population and evaluation of the wealth of the kingdoms of the crown of Castile that took place about the middle of the eighteenth century with a view to levying a single tax that would help to alleviate the tax confusion that the Spanish interior ministry had to face. Although the proposed "single tax" never materialized, today historians depend on the catastro as a first-rate source for learning about Castile in the eighteenth century. Recently it has been utilized to discover the presence of homes governed by women, that is, homes in which women were heads of households. See also Rebecca Haidt's discussion of the catastro in chapter 7 of this volume.

2. The Padrón of 1773 was a population count carried out in the city of Cádiz for military purposes; it tried to take a census of the entire masculine population. It only counted the heads of families and their sons, relatives, dependents, and male servants, including women who were the heads of families and whose families depended on them.

3. Archivo Diocesano de Cádiz, Varios, legajo 1854, año 1660.

4. For lawsuits in sixteenth-century Castile, see Cook and Cook; and Lorenzo Pinar. For lawsuits in sixteenth- and seventeenth-century Navarre, see Campo.

5. Archivo Diocesano de Cádiz, Varios, legajo 1856, año 1772.

6. Ibid., Viudedades, legajo 965, año 1795.

7. Ibid., año 1794.
8. Ibid., año 1818.
9. Archivo Histórico Nacional, Inquisición. libro 3721, expediente 24 (Tribunal de Sevilla, 1770–73).
10. Ibid., expediente 13 (Tribunal de Sevilla, 1777).

WORKS CITED

Birriel Salcedo, Margarita María. "Jefaturas de hogar femeninas en la ciudad de Granada (1752): I, Caracterización demográfica del hogar." In *Estudios en homenaje al profesor José Szmolka Clares*, ed. Antonio Luis Cortés Peña, Miguel Luis López-Guadalupe Muñoz, Francisco Sánchez-Montes González, and José Szmolka Clares, 591–604. Granada: Universidad de Granada, 2005.

Brucker, Gene. *Giovanni y Lusanna: Amor y matrimonio en el Renacimiento*. Madrid: Nerez, 1991.

Campo, J. "Los procesos por causa matrimonial ante el tribunal eclesiástico de Pamplona: Siglos XVI y XVII." *Príncipe de Viana* 202 (1994): 377–89.

Carbonell, Montserrat. "Las mujeres pobres en el Setecientos." *Historia Social* 8 (1990): 123–34.

Cavallo, Sandra, and Simona Cerrutti. "Onore femminile e controllo sociale della riproduzione in Piemonte tra sei e settecento." *Quaderni Storici* 44 (1980): 346–83.

Claverie, Elisabeth, and Pierre Lamaison. *L´imposible mariage: Violence et parenté en Gévaudan, 17e, 18e et 19e siècles*. Paris: Hachette, 1982.

Cook, Alexandra Parma, and Noble David Cook. *Un caso de bigamia transatlántica*. Trans. Carmen Aguilar. Madrid: Anaya-Mario Muchnik, 1992. Originally published as *Good Faith and Truthful Ignorance: A Case of Transatlantic Bigamy* (Durham, NC: Duke University Press, 1991).

D'Amelia, Marina. "Scatole cinesi: Vedove e donne sole in una societá d´ancien régime." *Memoria* 18 (1987): 58–80.

Dekker, Rudolf. *Childhood, Memory, and Autobiography in Holland: From the Golden Age to Romanticism*. Houndsmill, UK: Macmillan, 2000.

De la Pascua Sánchez, María José. *Mujeres solas: Historias de amor y de abandono en el mundo hispánico*. Málaga: Centro de Ediciones de la Diputación de Málaga, 1998.

———. "Social Reproduction and Alone Women Households: Cádiz in the 18th Century." Paper presented at "Women, Family, Private Life and Sexuality," fourth conference of the International Federation for Research in Women's History, Queen's University, Belfast, August 2003.

Demerson, Jorge, and Paula Demerson. *Sexo, amor y matrimonio en Ibiza durante el reinado de Carlos III*. Palma de Mallorca: El Tall, 1993.

Dubert, Isidro. "Los comportamientos sexuales premaritales en la sociedad gallega del Antiguo Régimen." *Studia Historica: Historia Moderna* 9 (1991): 117–42.

Elias, Norbert. *La sociedad cortesana*. Mexico City: Fondo de Cultura Económica, 1982. Originally published as *Die höfische Gesellschaft: Untersuchungen zur Soziologie des Königtums und der höfischen Aristokratie: mit einer Einleitung: Soziologie und Geschichtswissenschaft* (Neuwied, Germany: Luchterhand, 1969).

Farge, Arlette. *Vivre dans la rue à Paris au XVIIIe siècle*. Paris: Gallimard, 1979.

Fauve-Chamoux, A. "The Importance of Women in an Urban Environment: The Example of the Reims Household at the Beginning of the Industrial Revolution." In *Family Forms in Historic Europe,* ed. Richard Wall, 475–92. Cambridge: Cambridge University Press, 1983.

Hufton, Olwen. *The Poor of Eighteenth-Century France.* Oxford: Clarendon, 1974.

———. "Women without Men: Widows and Spinsters in Britain and France in the Eighteenth Century." *Journal of Family History* 9.4 (1984): 355–76.

Lorenzo Pinar, Francisco J. "La conflictividad social en torno a la formación del matrimonio (Zamora y Toro) en el siglo XVI." *Studia Historica: Historia Moderna* 13 (1995): 131–54.

Nader, Helen, ed. *Power and Gender in Renaissance Spain: Eight Women of the Mendoza Family, 1450–1650.* Urbana-Champaign: University of Illinois Press, 2004.

Palazzi, Maura. "Female Solitude and Patrilineage: Unmarried Women and Widows during the Eighteenth and Nineteenth Centuries." *Journal of Family History* 15.4 (1990): 443–59.

Perry, Mary Elizabeth. *Ni espada rota ni mujer que trota: Mujer y desorden en la Sevilla del siglo de Oro.* Trans. Margarida Fortuny Minguella. Barcelona: Crítica, 1993. Originally published as *Gender and Disorder in Early Modern Seville* (Princeton, NJ: Princeton University Press, 1990).

Poska, Allyson M. "When Love Goes Wrong: Getting out of Marriage in Seventeenth-Century Spain." *Journal of Social History* 29 (1996): 871–82.

Rial, Serrana. "Las mujeres solas en la sociedad semi-urbana gallega del siglo XVIII." *Obradoiro de Historia Moderna* 8 (1999): 169–97.

Rowlands, Alison. "To Wear a Virgin's Wreath: Gender and Problems of Conformity in Early Modern Germany." *European Review of History* 1 (1994): 227–33.

Ruggiero, Guido. "Più che la vita caro: Onore, matrimonio e reputazione femminile nel tardo Rinascimento." *Quaderni Storici* 66 (1987): 753–75.

Sanz, F. J. "Familia, hogar y vivienda en Burgos a mediados del siglo XVIII: Entre cuatro paredes, compartiendo armarios, camas, mesas y manteles." *Investigaciones Históricas* 22 (2002): 165–211.

Sarti, Raffaela. *Vida en familia: Casa, comida y vestido en la Europa moderna.* Barcelona: Crítica, 2003.

Wall, Richard. "Women Alone in English Society." *Annales de Demographie Historique,* 1981, 303–17.

9

An Enlightened Perspective on Hysteria in Eighteenth-Century Mexico

BEATRIZ QUINTANILLA-MADERO

> But in any case I wish to refer back to the experiences of sick women. Well recounted experiences [*experiencas bien hechas*] are always conclusive and do not leave those doubts and suspicions that reasoning can when it is not mathematically accurate.
> —JOSÉ IGNACIO BARTOLACHE, *El Mercurio Volante*, 25 November 1772

In this essay I analyze the portrayal of women in the eighteenth-century Mexican newspaper *El Mercurio Volante*, published by José Ignacio Bartolache y Díaz de Posadas, a physician, in 1772 and 1773. This newspaper is considered the first medical periodical to be published in the New World. One of the most fascinating issues, number 6, is devoted to women and entitled "Avisos sobre el mal histérico que llaman latido" (News of the hysterical illness called "palpitation"). The issue offers a detailed description of hysterical illness that is accessible to nonphysicians and provides a survey of important opinions of other well-known writers of the time. Bartolache's consideration of women's experience of hysteria represents a significant departure from other contemporary and traditional medical theories of the illness. He expresses his concern for women and their problems and speculates rationally on the possible origins and treatment of the disease, which he ascribes only to natural, not moral, causes. Before commenting specifically on *El Mercurio*, I shall discuss currently accepted medical definitions of hysteria and how this disorder has been viewed through the ages in order to evaluate changes in the perceptions about women and hysteria that took place among the enlightened men in Mexico during the eighteenth century.

What Is Hysteria?

Hysteria is a mental illness. It is well defined and has its own signs and symptoms. The medical profession now terms it *conversion disorder*,[1] so the term *hysteria* has come to be used in its adjectival form. It may be found in current classifications under "dissociative" or "somatoform" disorders (American Psychiatric Association; Organización Mundial de la Salud). The adjective *hysterical* characterizes a special type of personality, one that has some traits that are hysterical in nature. People with such traits might suffer a hysterical personality disorder.[2] Yet a third meaning might be given: *hysteria* is used to define a massive reaction suffered by a cohesive group in response to stressful or threatening events, for example, terrorist attacks. Several individuals in the group may display the same kind of symptoms in a given period of time. This phenomenon, called *mass hysteria* (Bartholomew and Wessely; Krack), can take as many forms as may be imagined, and usually symptoms do not have any organic correlate (Micale). Men might be particularly prone to *anxiety hysteria*, which has been seen mainly in military settings, where they might experience fear of poison gases or environmental pollutants (Bartholomew and Wessely). Cases of *battle hysteria* have also been observed in men (Patton).

Since ancient times, hysteria has been recognized as a unique medical entity with its own signs and symptoms. It could be said that it is one of the oldest diseases, and it has been described in different periods of history with little variation, at least with regard to its main signs and symptoms. There have been changes, however, in ideas about its cause, as well as in its clinical presentation, as if this were culturally determined. Hippocrates (ca. 460–377 BC) stated that every illness was related to an imbalance or corruption of the humors (Brain; Porter). But hysteria, as an almost exclusively female disease, was believed to be caused by the uterus, which wandered, like an animal, all over the body.[3] As uterus in Greek is *hysterus*, the illness was called *hysteria*. This belief about the "wandering womb" persisted into the seventeenth century (Brain). Even when anatomy was better understood and it was proved that the uterus was unable to wander, its responsibility as the cause for the illness was maintained until the nineteenth century. If the same kind of symptoms were seen in men, men would suffer *hypochondria*, but not hysteria (Boss).

Galen (AD 129–ca. 199), a Greek physician who practiced medicine in Rome, accepted Hippocratic conceptions and made his own contribution to the theory of hysteria (López Piñero). According to Galen, humoral imbalance was responsible for four types of "mental illness": frenzy, mania, melancholy, and fatuity. He supported the uterine origin of hysteria but denied that the uterus wandered about and that it was an animal. Enforced sexual abstinence was for him the principal etiology. He thought that a substance analogous to semen was produced inside the uterus. If this substance was retained, he believed, it could be poisonous and might cause illnesses such as hysteria. Similarly, men could suffer from hysteria if they retained sperm, and this retention was more serious (Veith; Williams).

Magic and superstition replaced learned medicine during the Middle Ages. Popular beliefs, folklore, traditions, demonic possession, sorcery, bewitchment, and the influence of the moon were melded with classic ideas about health. Even learned physicians would sometimes admit them as possible causes of disease. Demonic possession, which expressed itself predominantly in violent and bizarre behavior, was differentiated from physical illness. Treatments ranged from bleeding and purgatives to exorcisms and prayers. During the late Middle Ages and the Renaissance, the idea of demonic possession or sorcery gained strength. Women's susceptibility to demonic possession was attributed to their imperfect and weak nature. They were imperfect animals, inferior to men (Chodoff, "Hysteria"; Risse; Werner, Isaksen, and Malterud). Other disorders were associated with women's reproductive system and organs, mainly the uterus, where hysteria was believed to have its seat.

The Renaissance, however, brought a new attitude toward medicine. Original classic medical treatises were retrieved in order to find naturalistic explanations of the world and disease. While this focus on natural causes may seem like a return to antiquity, it was new in that there was an effort to give rational explanations to natural phenomena (Veith 116). This was an effort that had come to stay, and it would become especially strong during the Enlightenment. The uterus and its pathophysiological mechanisms were once again put forward as the cause for hysteria.[4] Besides the possible movement of the uterus, now uncertain for some physicians, its evil influence would be mediated through vapors ascending from the uterus to other organs and infesting them. In the eighteenth century "this belief gained such credence that subsequently . . . the term [*vapors*] not only became synonymous with hysteria, but was also descriptive of many lesser and insubstantial female behavioral peculiarities" (Veith 122n). Many other explanations flourished. Hysteria might be caused by seminal retention or spoiled seed; by menstruation or putrified menstruum; by bad and good odors; by vapors; by "sympathy" or the closeness of the diseased uterus to other organs; and by the "passions of the mind" (very strong and uncontrolled emotions) (Brain; Boss; Hare; Risse; Williams). But still witchcraft, sorcery, or even demonic possession was blamed, especially if the patient also had epileptic symptoms (García-Albea; Horta; Porter).

Another possible cause of the disease was the imagination, a faculty capable of producing physical changes in the organism. Following Paracelsus (ca. 1493–1541), John Baptista van Helmont, in the seventeenth century, believed the disease "was essentially 'imagined' but was not unreal" (Fischer-Homberger 620). Elaborating his notion of images produced by the spleen and the uterus, Helmont stated, "Uterine diseases do not arise from spoiled semen, but they are the fruits which follow the images" (qtd. in Fischer-Homberger 623). As Esther Fischer-Homberger explains, "If inadequate images [images produced solely by the female, not by the male] entered the uterus, they could lead to diseases of the hysterical imagination in a more limited sense. The uterus became the seat of pathogenic images" (623). Disease began as something immaterial but then was transformed into material reality through "an indomitable imagination, which cannot be submitted to volition, and is located in the spleen," Helmont explained (qtd. in Fischer-Homberger 620). The uterus was a second source for women, showing that in "a woman a double government does exist. . . . Under these conditions woman is a miserable creature. She is submitted to many diseases as a human being. But she is submitted a second time to these diseases on account of the essence of the uterus. She is up to this day punished twice, as if Eve had sinned doubly" (qtd. in Fischer-Homberger 621). The uterus as the prototype of an organ of imagination was physiologically predestined to receive imagination, the image of man (Fischer-Homberger; Risse). And because woman was only an "occasional animal," she was able to procreate the most "perfect" thing: man (Carbón).

By the eighteenth century, the prevailing conception of the origin of hysteria would gradually shift from the uterus to the brain, making hysteria a *nervous disease* in the literal sense (Brain; Webb et al.; Williams). Later, *nervous disorder* became synonymous with *psychological* disturbances. Hysteria has survived through the centuries. It has proven to be uniquely capable of adapting itself to the times, wearing different masks, mirroring "popular and cultural preoccupations that define each era and reflect unique social beliefs about the nature of the world" (Bartholomew and Wessely 300).

Bartolache and Hysteria in Eighteenth-Century Mexico

By the eighteenth century in New Spain, important enlightened authors were read and well known, and French was studied and spoken by well-educated people. But some physicians continued to believe that women were weak and in need of men's protection, that they were subject to the effects of imagination and vapors and even to demonic possession (Horta). Hysteria was the female disease par excellence, and besides all the causes already discussed, in some cases it was thought to be contagious.[5] Among these enlightened men in Mexico was José Ignacio Bartolache y Díaz de Posadas (Micheli). He was a Creole, born in Guanajuato to Spanish parents.[6] He studied philosophy at San Idelfonso College, a very distinguished and renowned Jesuit institution, and then received a scholarship to study theology at the Pontifical Seminar College in Mexico City. Later, he studied medicine at the Royal University of Mexico, and after being awarded his doctorate he published *El Mercurio Volante* in weekly installments for some months in 1772–73.[7] The journal came to an end when Bartolache ran out of money to support the cost. Each weekly issue discussed a different topic. Bartolache's opinions reflect what was known about medicine not only in Mexico but also in Spain and in other European countries. In his writings he quotes many authors—not only medical ones, such as Feijoo, Alzate, Paracelsus, Socrates, and Aristotle—and shows that besides being aware of the state of the art in medicine, he was familiar with classic medical texts.

Bartolache's enlightened attitude is reflected in his writings, in which he expresses his wish to be understood by everyone, writing in Spanish, not Latin. He specifically mentioned his intention to be read and understood even by women.[8] But since he was aware that he might be read by a medical audience as well, he quotes a large number of medical authors.[9] In the second issue of *El Mercurio Volante*, "Verdadera idea de la buena física y de su grande utilidad" (A true idea of good physics and its great usefulness), dated 28 October 1772, we find the following paragraph about women:

> I will say nothing in particular about women, . . . a sex that has been iniquitously abandoned and looked down upon as useless for the sciences and for no other reason than that men have wanted it like that. They [women] and simple, uneducated people may console themselves by knowing that they have a soul in their body that has been endowed with the same or maybe better powers than those of degree-holding students, who are so very respected because of their reputation. And by the way, they should know, to excuse any motives of envy, that Latin is necessary only to understand

Latin books, but not to think well or to understand sciences, which can be taught in every language. (*Mercurio* 14)

Bartolache's concern for women and their problems is especially apparent in issue number 6, "Avisos acerca del mal histérico que llaman latido," of 25 November 1772, one of the most important issues of the series.[10] There he describes hysteria methodically, as if he were describing the illness to other physicians, although he deliberately avoids technical terms. In some respects his description differs from previous descriptions of the illness,[11] and he makes interesting observations, especially on the possible causes of the disease. Bartolache's approach to the possible causes or treatment is clinical and rational. He believes only in natural causes.

Nevertheless, his description reflects many traditional views. For example, Bartolache assumes that hysteria is solely a woman's disease. Nothing in the paper suggests that he might have believed that men could suffer from the illness. He states:

> Although the fair sex represents half of the individuals of our species, their common and particular illnesses produce perhaps two-thirds of the plagues that affect humanity. A weak sex because of their own constitution, sickly and very much exposed to risk because of the destiny that God has given to them, they are afflicted with well-deserved punishment for their corruption. Because they are accustomed to soft treatment and delicacy by our gentleness, women are fastidious and spoiled and sensitive to the slightest annoyance. For all these reasons, physicians should treat women with the most particular care and attention. (*Mercurio* 55–56)[12]

Bartolache mentions some of the authors who in his opinion have written valuable treatises about women—Mercuriali, Ballonio, Mercado, Astruc, and Ramazzini. He then gives his own point of view with the authority of someone who has done "a great deal of study in the best books, who has carefully meditated on many things, and who has observed a large number of (female) hysterical patients" (*Mercurio* 60).

For Bartolache, three principal causes "among us" in Mexico are responsible for hysteria: "The first is the abuse of sweets and chocolate. The second, the tightened dress, because it supposes inaction or lack of exercise. The third, the perverted habit of going to sleep and getting up late" (*Mercurio* 60–61). This is a most interesting statement, in the first place because it gives us a clue as to what was thought to endanger one's health. Perhaps Bartolache had observed that chocolate was a stimulating beverage. However, Bartolache's enlightened compatriot José Antonio Alzate, wrote that although chocolate "is reputed to cause or increase melancholy" as well as "to cause nervous tremors, to lead to stupidity and other problems [as does coffee], it must be considered only as an indigestible beverage that increases hypochondriac humor" (Alzate y Ramírez 1:234–41).[13] In Britain at that time, stimulating beverages such as tea, coffee, and alcohol and eating too much meat and gravy were also mentioned as possible causes for the disease.[14] In New Spain, abusing sweets and chocolate and leading a sedentary life had been pointed out as dangerous habits by Farfan in the sixteenth century.

For Bartolache, burning cacao was not only dangerous to one's health; it was "a simple fashion introduced against good taste and health" (*Mercurio* 61). Corsets caused fainting because they impeded proper breathing. And exercise was necessary to expel bad humors from the body, by heat and sweat. Exercise was traditionally prescribed as a good method to "appease" women who suffered from hysteria (Boss; Risse; Veith). The habit of going to sleep late and getting up late was contrary to a temperate, orderly life, to which Bartolache gave enormous value. He strongly recommended the benefits of temperance in passions and emotions, a balanced diet, and exercise. He even dedicated four issues of *El Mercurio Volante* to a translation of a fifteenth-century essay by Luigi Cornaro about habits that promoted a long and healthy life.[15]

Bartolache cited the environment and poor public health as minor causes of hysteria. He discusses in some detail the problems that come from variations in the atmosphere of Mexico City, because "this land is at a very high elevation above sea level. Therefore, the air presses less upon our bodies and does not cause such a strong reaction of the solids against the humors in our bodies." The city, which is overpopulated, "abounds exceedingly in rubbish and bad vapors that make the air unhealthy and corrupted" (*Mercurio* 61). Miasmas and other dangerous exhalations—which in the case of Mexico may have come from the surrounding lakes—would corrupt certain areas, polluting the atmosphere and causing illness. The existence of microorganisms was not known at the time.

One of the largest cities in the world in Bartolache's day, as it is today, Mexico City was built by the Aztecs upon a lake. Many canals and some rivers surrounded or passed through it. Not all the houses had proper drainage, and most of the sewage and rubbish was thrown into the canals, the rivers, or the streets. Carriages drawn by horses, whose excrement contributed to unsanitary conditions, and slaughterhouses inside the city, with poor hygienic conditions, also contributed to the unhealthy environment. A main task of the authorities was to clean up the city and to maintain good air and water quality. Along with the civil authorities, the Protomedicato (Royal Medical Court),[16] proposed public-hygiene measures, such as using strongly perfumed plants to purify the air, cleaning streets and irrigation ditches, and even digging deeper graves. Another public measure was to send back to their hometowns healthy foreign Indians who were found wandering around and to keep the ill ones in hospitals (Rodríguez).

Bartolache observed that at the beginning of a hysterical attack "the woman feels in her stomach a very unpleasant weakness or hunger sensation and fainting that cannot be appeased by any kind of soft and liquid food but is helped by bitter foods and spirit" (*Mercurio* 56–57).[17] He specifically mentions the influence of odors, and he notes that "some aromatic and soft odors are very uncomfortable for the patients, as are some fruits, such as pineapple, watermelon, pears, and others. There are, however, some patients for whom the cause of palpitation [*latido*] is anything with a bad odor" (*Mercurio* 57).[18] Early phases of the attack were characterized by "cold in the extremities, buzzing in the ears, confused head, knotted throat, lack of energy or aptitude for any action, and proneness to sleep."[19] But if the illness lasted longer, more serious symptoms would appear, such as "convulsive tremors, breathing difficulties, anxiety, sights, tearfulness, an acute headache that is named the nail [*clavo*]."[20] "Mood swings, contortions of the limbs, jumps, and gestures that seem as if someone had bewitched them" (*Mercurio* 57) were also described.[21] Convulsive tremors and epileptic fits were confused, although sometimes they could be differentiated from hysterical attacks because in an epileptic fit, loss of consciousness was observed (Horta; Pearce).[22]

Behavioral, emotional, and psychological problems were other sources of symptoms, such as "perturbation of ideas and fears of having very serious illnesses patients heard reported by others. A fear of dying and other peculiar habits were observed, and got worse as the illness [went] on"; "vehemently felt passions (*rage, sadness*, etc.)" were considered triggers of the illness and worsened the clinical picture (*Mercurio* 57). Authors referred to them as the "passions of the mind" (Boss; Brain; Risse; Williams). Different phases of the illness were observed, because hysterics were not always indisposed, but exhibited very strong symptoms of their illnesses on some occasions more than others. "Poor hysterics go through very bad times when they are fasting, during their pre-menstrual period, or the phases of the moon," Bartolache observes (*Mercurio* 57), noting that women believed that the suppression or diminution of their menstrual cycle caused their illness. Bartolache disagreed, and in an effort to teach women, with obvious pride he assured his readers that "physicians do know that, if not always, at least in the majority of the cases, . . . the suppression or diminution [of menstruation] may be considered an effect of another illness, which should be investigated and cured" (*Mercurio* 63). Hysterical symptomatology was so bizarre and difficult to manage that he advised physicians to learn "how to get along with their patients in order to help them put up with their uncomfortable annoyance" (*Mercurio* 57). He gave special advice to physicians on how to avoid being blamed as bad doctors because of the rare success that accompanied the treatment of such cases.

Bartolache was aware that hysteria was mainly a women's illness. Perhaps he was inclined to write about hysteria because, in addition to being a "very serious and prolific illness [that was] difficult [to] cure," hysteria had come to represent a huge sanitary and social problem. He describes it as a problem that "especially here in America [Mexico, New Spain] has become a more common plague, particularly for upper- and middle-class people born and raised in a comfortable life; so it is gaining ground and inflicting damage on almost the most noble portion of this sex."[23] He even insists that "[i]n Puebla de los Ángeles and here in Mexico [City] it deserves to be named an endemic illness, . . . and indeed it is" (*Mercurio* 58).

During the eighteenth century a "hysterical epidemic" was observed in Mexico and in other parts of Spanish America, and many women of every condition were afflicted. In order to give his reader an idea of the situation, Bartolache provides some rough statistics: "Without any exaggeration, we can make the account that from every ten lay people only four, and from that same number of nuns only two, will be free of hysterical sickness." But Bartolache believed that the problem could get worse, for he was convinced that hysteria was a hereditary illness: "As it is demonstrated every day by reason and experience, the same kind of hysterical daughters are born from hysterical mothers, and because of this it is very easy to perceive how much this painful illness will be propagated and how very important it would be to try to cure it and to prevent it" (*Mercurio* 58).

The very high incidence reported among nuns might be explained by a problem that arose mainly in Mexico City and in Puebla de los Ángeles when their respective archbishops, Francisco Fabián y Fuero and Francisco Antonio Lorenzana, trying to enact ecclesiastic reform, began to reform nuns' convents in 1769. Most of the nuns were wealthy women from the aristocracy, among whom retiring to a conventual life was a highly respected practice. Nuns were accustomed to having their own rooms, their own servants, and other privileges. A dowry would be given upon their entering the convent to provide for their maintenance, but their families or important citizens who were renowned as patrons of a convent also helped with the costs. Often the number of servants who worked and lived in the convents was three times the number of nuns. The number and size of the convents, or the amount of money that wealthy patrons could give, was a sign of the power and wealth of the city. The convents were important social institutions in colonial Mexico, and much of the life of the cities centered around them (Bartolache, *Mercurio*; González Morales; Lavrin).[24]

The order of the archbishops, which took effect in the last part of the eighteenth century, was that the nuns should live according to stricter rules. They were restricted to community life, living, eating, praying, and sleeping together, giving up their privileges, and reducing the number of servants and attendants they kept with them. The nuns protested vigorously, but their protests were ignored, and they were forced to change their way of life. The civil population and the convent patrons also were against these stricter rules, which led to a very serious civil and religious problem.[25] The dispute was finally resolved when a double system of norms was permitted: the strictest rules would apply only for the new nuns (Bartolache, *Mercurio*; Lavrin). Under these circumstances many nuns fell sick. One of the most frequently observed illnesses consisted in a kind of convulsion or fit, with tremors and other unexplained symptoms. Convent authorities and physicians were confused and did not know whether to attribute the symptoms to hysteria, epilepsy, or even demonic possession. That is why Bartolache gives such a high estimate of the number of nuns with the disease and refers to them specifically; perhaps he also thought that in view of the rise in the number of cases seen in the entire female population, it was important to write something about hysteria.

Bartolache avoids referring to causes other than natural ones, however basic they were. He supported Hippocrates' theory about the uterine origin of the disease but did not accept the possible wandering of the uterus. Nor does he talk specifically about "vapors," but he admits that "hysteric sickness might have its origins in some kind of uterine irritation that infests the brain, the nerves, and also the muscles, firstly those that are needed for vital movements and in its outcome affecting those that are needed for voluntary movement" (*Mercurio* 57–58). This "infestation" of the brain was also mentioned by Horta, although he did not refer to the uterus (García-Albea; Horta).

Desiring to be read by women, Bartolache announces that he will "reduce this matter to some general points or maxims that may help as a guidance to all female hysterical patients [*las histéricas*] without exception, leaving every other matter to the good behavior and discretion of their physicians" (*Mercurio* 59). His advice is quite simple; in the first place he recommends avoiding predisposing factors, for example, "using chocolate with great moderation, and even more with sweets" (*Mercurio* 61). He also recommends exercise, a traditional treatment for hysterics (Boss; Risse). Bartolache explains that even nuns might be able to perform some simple exercises. His advice is "to hold one's breath and shake the body a number of times before breakfast. In this way the lungs are agitated, along with almost all the muscles, and blood circulation is accelerated in the veins and arteries, which is the aim of corporal exercise" (*Mercurio* 62). He also gives instructions on how to assure good-quality indoor air, and along the same line he advises nuns who sleep in common dormitories to crack the windows slightly, "so that they will have the required ventilation all night long." By this measure, they would avoid having the air infested with "many pounds of vapor enclosed in that room" (*Mercurio* 62–63), which results from the exhalation of humors by the body during the night.

Bartolache dismisses popular beliefs about the illness, ridiculing those who trusted in the efficacy of current remedies:

> Let us speak without deceiving ourselves: against hysterical illness there is very little that purgatives, vomiting, bleedings, pills, and other prescriptions can do. The liquors that are prepared with antihysterical drugs, if there are truly such, may help a little at the very beginning, but if taken continuously they will worsen the illness. Other tranquilizers and sedatives must be used for life, and the doses will be constantly augmented; but none of these works against the root cause nor diminishes the illness, and because of this alone we should mistrust such aids. (*Mercurio* 63)[26]

Eliminating the causes that restrained menstruation instead of merely trying to produce it was also strongly recommended. At the end of issue number 6 Bartolache warned women not to trust midwives or any of their remedies, which he included among popular remedies of the time, nor to "abandon themselves to the midwives' indiscretions in their pregnancies and childbirth" (*Mercurio* 64).

Bartolache's issue of *El Mercurio Volante* devoted to hysteria and the opinions of other contemporary physicians, such as Horta, about epilepsy reveal how women were seen in eighteenth-century Mexico. Although they were still viewed as fragile, prone to disease, and capable of being possessed or bewitched, as Horta suggests, Bartolache's writings reflect an important change in learned men's attitudes toward women. He shows respect for them, he is preoccupied with their sorrows, and he writes for them in Spanish, without caring what others might think of his doing so. In fact, his issue number 6 is devoted to all women. It is not written for a medical audience, but for everyone. In that and other issues of the *Mercurio* we can see how new ideas were introduced in Mexico. His modern approach is firm, and he rejects the idea that hysteria is a mysterious disease with transnatural causes or that it is connected to women through witchcraft. He does not give importance to the imagination as a cause for the disease, as had been common in other centuries, nor does he think that it is caused only by the influence of the uterus. Rather, his aim is to understand the illness rationally, to discover its natural and medical causes, and to make it understandable for others, giving simple and logical advice for everyone, especially women. Bartolache was also well ahead of his time in proposing sanitary and preventive measures to manage the problem, even before there was knowledge of microorganisms and before technology had been developed to investigate and diagnose disease. Bartolache's *Mercurio Volante* represents an empirical, enlightened approach to the medical interpretation of women's experience of illness.

NOTES

1. The term *conversion* was introduced after Freud's work (Brain; Chodoff, "Diagnosis"; Illis).

2. Current psychiatric classifications use the term *conversion* to refer to those psychological conflicts that are *converted* into organic symptoms unconsciously. These problems may be denied by the patient (Organzación Mundial de la Salud). The symptoms are not intentionally produced or feigned. The symptoms or deficits affect voluntary motor or sensory functions, suggesting a neurological or other general medical condition (American Psychiatric Association).

3. As stated in Plato's *Timaeus*, "The womb is an animal which longs to generate children. When it remains barren too long after puberty it is distressed and sorely disturbed and, straying about in the body and cutting off the passages of the breath, it impedes respiration and brings the sufferer into the extremest anguish, and provokes all manner of diseases besides. (The disturbance continues until the womb is appeased by passion and love). Such is the nature of women and all that is female" (qtd. in Chodoff, "Hysteria" 546).

4. Pathophysiological mechanisms of the uterus were advanced by Farfan, Jorden, Weyer, Willis, Harvey, Helmont, and others (Brain; Veith).

5. Joseph Raulin, in his 1758 *Traité des affections vaporeuses du sexe, avec l'exposition de leurs symptômes de leurs différentes causes, et la méthode de les guérir*, says of hysteria, "This illness in which

the women invent, exaggerate, and repeat all the different absurdities of which a disordered imagination is capable, is sometimes epidemic and contagious" (qtd. in Veith 169).

6. Biographical notes have been taken mainly from José Antonio de Alzate, a contemporary of Bartolache's who published a eulogy, "Elogio Histórico del Dr D José Ignacio Bartolache," in Mexico on 3 August 1790, only one month after Bartolache's death (Alzate y Ramírez 1:405–13; see also Moreno).

7. The complete title was *El Mercurio Volante, con noticias importantes y curiosas de Física y Medicina* (The Flying Mercury, with important and curious notices about some matters of Physics and Medicine).

8. Bartolache, *Mercurio* 14. Most quotations from Bartolache are from issue number 6, about hysteria, except a paragraph that corresponds to issue 2, which is specifically indicated. All translations from original texts are mine.

9. "The physicians, to whose censure I am subject, will judge with impartiality whether there is anything useful in the content of this paper. But in any case, I would like to refer to sick women's experience" (ibid., 56).

10. I have used for this study both the original paper (Bartolache, "Avisos") and the modern transcription of Roberto Moreno (Bartolache, *Mercurio* 55–64).

11. See Risse.

12. In referring to women's "destiny," Bartolache generalizes to explain why, in his opinion, women are more exposed to risk than men, saying that although it is based in the body, women's weakness may also be taken as a spiritual explanation for physical illnesses. The theory of women's weakness comes from the Bible, where Eve was tempted by the devil due to her fragility. For more on the traditional interpretation of Eve, see the introduction to this volume.

13. Writing some years after Bartolache, Alzate still subscribes to the theory of humors.

14. See Risse.

15. The issues were 11–14, all in January 1773.

16. The Royal Medical Court certified physicians and other sanitary professionals. It could make rules on sanitary issues, procedures, and certification requirements.

17. Symptoms such as diarrhea, vomiting, or abdominal pain were usually observed, as they are today (Boss; Guze and Perley).

18. Odors have been related to epileptic aura.

19. A knotted throat was defined in the *Oxford English Dictionary* in 1794 as "a choking sensation, as of a lump in the throat to which hysterical persons are subject." The term *globus hystericus* (from the Latin. *globus* [lump] and the Greek *hystericus* [related to the uterine axis]) was coined by John Purcell in 1707 to describe the condition, which was regarded as an affliction solely of women (Brain; Webb et al.).

20. The *clavus hystericus* was a special form of headache described in hysterical patients as a most "vehement pain in the head" (Birket-Smith; Boss; Williams).

21. This is Bartolache's only reference to probably unnatural phenomena.

22. The convulsive tremors, contortions of the limbs, and so on, mentioned here were known as the "fits of the mother" (Boss; Brain; Farfan; Risse).

23. Hysteria was thought to be an upper- and middle-class women's illness, most frequent among widows and spinsters. However, Risse's interesting publication shows that it was observed in women of every class.

24. See Elisa Sampson Vera Tudela's discussion of the pressures caused by convent reform in chapter 5 of this volume.

25. This problem was also observed in Lima, Peru (Lavrin).

26. Opium was the most frequently used tranquilizer.

WORKS CITED

Alzate y Ramírez, José Antonio de. *Gacetas de literatura de México*. 4 vols. 1788–95. Puebla, 1831.

American Psychiatric Association, Task Force on DSM-IV. *Diagnostic and Statistical Manual of Mental Disorders: DSM-IV-TR*. 4th ed. Washington, DC: American Psychiatric Association, 2000.

Bartholomew R. E., and S. Wessely. "Protean Nature of Mass Sociogenic Illness: From Possessed Nuns to Chemical and Biological Terrorism Fears." *British Journal of Psychiatry* 180.4 (2002): 300–306.

Bartolache, José Ignacio. "Avisos acerca del mal hysterico, que llaman latido." *Mercurio Volante con Noticias Importantes i Curiosas Sobre Varios Asuntos de Física y Medicina* 6 (1772): 41–48.

———. *Mercurio Volante (1772–1773)*. Ed. Roberto Moreno. Mexico City: Universidad Nacional Autónoma de Mexico, 1993.

Birket-Smith, M. "Somatization and Chronic Pain." *Acta Anaesthesiologica Scandinavica* 45.9 (2001): 1114–20.

Boss, J. M. "The Seventeenth-Century Transformation of the Hysteric Affection, and Sydenham's Baconian Medicine." *Psychological Medicine* 9 (1979): 221–34.

Brain, Russell. "The Concept of Hysteria in the Time of William Harvey." *Proceedings of the Royal Society of Medicine* 56 (1963): 317–24.

Carbón, Damián. *Libro del arte de las comadres o madrinas y del regimiento de las preñadas y paridas, y de los niños*. 1541. Trans. Francisco Susarte Molina. Alicante: Universidad de Alicante, 1995.

Chodoff, Paul. "The Diagnosis of Hysteria: An Overview." *American Journal of Psychiatry* 131.10 (1974): 1073–78.

———. "Hysteria and Women." *American Journal of Psychiatry* 139.5 (1982): 545–51.

Farfan, Agustín. *Tratado breve de medicina y de todas las enfermedades, que à cada passo se ofrecen*. 1592. Facsimile ed., Valladolid: Maxtor, 2003.

Fischer-Homberger, Esther. "On the Medical History of the Doctrine of Imagination." *Psychological Medicine* 9 (1979): 619–28.

García-Albea, E. "El *Informe médico-moral de la penosissima y rigorosa enfermedad de la epilepsia* (1763), del hispano Pedro de Horta, el primer tratado americano sobre la epilepsia." *Revista de Neurología* 26.154 (1998): 1061–63.

González Morales, A. "Dolor y sensualidad: Vida cotidiana de una monja iluminada en Puebla." *Elementos* 46.9 (2002): 51–58.

Guze, S. B., and M. J. Perley. "Observations on the Natural History of Hysteria." *American Journal of Psychiatry* 119 (1963): 960–65.

Hare, E. "The History of 'Nervous Disorders' from 1600 to 1840, and a Comparison with Modern Views." *British Journal of Psychiatry* 159 (1991): 37–45.

Horta, Pedro de. *Informe médico-moral de la penossisima y rigorosa enfermedad de la epilepsia.* 1763. Facsimile ed., Alcalá de Henares: Universidad de Alcalá de Henares, 1994.

Illis, I. S. "Hysteria." *Spinal Cord* 40 (2002): 311–12.

Krack, P. "Relicts of Dancing Mania: The Dancing Procession of Echternach." *Neurology* 53.9 (1999): 2169–72.

Lavrin, Asunción. "Religiosas." In *Ciudades y sociedad en Latinoamérica colonial*, ed. Louisa Schell Hoberman and Susan Midgen Socolow, 175–213. Buenos Aires: Fondo de Cultura Económica, 1992.

López Piñero, José María. *La Medicina en la Historia.* Madrid: La Esfera de los libros, 2002.

Micale, Mark S. "Hysteria and Its Historiography: The Future Perspective." *History of Psychiatry* 1 (1990): 33–124.

Micheli, A. de. "La medicina y la Ilustración en la Nueva España." *Gaceta Médica Mexicana* 134.3 (1998): 343–49.

Moreno, Roberto. Introduction to *Mercurio Volante (1772–1773)*, by José Ignacio Bartolache, ed. Roberto Moreno, v–xlviii. Mexico City: Universidad Nacional Autónoma de Mexico, 1993.

Organización Mundial de la Salud. *CIE-10: Trastornos mentales y del comportamiento; Descripciones clínicas y pautas para el diagnóstico.* Madrid: Meditor, 1992.

Patton, M. A. "An Early Case of Battle Hysteria." *British Journal of Psychiatry* 138 (1981): 182–83.

Pearce, J. M. S. "Early Accounts of Epilepsy: A Synopsis." *Journal of Neurology, Neurosurgery and Psychiatry* 64.5 (1998): 679–82.

Porter, Roy. *The Greatest Benefit to Mankind: A Medical History of Humanity.* New York: Norton, 1998.

Risse, G. B. "Hysteria at the Edinburgh Infirmary: The Construction and Treatment of a Disease, 1770–1800." *Medical History* 32 (1988): 1–22.

Rodríguez, María Eugenia. *Contaminación e insalubridad en la Ciudad de México en el siglo XVIII.* Monografías de Historia y Filosofía de la Medicina, 3. Mexico City: Departamento de Historia y Filosofía de la Medicina, Facultad de Medicina, Universidad Nacional Autónoma de México, 2000.

Veith, Ilza. *Hysteria: The History of a Disease.* Chicago: University of Chicago Press, 1965.

Webb, C. J., Z. G. G. Makura, J. E. Fenton, S. R. Jackson, M. S. McCormick, and A. S. Jones. "Globus Pharyngeus: A Postal Questionnaire Survey of UK ENT Consultants." *Clinical Otolaryngology and Allied Sciences* 25 (2000): 566–69.

Werner, A., L. W. Isaksen, and K. Malterud. "'I am not the kind of woman who complains of everything': Illness Stories on Self and Shame in Women with Cronic Pain." *Social Science and Medicine* 59 (2003): 1035–45.

Williams, Katherine E. "Hysteria in Seventeenth-Century Case Records and Unpublished Manuscripts." *History of Psychiatry* 1.4 (1990): 383–401.

PART III
REPRESENTATIONS OF WOMEN
Between Rational Equality and Sensibility

The essays in this final part deal with artistic and literary representations of women and their real or imagined connection to women's experience, the cultural imaginary of gender. The Enlightenment penchant for classifying social roles and castes established categories that became new stereotypes defining women according to class and race. Lucy Harney analyzes how the caste systems of eighteenth-century Cuba were informed by Enlightenment political and social theories of social responsibility and class difference. Her study of the legacy of Enlightenment thought in colonial discourse is based on Cirilo Villaverde's short story "Cecilia Valdés" and shows how Enlightenment ideas of race and gender were a crucial step in late nineteenth-century reworkings of class and race in the context of Spanish American nationalism and identity. Following Harney's analysis of the centrality of representations of cultural constructions of gender to national identity, Catherine Jaffe discusses how representations of women readers in late eighteenth-century Spanish periodicals reflect the ambivalent relation of women to the modernizing project of Enlightenment. She shows how these representations critique women readers and establish women's reading as an inferior intellectual practice, revealing discomfort with the necessary shift in power relations implied by women's literacy and accession to culture. Ana Rueda looks at the representation of the motif "virtue in distress" in the Spanish sentimental novel and theorizes that novels and conduct manuals attempted to inculcate "moral sentiments" in their female readers. But the moral lesson could be read ambivalently, and sensibility could arouse passion, a key insight for the study of the evolution of the modern novel and gender discourse in the nineteenth century, when sensibility was discredited as a moral force under the pressures of defining national identity. Janis Tomlinson closes the volume by approaching one of the most highly charged debates about female "nature" and gender difference, centered on a woman's role and duties as mother, through a study of works by Francisco de Goya. In her analysis of drawings, tapestry cartoons dating from 1776–92, portraits of women of the mid- to late 1780s, and etchings from the series *Desastres de la Guerra* (1810–20), Tomlinson finds that the artist borrowed a rhetorical technique from Enlightenment essays that emphasized model behavior through juxtaposition. She finds that Goya was aware of changing social roles but remained ambivalent regarding "ideal" models of women, such as that of motherhood. But Tomlinson also shows that certain attitudes and types, such as *marcialidad* (an uninhibited, outspoken manner) and the *maja*, were assertive expressions of modernity for women. Thus, the top-down pattern of class influence described by María Victoria López-Cordón Cortezo in chapter 6 could also function in reverse. Tomlinson concludes that Goya's representation of women's heroism during the War of Independence suggests a new vision of femininity made possible by the Enlightenment and the new attention it brought to women's lives.

10

The Enlightenment Origins of Cuba's Iconic *Mulata*

LUCY D. HARNEY

*I*n Cuban letters and popular culture, there is no symbol more evocative of the racial, sexual, and social dimensions of women's experience than the *mulata*. In *Sugar's Secrets: Race and the Erotics of Cuban Nationalism* Vera Kutzinski maintains that "the iconic mulata is a symbolic container for all the tricky questions about how race, gender, and sexuality inflect the power relations that obtain in colonial and postcolonial Cuba." She notes that through various idealized constructions the "half-breed race . . . has been discursively engendered in Cuba since the early 1800s," the first literarily significant representation appearing in Cirilo Villaverde's original short story "La primitiva 'Cecilia Valdés'" (Kutzinski 6–7). The widespread identification of the *mulata* with Cuban national identity has pervaded Cuban letters for the past two centuries, finding frequent—some would argue obsessive—expression in the works of José Martí, Alejo Carpentier, Nicolás Guillén, and Reinaldo Arenas, among many others. First published in 1839, Villaverde's short story is often dismissed as a rough draft of the second and third chapters of the final novelized version, *Cecilia Valdés; o La Loma del Ángel* (1882), a work that Jean Lamore describes as "a founding text for [Cuban] nationalism" (17).[1] However, I would argue that while the story shares with the novel its characters and basic plot, it derives from and exemplifies a distinct literary tradition and social outlook rooted in the eighteenth century. The purpose of this essay is to examine Villaverde's short story, both on its own terms and in comparison with the 1882 novel, to demonstrate the earlier work's affinities with neoclassical narrative modes as well as with Enlightenment models of race, gender, and society. These considerations bring into relief many literary and social echoes of eighteenth-century thought that persisted into the nineteenth century, thereby providing a conceptual bridge of sorts between Enlightenment principles and early nineteenth-century representations of the marginalized female's experience in Cuba.

In her consideration of nineteenth-century Cuba's growing disaffection with Spain, Sherry Johnson maintains that "the ideology of *cubanidad* [Cubanness] took its root in eighteenth-century demographic and social forces" (190). The ideology to which Johnson refers, one in which "identification with Spain was replaced with pride in being Cuban" (180), can be discerned in the introductory paragraph of Villaverde's original short story: "every people has its unique nature, its distinct inclinations, habits, and customs" (no. 1).[2] This presumption of a communal identity—in a phrase that could as readily have come from a *cuadro de costumbres* (portrait of customs) by a Spanish romantic writer such as Mesonero Romanos or Larra—takes on greater significance given its colonial context. The Rousseauist gesture with which Villaverde implicitly subsumes Cuba's various colors, castes, and classes, irrespective of national origin, within the notion of *pueblo* is underscored by his reference to the "sacred debt" that the individual "has contracted with society" (no. 1).

Villaverde's humanist rhetoric is calculated. A disciple of Félix Varela (Johnson 178), the young Villaverde considered himself a product of the new philosophy and experimental sciences that had only recently driven Scholasticism from the Cuban academy when he obtained his law degree in 1834 (Leal 236–37). During his many years of exile in the United States, beginning in the late 1840s, Villaverde would publish several periodicals, including *La Ilustración Americana,* committed to progressive causes such as independence for Cuba and the abolition of slavery (Luis 106–7). Plantation slavery is depicted in great detail in the 1882 novel, which is frequently characterized as abolitionist, although this interpretation is not unanimous.[3] In the short story, however, slavery is not at issue. Also absent from the story are numerous elements of the novel's intricate social matrix, which includes many historical personages and references to significant political, social, and economic events.[4] The disparity in length and historical complexity between the novel and the story should not, however, lead one to conclude that the shorter work is merely a preview of the longer. The story has its own stylistic and generic affiliations, as well as its own social philosophy.

Mode, Style, and Genre

Villaverde considered his novel an expression of realist *costumbrista* aesthetics. He subtitled his 1882 edition "Novela de costumbres cubanas" and in its prologue affirms: "I pride myself on being, above all, a realist writer" (Prologue 49–50). Beyond its acknowledged inspiration in the historical works of Walter Scott and

Alessandro Manzoni, Villaverde's novel evinces similarities to Spanish *costumbrista* writers of the second half of the nineteenth century (e.g., Fernán Caballero, Pedro Antonio de Alarcón, and José María de Pereda), as well as to the realism and naturalism of Balzac, Pérez Galdós, and Pardo Bazán, who are also concerned with folkloric and ethnographic authenticity and whose works can likewise be said to represent an outgrowth of Enlightenment ideas and artistic practices. However, Villaverde's short story, written some forty years earlier, is a more direct product of Enlightenment literary values. Regarding its many undeniable *costumbrista* traits found in references to culturally specific artifacts of urban Havana, such as the various fruits—*pasas, plátano, mamey, guayaba*—that the mischievous young Cecilia is often seen to pilfer from street vendors (no. 1) and the catalog of religious souvenirs and icons—*estampas, reliquias colgadas, samblases, cruces de cartón, guano bendito*—littering the shack of Cecilia's devout grandmother (no. 2), the question remains whether the story might best be understood as belonging to the *costumbrista* tradition practiced by Villaverde's Spanish contemporaries, as in Larra's *Artículos* (1835–37), the *Escenas matritenses* (1836–42) of Mesonero Romanos, or Estébanez Calderón's *Escenas andaluzas* (1847). Villaverde's story, I suggest, represents an earlier, Enlightenment phase of *costumbrista* writing, in which minute descriptions and typological formulations serve more often to convey moral exempla than to evoke the picturesque nostalgia and mordant social satire prevalent in nineteenth-century *costumbrismo*.

As Russell Sebold has observed, the *costumbrista* mode began long before its acknowledged heyday in the nineteenth century. He points to its roots in the sensationalism of the eighteenth century, which ensured that "all literary trends of the time tended toward a more objective and documented representation of the social framework of human life" ("El subtexto" 7). Sebold emphasizes the Enlightenment's prolongation of the seventeenth-century tendency "to reason from the general to the particular" and thus to avoid the problem of the individual's relationship to the milieu. The implied privileging of preconception over observation is reflected in a tendency toward typological representations of literary characters (Sebold, "Enlightenment" 113). Citing Américo Castro's concept of a distinctive "egocentric pantheism" as the hallmark of romanticism, Sebold argues that the significant development from neoclassicism to romanticism, which he characterizes as "evolutionary rather than revolutionary," yields an "egocentric Romantic metaphysic" ("Enlightenment" 117–18).

If, as Sebold suggests, this principle of individuation differentiates neoclassicism from romanticism, then the universalism of Villaverde's story may be usefully contrasted with the individuation of his novel. An appeal to universality frames the story with a generalized introduction and a fablelike ending. The story's introductory paragraphs, omitting specific references to characters or setting, express a broad social vision that defies regional specificity, alluding instead to general notions of society, social progress, and humanitarianism. This contrasts with the novel's first chapter, which launches the reader directly into the action of the events surrounding Cecilia's birth while precisely identifying characters, time, and place.

The story's introduction emphasizes the responsibility of the privileged classes to protect society's less fortunate members, warning that punishment awaits those who instead seek to exploit the innocent. The narrator indicts the system of charity that allows unwanted children to be left in orphanages, thus depriving them of the parental guidance and proper instruction necessary to their prosperity. The narrator then informs us that his recollection of Cecilia's plight has caused him to reflect along such lines: "These reflections occurred to us upon our remembering that . . . almost daily we used to encounter a young girl . . ." (no. 1). While the narrator's claim suggests a movement from the particular to the general, the story's opening rumination on society and its ills seems to set the stage for the presentation of Cecilia's experience as an exemplum of exploited innocence, suggesting the general-to-specific pattern described by Sebold, an orientation reminiscent of the homiletic tradition embraced and adapted by eighteenth-century writers and later rejected by realist writers.

In contrast to the novel's detailed depictions of many of Villaverde's own "friends, classmates, acquaintances, relatives, etc." (Nora and Friol 100), the story affiliates its characters on the one hand with the fabulist tradition in Hispanic letters—from the medieval period's Don Juan Manuel to the eighteenth-century *fabulistas* Samaniego and Iriarte—and on the other hand with the Theophrastian characterology that is one of the Enlightenment's more striking literary partialities (as reflected in the reception and influence of La Bruyère). Cecilia, the typical unsuspecting young beauty, falls prey to Leocadio Gamboa, the quintessential rakish *señorito*. The narrator compares Cecilia to "the dove just leaving the nest." Like the fledgling who tries out "her weak wings beneath the heavens," she is tracked in her flight by the "round, fixed eyes of the kite" as the bird of prey swoops down "to devour her between its talons!" (no. 3).

In an effort to dissuade Cecilia from running off to dances and parties, her grandmother recounts a cautionary fable in which a young girl named (pointedly enough) Narcisa, attracted by the music of a dance, runs off without permission. On the way, Narcisa encounters a handsome young man who offers to accompany her. As he leads her along, however, his skin begins to grow dark like coal, the hairs on his head stand up like wire, and his teeth project outward like a boar's tusks. Two horns sprout from his forehead, a long tail drags behind him, and fire spews from his mouth. As Narcisa shrieks in terror, the demon, burying his claws in her throat, picks her up and climbs to the top of Angel's Tower, which (the grandmother reminds Cecilia) has no cross. From there Narcisa is hurled down into a bottomless pit. Ña Chepa spells out the moral: "this is what happens to girls who fail to follow the advice of their elders" (nos. 2–3).

In the story, this cautionary fable evokes a somber fairy-tale atmosphere, preparing for the wistful sadness of the story's ending, in which the unhappy ña Chepa, "beset by grief," dies a few days after the disappearance of her beloved Cecilia. In the novel (87–88), the grandmother's admonitory tale constitutes only one of Chepa's many (ultimately futile) attempts to keep Cecilia away from Leonardo (Leocadio in the story), who, unbeknownst to Cecilia, is her half-brother. In the story, which likewise intimates the danger of incest (as when Cecilia's visit to the Gamboa home provokes a suspicious consternation in both parents [no. 1]), this drama is never developed explicitly. Instead, the story concludes with the disappearance of Cecilia, who "asked permission to go to a dance and never returned" (no. 1). The narrator eerily suggests that Cecilia, by ignoring her grandmother's warnings and taking up with Leocadio, may have suffered a fate comparable to Narcisa's. The story's ending thus brings into relief an exemplary (and structurally central) function for Chepa's warning. The didactic quality of the grandmother's cautionary tale is somewhat blunted in the novel by Chepa's advising Cecilia (one passage earlier) to marry a white man at all costs (86). By contrast, an unmistakably gnomic quality is conferred with the analogy between Cecilia's disappearance at the end of the story and Narcisa's fate in the framed tale.

The admonitory effect of the story's intercalated fable is prepared by the opening passage's condemnation of those writers, especially French ones, who perceive society as "an unnatural beast, a sphinx, a great monster that devours itself." However, declares the narrator, in a society that is "well-bred, Christian, and educated," injustice is generally the work of "a small fraction of its individuals . . . but not all of it." Those responsible for maintaining "the continual and progressive course" of society are "those with the education and the means." With the rest of society, this informed elite contracts a sacred duty that obliges its members to "lead [society] in a laudable and humanitarian direction." Corruption, then, cannot be blamed on society at large, "which often lets itself be led like a sheep to the fold, and not infrequently to the wolf's claws" (no. 1).

This paternalistic stance, assuming leadership of an ignorant populace to be incumbent upon the educated classes, as described by Lucienne Goldmann (57, qtd. in Miller 1071), typifies Enlightenment political theory and articulates with the image of society as a herd of innocent sheep that may either be led to the safety of the fold or fall into the clutches of the wolf. This fundamentally pastoral motif invokes both the Christian tradition of the savior as shepherd of his flock and the medieval and Renaissance pastourelle's conventional portrayal of the innocent shepherdess beset by the seductive noble. In Spanish literary history a prominent example of this theme presents the most infamous sexual predator of them all—Don Juan—seducing, in a piscatorial variation, the poor fisher-girl Tisbea ([Molina] 158–63).

The essence of pastoral, notes William Empson, is the representation of "the lives of 'simple' low people to an audience of refined wealthy people, so as to make them think first 'this is true about everyone' and then 'this is specially true about us'" (195–96). Extrapolating from Empson's distillation of the core pastoral motif, we might classify Villaverde's short story as a specimen of urban pastoral in which, by an analogical transference from countryside to town, lower-class innocence and simplicity are contrasted with upper-class duplicity and depredation.[5] The artless shepherdess and the libidinous knight of earlier centuries are readily recast in the Cuban context in the form of the naive *mulata* and the spoiled and predatory *señorito*.

An essential difference between the story's vision and purpose and those of the novel can be inferred from Villaverde's own disclaimer in the novel's prologue, in which he justifies his realist project: "I recognize that it would have been better for my work if I had written an idyll, a pastoral romance . . . but this, though more entertaining and edifying, would not have been the portrait of any living personage, nor the description of the customs and passions of a flesh-and-blood people" (Prologue 50). The story, however, resembles precisely the sort of moralistic pastoral ballad rejected by Villaverde as the model for the later work.

Social Philosophy, Gender, and Race

Eighteenth-century political and social theory was contradictory in its attitude toward hierarchy, reaffirming egalitarian ideals while supporting the institution of the enlightened despot. The notion of responsible guardianship as an element indispensable in maintaining social order and justice explains the Enlightenment's often paradoxical understanding of the social elite. Villaverde's short story seems to participate in this paternalist social vision. In condemning the upper class's dereliction of duty, Villaverde assigns that class a preemptive competency and responsibility, while minimizing the accountability of the lower classes.

The story's division between a passive society and a responsible elite recalls Locke's observation that men put themselves "into Society" in order to establish "an Authority, a Power on Earth," that will protect them from the violence of their fellow men (300). Similarly, Montesquieu recommends the pragmatic utility of a certain degree of social inequality, observing that in nature "all men are born equal, but they cannot continue in this equality." Society makes them unequal, with equality restored only by "the protection of the laws" (52). Thomas Paine's *Common Sense* contrasts society, "produced by our wants," and government, springing from "our wickedness." Society of every kind is thus "a blessing," but even the best government is only "a necessary evil" (7). These sentiments echo Rousseau's famous declaration that "man is born free but is everywhere in chains," leading to his notion of a civil state in which the spirit of justice replaces instinct and in which "duty takes the place of physical impulses and right of appetite" (387).

These social premises provide an ethical and political backdrop to Villaverde's earliest characterization of his iconic heroine. Cecilia is, the narrator declares, "so pure, so delicate, so playful" that she seems "the ideal creation of the enamored poet." Because her only school is the city itself, her "tender heart" is deprived of "all the virtues that beautify the existence of a good woman." Instead she is subjected to "the most corruptive lessons in the world" and the most harmful examples of "lasciviousness and immodesty that an uncouth and degenerate people display on a daily basis" (no. 1). In accordance with the unambiguous typology of much Enlightenment narrative, the Cecilia of the story is as blameless as Leocadio is culpable.

This moralistic simplicity is considerably attenuated in the novel, where the upper-class aggressor is characterized somewhat more sympathetically (smitten by Cecilia, manipulated by his mother, etc.), while Cecilia's complicity is more clearly suggested. As Cécile Leclercq demonstrates, Villaverde's novel depicts the plight of the *mulatos* as an intermediate caste subject to the "powerful ambivalence of being racially, psychologically, and culturally marginal," yet driven to interiorize "the values of the dominant class" and obsessed by "yearning for upward social mobility" (415). Social climbing particularly characterized *mulatas*, who saw in relations with white males the possibility of escaping oppressive social and economic circumstances.

In the novel, suggests Leclercq, Cecilia's "yearning for social advancement" makes her the typical "gold-digging *mulata*," readily seduced by "wealthy white men." Villaverde shows such women to be "fragile" and "of scant virtue." Because they are "desirous of climbing and bettering their condition," they are the predestined concubines of men of "superior" race. The Cecilia of the novel engages in calculations that may be termed "the mulata's wiles, since her love for Leonardo is inspired by social motives, and by eagerness for upward mobility" (Leclercq 416). This understanding of Cecilia's situation contrasts sharply with the story wherein she is described as "a lamb at her sacrificer's feet" (no. 3).

In the novel, Villaverde is at great pains to describe the real social pressures and constraints faced by early nineteenth-century Cubans. As Verena Martínez Alier observes, the system Villaverde depicts is pervaded by hypergenation, the tendency toward "procreation between upper-class men and lower-class women." The liaisons established within this unofficial regime were necessarily extralegal, according to an unstated but rigidly observed rule whereby upper-class men's personal honor and their families' honor were not affected by concubinage but were compromised by formalized marital unions with lower-class women, especially women of color (118).

Villaverde's short story only hints at the specific workings of this unofficial social regime in Cuba, highlighting instead Cecilia's membership in the victimized masses of humanity, the defining characteristics of which are understood to vary only incidentally among cultural loci. The story, notes Leclercq, exonerates Cecilia of any biological defect on which her "moral frivolity," her "footloose character," or her "desire to live better dressed" might be blamed. Instead, the girl's "psychological disorientation" is attributed to a lack of domestic supervision and scholastic instruction (Leclercq 415). Wandering the city at will, this innocent but headstrong girl excites "illicit hopes and desires in boyish hearts." Cecilia, the narrator laments, lacks a certain "category of instruction" and "virtues which might be transmitted and sown in a childish heart so as to reap a harvest of virtues, the only ones capable of garnering happiness and success." These things ña Chepa, "sad woman of the masses," cannot provide even for herself, let alone for someone else (no. 3).

The essential innocence of the underclass, of which Cecilia is emblematic, and its impressionability (core tenets of the Enlightenment) are underscored in the story by Villaverde's narrator, who explains that although Cecilia is "of a kind and peaceful nature," her continual exposure to the life of the streets causes her to succumb to the allure of "luxury," which flatters her "vanity and her pride." Without moral and worldly guidance, bereft of "moral examples," and too often exposed to "vulgar scenes," she is merely another of the "poor, disoriented girls" who are the favorite prey of Leocadio, "the great seducer" of such girls (no. 3).

Leocadio, the typical *señorito,* is profiled by Leclercq as "rich, lazy, a bad student, arrogant, and harsh-natured." A "spoiled brat" and a spendthrift, Leocadio amuses and fulfills himself by humiliating people of lower status, especially women (Leclercq 416). Born to a "rich, if not quite noble family," Leocadio is destined for the legal profession, one of only three careers to which one "rich and with ample pretensions to nobility" might aspire. More enamored of leisure than of his studies, he leaves school with a bachelor's degree but without being "a man of letters." One may say of him what is said of many such young men, "that although they entered school, school did not enter them" (no. 3).

In this portrait of the rake Leocadio one detects the pedagogical bias of Enlightenment liberalism, which repudiated the upper class's traditional scorn for hard work and self-improvement. Martínez Alier documents the growing prevalence in nineteenth-century Cuban society of an entrepreneurial ethic that extolled "the prestige of hard work," while emphasizing the importance of education. Families judged their daughters' suitors on the basis of compliance with notions of the "industrious life" (Martínez Alier 85). For the new "Cuban entrepreneurial class," which held in contempt "the purchasers of titles and nobility," the ideal was the "active man," whose honors should be conferred "in accordance with a person's abilities and virtues and not on account of his birth" (86).

In the novel, Leonardo is shown to disdain his father's attempts to acquire a noble title, arguing that "nobility purchased with the blood of the Negroes" that his father and "the rest of the Spaniards kidnapped in Africa to condemn them to eternal slavery" was not nobility but infamy and that aristocratic titles were "the greatest disgrace of all" (622). Even conceding that Leonardo's opinions on such issues often seem an expression more of petulant defiance than of a deeply felt belief, it is important to note that such social commentary is entirely absent from the short story's characterization of Leocadio. Havana's most prominent *petimetre* (fop)—with his "touch of the learned and eloquent fellow," his carriage ("the lightest and most flamboyant"), his horse ("the handsomest"), and his driver ("the most elegant of mulattoes") (no. 3)—Leocadio typifies one of Hispanic *costumbrismo*'s stock figures, referred to in numerous popular and journalistic texts from the late eighteenth and early nineteenth centuries (Montgomery 39–61).

This idle, pretentious, and philandering wastrel encounters the fourteen-year-old Cecilia at a party, playing the harp with "skill and grace," dazzling everyone with her "sweet and harmonious voice." Hearing her performance, Leocadio wants to possess the "silken hand" that plucks the harp strings, the voice that yields such "harmonious torrents," and the "tender heart" that directs both hand and voice (no. 3). These typological characterizations give the narrative a fairy-tale aspect, with Cecilia becoming a sort of Little Red Riding Hood to Leocadio's Big Bad Wolf. Cecilia's charms compel him to fixate on her as his next victim, and she is no less dazzled by his "elegance, glamour, and swagger." Blinded by an overwhelming passion, she readily succumbs to Leocadio, who is portrayed as "smug in his triumph" (no. 3).

In its depiction of the complex motivations and interactions among the citizens, servants, and slaves of colonial Cuba, Villaverde's novel presents detailed and intricate portraits that highlight the social privileges and prohibitions (as he perceived them) for Cuban girls and women pertaining to various racial and social categories of the day. In the story, however, Cecilia's gender and color serve, I would suggest, only the incidental function of positioning her socially among the most vulnerable members of society. Because her mother is a *mulata*, Cecilia's Creole father will not recognize her as his daughter. This leads to her growing up without proper instruction, since her aging and impoverished grandmother lacks the resources and authority to educate and control her. The fact that she is female makes her a sexual target for men of all classes. Cecilia's lack of education in turn makes her susceptible to the designs of roving predators like Leocadio. The story's emphasis, however, is on what Villaverde perceived to be the universal phenomenon in which the morally obligated stewards of society exploited the masses for their own perverse pleasure.

When Cecilia first appears in the short story, she is only ten years old, but she already reveals "that softness of contours, that impeccable finish characteristic of Greek statues." Such features, we are told, "are common in southern climes." The face, "a paragon of beauty," is framed by thick, black hair. The broad, smooth forehead, the arched eyebrows, the delicate, straight nose, and the large, dark eyes lend a certain "dash and sparkle." Although there are some racial overtones here, racial details abound in the novel's introduction of the young Cecilia:

> [O]ne could see in the coloring of the face that while still ruddy, it nonetheless had too much of the ocher in its complexion. . . . To which race, then, did this girl belong? It would be difficult to say for sure. However,

the knowledgeable eye could not overlook the dusky edge or ridge that outlined her lips, nor the way the brightness of her face ended at the hairline in a kind of penumbra. Her blood was not pure, and one could be certain that somewhere back in the third or fourth generation it was mixed with that of the Ethiopian. (73)

Here Villaverde indulges (either through his own voice or in an attempt to characterize a social mind-set, as he views it) the sort of racial delectation evocative of nineteenth-century ethnological writing (cf. De Hostos). This concern with the physical discernibleness of racial mixing, along with the presumptive correlation between personal character and outward physiognomy, is reflective, according to Martínez-Alier, of a status system in nineteenth-century Cuba in which "colour or [sic] physical appearance are conceived not as attributes conclusive in themselves but as mere outward 'signs' of a deeper condition" (72, 75–76; see also Stinchcombe 159–71).

Such racial theories were anything but new in the nineteenth century. Rebecca Haidt reminds us, citing Deidre Lynch, that "in Spain as in England or France the body was perceived during the eighteenth century as 'discursive, a telltale transcript of the identity it housed'" (Haidt 5).[6] Juan Gelpí (55) points out the influence on nineteenth-century novelists of anatomical theories such as those of the eighteenth-century Swiss theologian Johann Caspar Lavater, which postulated "a link between facial anatomy and moral character." He cites the instance in the novel in which Villaverde's narrator describes the young Cecilia as having a small mouth and full lips, "indicating more voluptuousness than strength of character" (qtd. in Gelpí 55). In the same passage from the novel, it is suggested of Cecilia's face that "it would have been perfect had her expression only been less malicious, if not malignant" (73). Villaverde's story, however, suggests a universal morality rather than engaging in the deductive empiricism (or pretensions to such) that would come to find such resonance among realist and naturalist writers.

Pointed references to physical evidences of Cecilia's race are far less emphatic in the short story. For example, one rumor as to her parentage suggests simply, without speculation as to race, that she had been the product of an indiscretion committed by a noble woman with "a certain petty military officer." According to the best information, though, she was the daughter of a "a young *mulata* seduced by a gentleman" and is thus "part noble, part plebeian, a thing which is and is not" (no. 1). Although her racial origins are here (accurately) identified, note that the emphasis is on the social designations that emanate from the color and status of her parents. By the age of fourteen, the story tells us, Cecilia is known as the "virgencita de bronce" (little bronze virgin) because of her beauty and her "dusky hue." However, while *virgencita de bronce* is used synonymously for Cecilia throughout the novel, the Cecilia of the story is just as often referred to by her many admirers as a "seraph." The narrator adds that, for the opportunistic Leocadio, Cecilia is "like a siren of the seas, like a sylph of the clouds," Greco-Roman allusions not traditionally associated with dark, exotic beauty.

On the question of race, both Villaverde's short story and the later novel fall on the liberal side of a conceptual divide in the life sciences of the late eighteenth and early nineteenth centuries. Arthur O. Lovejoy points out two modes of biological thought. The more rigid maintained a taxonomy of "sharp divisions, clear-cut differentiations." The other, more temperate mode regarded the concept of species as "a convenient but artificial setting-up of divisions having no counterpart in nature" (Lovejoy 227). This notion of the "scientific inadmissibility of the concept of species" assumes imperceptible gradations between natural orders and the consequent artificiality of divisions among human groups (231). Villaverde adheres to the latter mode of thought among the natural historians and social philosophers of the late eighteenth and early nineteenth centuries. Although he particularizes racial types and blends with their corresponding cultural markers, Villaverde refrains from the rigid classification proposed, for example, by Linné, the founder of modern systematic biological nomenclature.

Linné describes "Negroes" as "crafty," "indolent," "negligent," and "governed by caprice" (in contrast to the European's being "governed by laws") and assigns them such physical attributes as "frizzled" hair, "flat" noses, and "tumid" lips (Linné 13). Villaverde likewise diverges from David Hume's racial classification of four or five distinctly separate human species, as well as from his assertion of the natural inferiority of all nonwhite races, none of which are capable, according to Hume, of "ingenious manufactures" or of arts and sciences in general (Hume 33). Similarly far from the Cuban author's racial ideas, Kant perceives race in terms of pure stocks, so that "Negroes and Whites are ... different races ... [that] generate between them children that are necessarily hybrid, or blendlings (mulattoes)" (40). Kant, like Hume, assumes that racial crossbreeding constitutes an anomalous mongrelization of natural kinds (41).

More akin to Villaverde's racial theory are the ideas of James Beattie, whose refutation of Hume points out that the latter—along with others who correlate race with natural aptitudes or weaknesses and thus with predisposition to servitude—forgets the Greeks, "for many ages doomed to that slavery, which . . . nature had [supposedly] destined them to impose on others" (34). In line with the liberal didacticism mentioned earlier, Beattie reminds us that the ancient inhabitants of Great Britain and France were "as savage . . . as those of Africa and America are to this day." He summarizes his critique of Hume in pedagogical terms: "One may as well say of an infant, that he can never become a man, as of a nation now barbarous, that it can never be civilized" (35). Blaming the social elite in much the same manner as Villaverde, Beattie argues that many Negroes, though reduced to servitude, "become excellent handicraftsmen, and practical musicians, and indeed learn everything their masters are at pains to teach them, perfidy and debauchery not excepted" (36). Foreshadowing Villaverde's portrait of Leocadio, Beattie condemns "fashionable duelists, gamblers, and adulterers" as shocking examples of the Europeans' "brute barbarity" and "sottish infatuation." To deny the moral truth of this contrast is to deny "the sacred rights of mankind" (37).

Beattie's racial views are shared by the eighteenth-century encyclopedist Antonio de Alcedo, whose *Diccionario geográfico-historico,* under the heading "Negro," deplores the transportation of Africans to American shores, "where they are treated with the greatest harshness and inhumanity, as if they were not of the rational species . . . and as if this part of humankind must be bereft of the privileges of humanity by reason of the different color that gives them their name" (306). *Mulato* is glossed as "a caste of people in America," the product of "the mixing of a black mother and white father, or black father and white mother." Mulattoes, a numerous caste in the New World, are described as being "like the fruit of European dissipation and the lasciviousness of black women." The culpability of black women, however, is attenuated by the "domination" to which female slaves are subjected by their white masters.

Alcedo, unlike the reactionary racial theorists, does not regard this mixed category as suspect merely because of its hybridity. Mulattoes, indeed, are generally "well-built, of good stature, vigorous, strong, industrious, very valiant and intrepid, possessed of great vivacity." This sympathetic description, like Villaverde's, allows for certain characteristic proclivities. Mulattoes are, Alcedo informs us, "given over to pleasure, fierce, cunning, and capable of committing the worst wrongdoing without compunction" (483). Similarly, Villaverde, in the story, informs us regarding Cecilia's love of dance music that "in this she did not belie her race" (no. 3).

For Alcedo, however, as for Villaverde, the condition of *mulatas* is attributed principally to paternal irresponsibility and deficient education. Because most mulattoes are born to slave women, the law, if strictly applied, would normally classify them also as slaves. However, since they are commonly sired by their mothers' masters, they are freed, then "raised from the earliest age in every kind of vice" (483). Despite the "bad qualities" to which mulattoes are prone, some, evincing "decency and virtue," have distinguished themselves, showing by their accomplishments "the little effect that color has on mental qualities" (484). Alcedo represents an ethical tradition whose champion was the enlightened despot Carlos III, "whose pious heart is a protector of all mankind" (490). Lerner argues that Alcedo's ethical perspective on race and slavery reflects a traditional Catholic approach to social problems, an approach that came to be privileged at certain moments and by certain monarchs, popes, and other notables determined to live up to the humanitarian image of an enlightened century (Lerner 90–91).

This is the ethical viewpoint—humanitarian and egalitarian, but with a somewhat contradictory perception of the moral and ethical deficiencies of admittedly oppressed racial types—suggested by Villaverde's story, which places so much importance on the responsibility of the ruling elite and on the moral dereliction of its disreputable members, of whom Leocadio is typical. The story, much more integrally than the novel, encapsulates several Enlightenment themes and modes: the educability of man, underscored by the tragic deprivation of those with no access to instruction; the notion of noblesse oblige, which serves to prolong the authoritarian paternalism that motivates Enlightenment liberalism; the folkloric and exemplary effect, reinforced by the brevity of the piece, its fairy-tale tone, and its universalist orientation, which clearly separates the ethical types represented by the innocent Cecilia and her amoral seducer; and finally, an incipient feminism, implied by the story's sympathy for the helplessness of the female protagonist and its condemnation of the gender-specific power of her oppressor. Whereas the novelized representation of Cuba's most famous fictional *mulata* explores the individuated experience of an exploited, if complicit, young woman, in the story Villaverde crafts a representation of Cecilia's experience that is best understood through the universalist typologies of victimization and paternalism characteristic of an Enlightenment view of the social plight of the *mulata*.

NOTES

1. Both Lamore and William Luis believe the short story to be an early version of the second and third chapters of the 1882 novel. Shortly after the appearance of the short story of 1839, Villaverde published the first eight chapters of the novel *Cecilia Valdés*, which incorporates almost verbatim the

text of the short story but also can be said to look ahead stylistically and thematically to the 1882 version. All references to Villaverde's novel are to Jean Lamore's 1992 edition of the 1882 version. Unless otherwise indicated, all translations from Spanish to English from Villaverde and from secondary texts are mine.

2. Villaverde's short story "Cecilia Valdés" was originally published in two parts in the Havana journal *La Siempreviva* in 1839. It was reprinted as "La Primitiva 'Cecilia Valdés'" in three installments in the Havana journal *Cuba intelectual* in 1909. All references to the story are to the 1909 reprinting. Since the journal lacks pagination, I refer to the installments by number as follows: no. 1 (June), no. 2 (July), and no. 3 (August).

3. For a summary of recent critical stances regarding Villaverde's position on slavery in *Cecilia Valdés* (1882), see Harney, "Soy mestiza" 113–16.

4. Villaverde viewed himself as a chronicler in his final edition of *Cecilia Valdés*, published when the events depicted in the novel (which took place between 1812 and 1831), as well as its social and political context (e.g., the years of the Vives government, 1823–32), were retreating ever further into the past. He wrote that he felt compelled to finish the novel in New York after so many years despite his preoccupation with "the militant politics" of the later nineteenth century because "the memory of the homeland drenched in the blood of its finest sons . . . demanded of those who truly loved her a faithful portrait of her existence . . . before her death or exaltation to the ranks of free peoples (liberation) should forever alter those traits characteristic of her prior physiognomy" (Prologue 49).

5. See Harney, "Zarzuela."

6. See Lynch 116.

WORKS CITED

Alcedo, Antonio de. *Diccionario geográfico-histórico de las Indias Occidentales o América*. Vol. 3. Madrid: Blas Román, 1788.

Beattie, James. "A Response to Hume." In *Race and the Enlightenment: A Reader*, ed. Emmanuel Chukwudi Eze, 34–37. Oxford: Blackwell, 1997.

De Hostos, Eugenio. "El Cholo." *La Sociedad* (Lima), 23 December 1870. Reprinted in Eugenio De Hostos, *Obras completas*, 20 vols. (Havana: Cultural, 1939), 7:151–56.

Empson, William. *Some Versions of Pastoral*. 1935. London: Hogarth Press, 1986.

Gelpí, Juan G. "El discurso jerárquico en *Cecilia Valdés*." *Revista de Crítica Literaria Latinoamericana* 34 (1991): 47–61.

Goldmann, Lucien. *The Philosophy of the Enlightenment*. Trans. Henry Maas. Cambridge, MA: MIT Press, 1973.

Haidt, Rebecca. *Embodying Enlightenment: Knowing the Body in Eighteenth-Century Literature and Culture*. New York: St. Martin's, 1998.

Harney, Lucy D. "'Soy mestiza y no lo soy': Gonzalo Roig's Musical (Re)Vision of *Cecilia Valdés*." In *Music, Writing, and Cultural Unity in the Caribbean*, ed. Timothy J. Reiss, 111–28. Trenton, NJ: Africa World Press, 2005.

———. "*Zarzuela* and the Pastoral." *MLN* 123.2 (2008): 252–73.

Hume, David. "Of National Characters." In *Race and the Enlightenment: A Reader*, ed. Emmanuel Chukwudi Eze, 30–33. Oxford: Blackwell, 1997.
Johnson, Sherry. *The Social Transformation of Eighteenth-Century Cuba*. Gainesville: University Press of Florida, 2001.
Kant, Immanuel. "On the Different Races of Man." In *Race and the Enlightenment: A Reader*, ed. Emmanuel Chukwudi Eze, 38–48. Oxford: Blackwell, 1997.
Kutzinski, Vera M. *Sugar's Secrets: Race and the Erotics of Cuban Nationalism*. Charlottesville: University of Virginia Press, 1993.
Lamore, Jean. Introduction to *Cecilia Valdés o La Loma del Ángel*, by Cirilo Villaverde, ed. Jean Lamore, 9–56. Madrid: Cátedra, 1992.
Leal, Luis. "Féliz Varela and Liberal Thought." In *The Ibero-American Enlightenment*, ed. A. Owen Aldridge, 234–42. Urbana: University of Illinois Press, 1971.
Leclercq, Cécile. *El lagarto en busca de una identidad: Cuba; Identidad nacional y mestizaje*. Madrid: Iberoamericana; Frankfurt am Main: Verfuert Verlag, 2004.
Lerner, Isaías. "The *Diccionario* of Antonio de Alcedo as a Source of Enlightened Ideas." In *The Ibero-American Enlightenment*, ed. A. Owen Aldridge, 71–93. Urbana: University of Illinois Press, 1971.
Linné, Carl von. "The God-given Order of Nature." In *Race and the Enlightenment: A Reader*, ed. Emmanuel Chukwudi Eze, 10–14. Oxford: Blackwell, 1997.
Locke, John. *Two Treatises of Government*. Ed. Peter Laslett. 2nd ed. Cambridge: Cambridge University Press, 1967.
Lovejoy, Arthur O. *The Great Chain of Being*. Cambridge, MA: Harvard University Press, 1936.
Luis, William. *Literary Bondage: Slavery in Cuban Narrative*. Austin: University of Texas Press, 1990.
Lynch, Deidre. "Overloaded Portraits: The Excesses of Character and Countenance." In *Body and Text in the Eighteenth Century*, ed. Veronica Kelly and Dorothea von Mücke, 112–43. Stanford, CA: Stanford University Press, 1994.
Martínez Alier, Verena. *Marriage, Class, and Colour in Nineteenth-Century Cuba*. 2nd ed. Ann Arbor: University of Michigan Press, 1989.
Miller, Paul B. "Enlightened Hesitations: Black Masses and Tragic Heroes in C. L. R. James's *The Black Jacobins*." *MLN* 116.5 (2001): 1069–90.
[Molina, Tirso de]. *El burlador de Sevilla*. Ed. Alfredo Rodríguez López-Vázquez. 8th ed. Madrid: Cátedra, 1996.
Montesquieu, Charles de Secondat, baron de. *The Spirit of Laws*. Trans. Thomas Nugent. Rev. J. V. Prichard. In *Great Books of the Western World*, 38:1–315. Chicago: Benton, 1952.
Montgomery, Clifford Marvin. *Early Costumbrista Writers in Spain, 1750–1830*. Philadelphia, 1931.
Nora, María Luz de, and Roberto Friol. "Cartas de Cirilo Villaverde a Julio Rosas." *Bohemia* (Cuba) 57.40 (1965): 100–101.
Paine, Thomas. *Common Sense*. Ed. Isaac Kramnick. 2nd ed. Harmondsworth: Penguin, 1976.
Rousseau, Jean-Jacques. *The Social Contract*. Trans. G. D. H. Cole. In *Great Books of the Western World*, 38:387–439. Chicago: Benton, 1952.
Sebold, Russell. "Enlightenment Philosophy and the Emergence of Spanish Romanticism." In *The Ibero-American Enlightenment*, ed. A. Owen Aldridge, 111–40. Urbana: University of Illinois Press, 1971.

———. "El subtexto costumbrista de las *Noches lúgubres*, de Cadalso." *Dieciocho* 21.1 (1998): 7–19.
Stinchcombe, Arthur. *Sugar Island Slavery in the Age of Enlightenment*. Princeton, NJ: Princeton University Press, 1995.
Villaverde, Cirilo. *Cecilia Valdés o La Loma del Ángel*. Ed. Jean Lamore. Madrid: Cátedra, 1992.
———. "La primitiva 'Cecilia Valdés.'" *Cuba Intelectual, Época Segunda*, nos. 1–3 (June–August 1909).
———. Prologue to *Cecilia Valdés o La Loma del Ángel*, ed. Olga Blondet Tudisco and Antonio Tudisco, 47–51. New York: Las Américas, 1964.

11

Doña Leonora's Library
Women's Reading from the Spectator *(1711) to* El Semanario de Salamanca *(1795)*

CATHERINE M. JAFFE

A letter published in the *Semanario de Salamanca* in 1795 recounts a visit to an eccentric widow, Leonora, a lady who shuns the world, surrounds herself with books, and builds grottos and gardens to re-create the atmosphere of her favorite romances.[1] The amused gentleman narrator describes the physical appearance of the library and records the book titles in his pocketbook. This letter is an unacknowledged translation of Joseph Addison's portrait of Leonora and her library in the *Spectator* on 12 April 1711 (Addison and Steele, *Spectator* 152–59). Its republication eighty-four years later in an entirely different social and cultural environment testifies to the growing Spanish interest in enlightened practices of sociability and education and signals the evolving role of Spanish women in the world of letters. The *Semanario Erudito y Curioso de Salamanca* (1793–98), a vehicle of *ilustrado* thought, printed articles, letters, and essays discussing the purpose of women's education and offering advice to its female readers (Rodríguez de la Flor 104–12). The letter about Doña Leonora manifests disdain for women's intellectual pretensions and a desire to protect women from what were considered harmful effects of reading fiction (Bolufer Peruga, *Mujeres* 304–5). The reappearance of Addison's literary portrait in 1795 attests to an ambivalent acceptance of the connection between women and reading. This portrait of a woman and her books is inscribed in the genre of periodical literature, which itself was complicit in the evolving cultural understanding of women's reading.

During the final decades of the century the periodical press, including publications like the *Semanario de Salamanca*, expanded dissemination of reading matter for both instruction and entertainment and had a significant impact on the debate regarding division of gender roles. Wider access to print culture stimulated the efforts of censors to control access to books; Enlightenment writers worried about the effects of growing literacy and attempted to regulate reading matter for distinct classes of readers. In Spain, the broad social transformation known as the *Ilustración* established in principle that women were not inferior and had a right to education, yet it left ambiguous the appropriate limits of their instruction. Such reservations about literacy betrayed an awareness of the implicit link between knowledge and power (Bolufer Peruga, *Mujeres* 399, 165). We must also bear in mind that women readers constituted only a small percentage of the female population. In Spain at century's end (1787–1805) women's literacy, notoriously difficult to calculate, is estimated to have been 13.46 percent, compared with 27 percent for women in France and 49.90 percent for men in Spain (Soubeyroux 167). The evolution of women's accession to literacy, the description of their reading practices, and the semiotic dimensions of the representation of the woman reader remain relatively unexplored aspects of a complex history of reading and its social significance during the eighteenth century in Spain (Infantes 336–37).

While reading novels was increasingly associated with women, the periodical press also looked to female readers to develop its market. The *Semanario de Salamanca* and similar publications are therefore an important index of evolving attitudes toward female readers. Early in the century, Joseph Addison and Richard Steele's *Spectator* (1711) had developed a part fictional, part real correspondence with women subscribers as an audience-building technique, a "conceit of community" (Shevelow 47). This personalized "spectatorial" technique was extremely influential in Europe, where it was often known through French translations, and was later adopted in the popular periodicals of Spain.[2] Spanish periodicals modeled on the *Spectator*, such as *El Pensador* (1762–67) and *El Censor* (1781–87), published essays and letters that discussed how education would benefit women, which kind of woman stood to gain the most from suitable instruction, and the appropriate reading practices for women (Kitts 60–96, 178–81). Although the *Spectator* was well known on the Continent through its numerous French translations, in Spain during the first half of the century a receptive audience of bourgeois readers with a secular world-view did not exist for such publications (Guinard 75). The *Spectator* was hardly known in Spain before midcentury. Feijoo mentions it in 1745, and it was banned by the Inquisition in 1750 (Guinard 160–69). In Spain the "spectator" model finally found a public, first with *El Pensador* and similar periodicals (1750–70) and then, especially in the 1780s, with a "second generation" of *Spectator*-type periodicals, such as *El Censor* (Guinard 291–93).

Although the *Spectator* may have been known in Spain mostly through its

French translations and was not found in noble libraries (Guinard 160–61), at least two important figures of the Spanish Enlightenment, the Salamancan poet Juan Meléndez Valdés and the writer and statesman Gaspar Melchor de Jovellanos, owned volumes of the periodical in English (Aguilar Piñal 132; Demerson 119). A comparison of the original English *Spectator* article about Leonora's library, a French translation of 1754,[3] and the Spanish version from the *Semanario de Salamanca* shows that the Spanish translator appears to have based his article on the English original. The Spanish version has uniquely "Spanish" elements that were additions or changes to the English, such as different book titles, and retains words, parts of descriptions, and a book title—"Novelas exemplares (o escandalosas) de Doña María de Zayas" (11) ("A Book of Novels" [155])[4]—that the French version omits.

Doña Leonora's Library

Because the Spanish version is a fairly faithful rendering of Addison's original letter and does not appear to be based on a French translation, its few deviations from its English source help us to perceive the dimensions of the woman reader in the literary imagination of the day. Typically, the Spanish translator "Hispanicized" the text by substituting certain names with Spanish parallels (Guinard 169). In the *Spectator* letter, Addison's narrator describes a visit undertaken on behalf of his friend Sir Roger, a "spectator" who frequently appeared in the English periodical, to a lady living in retirement in the country. The Spanish version adds an explanation of why the narrator visits her so early in the morning: "ignorando si esta Dama, a quien llamaré *Leonora*, era de las que el corto rato que están visibles lo pasan entre una nube de visitas diarias, entre quienes haría yo un papel ridículo, y no hallaría oportunidad para entregarle la carta, que creía que contuviese materias de importancia; fui a su casa a hora que estaba la Dama aun en el tocador" (9) [not knowing if this Lady, whom I shall call *Leonora*, was one of those who spend the short while they are visible amidst a cloud of daily visits, among whom I would play a ridiculous part, and believing the letter to contain matters of some consequence, I went to her house at an hour when she was still at her dressing-table].[5] Unlike in the English version, this introduction to Leonora, appearing before the description of her library, associates her explicitly with the frivolous pursuits of fashionable women, indicating that the translator felt some need to explain a perceived difference in manners and practices of sociability to his Spanish audience.

While waiting to see her, the author is shown into what is described as "la *Librería de la Señora*" ("her *Lady's Library*"). The narrator's curiosity is aroused, one supposes, because a lady's library was a rarity, and so he inspects the room and makes a list of the books he finds there. The books are arranged in piles and ordered by size. They form colorful architectural shapes that are framed by items of domestic ware such as vases and teacups:

> Al estremo de los tomos *en folio* había unos jarrones de Porcelana, colocados en un estante de una arquitectura noble: los tomos *en quarto* estaban separados de los *en octavo* por una fila de vasos más pequeños, que formaban una hermosa pirámide: los, *en octavo* estaban sujetos por una porción de tacitas para té de todos tamaños, colores y figuras, dispuestas de tal manera, que parecían un pilar seguido, entallado de la más delicada escultura, y manchado de los matices más varios y deliciosos. (9–10)

> At the End of the *Folio's* (which were finely bound and gilt) were great Jars of *China* placed one above another in a very noble piece of Architecture. The *Quarto's* were separated from the *Octavo's* by a pile of smaller Vessels, which rose in a delightful Pyramid. The *Octavo's* were bounded by Tea Dishes of all Shapes, Colours and Sizes, which were so disposed on a wooden Frame, that they looked like one continued Pillar indented with the finest Strokes of Sculpture, and stained with the greatest Variety of Dyes. (153)

The narrator describes the section of pamphlets and papers as forming "un cuadro, compuesto del más hermoso grotesco, que vi jamás, y formado de leoncillos, arbolitos, caracoles, y otras mil figuras estravagantes, todas de Porcelana" (10) ("one of the Prettiest Grotesque Works that ever I saw, and made up of Scaramouches, Lions, Monkies, Mandarines, Trees, Shells, and a thousand other odd Figures in *China* Ware" [153]). The author's description of the scene as "grotesque" makes incongruity, lack of proportion, and exaggeration the metaphorical tenor of his portrait.

The contrasting placement of heavy books with china teacups physically reinforces the startling, humorous, and ultimately untenable conjunction of *Lady* and *library*, and the opposition of porcelain and books underlies the thematic intent of the portrait. According to Elizabeth Kowaleski-Wallace, china was often deployed "as a defining trope for femininity" (53) in the eighteenth century. Its superficiality offered a "blank textual surface upon which culture could write its notions of gender," and it was a material that had no meaning or use until it was molded to a purpose (54). The teacup's emptiness and delicacy links it to the superficiality of Leonora's literary endeavors and genders them as feminine. Furthermore, porcelain's relation to mercantilism, consumerism, and the display of wealth in the domestic economy connects Leonora to the transformation that took place during the century from the representation of woman as object to her representation as desiring subject (56). The piles of china relate their owner to the commercialization of culture. Daniel Defoe, in his *Tour through Great Britain* (1724–26), remarked on the cult of acquiring china in England at the end of the previous century in imitation of Queen Mary: "the custom or humour of furnishing houses with China-ware, which increased to a strange degree afterwards, [the common people] piling their China upon the tops of cabinets, scrutores, and every chimney piece, to the tops of the ceilings, and even setting up shelves for their china-ware" (qtd. in Barker-Benfield xxiv). Since Leonora's own words are not reported by Addison's narrator, and since she appears only briefly in the narrative, her library—its books and their arrangement—represents her subjectivity and desires.

The fanciful placement of the books in architectural shapes alongside pillars of china cups juxtaposes solidity and precariousness, while the emphasis on appearance over content suggests that these books are just for show. Moreover, some books, the visitor discovers, are made of wood. He declares, "Me agradaron sobre manera tan estrañas y tan varias clases de adornos, tan oportunos para una Dama, como para un Literato, y me hicieron dudar al principio, si estaba en una gruta, o en una Librería" (10) ("I was wonderfully pleased with such a mixt kind of Furniture, as seemed very suitable both to the Lady and the Scholar, and did not know at first whether I should fancy my self in a Grotto, or in a Library" [153–54]). Both versions emphasize that the lady had probably read very few of the books she had collected, but had acquired them because she had heard them discussed or had met the authors.

The incongruent grouping of roles and reading practices, "Dama" and "Literato" ("Lady" and "Scholar"), echoes the mutually exclusive spaces of "Grotto," a constructed fantasy in which to imitate fictional characters, and "Library," the authoritative, masculine space of study and retreat from feminized domestic spaces. In the "Grotto" one plays or dreams or creates; in the "Library" one works. In the "Lady's Library" fancy and imagination prevail over serious study; selection is based on gossip and fashion rather than on intellectual principle. Addison's description of Leonora's library blends form, surface, and function suggestively, with an eye to the banal diminishment of the iconic symbols of learning and culture—the book and the library—and thus projects an ironic (de)valuation of the person who uses them and reveals "an intent to ridicule feminine intellectual pretensions, such as the wide, diverse, and somewhat erratic reading enabled by the growth in literacy and new, more easily accessible formats" (Bolufer Peruga, *Mujeres* 305). It is a powerful literary portrait of traditional attitudes toward the relation between women and letters.

The list the author makes of Leonora's books is contextualized and determined by the library's eccentric, superficial principle of organization. In the Spanish version, some titles have been altered slightly and some have been replaced with Spanish titles. A number of authors from the original English list, such as Newton and Locke, have been deleted, while others have been added, such as Buffon and Condillac. In his *Entretiens sur la pluralité des mondes* (1686) Fontenelle, also a new addition, set out to make the Copernican system comprehensible to all readers by couching his exposition as a series of conversations in a moonlit garden between a philosopher and an aristocratic lady. No doubt the author of the *Semanario de Salamanca* article was attracted to Fontenelle's book because of its appeal to the female reader through the eroticized relationship between the male teacher and the female student. Among the new Spanish authors on the list are Juan Pablo Forner, who argued in his *Discursos* that virtue rather than natural science should be the study of man (Sarrailh 480–81), and Manuel Antonio Ramírez y Góngora, whose *Óptica del cortejo* roundly condemned the social practice of the *cortejo*, the gallant companion of a married lady (Rueda 255).[6]

Conduct manuals and guides to matrimony have been replaced with Spanish titles, such as Fray Luis de León's *La perfecta casada* (1583) and the Spanish translation of Fénelon's *Traité de l'education des filles* (1687). Among the books that appear on both the English and the Spanish list are translations of classical texts such as Virgil, a dictionary, a spelling book, D'Urfé's "Tales in Verse," and luxury, gilt collections of authors (although the English version specifies that the "Classical" authors are in wood). "A Book of Novels" from the English version is given as María de Zayas's extremely popular seventeenth-century "Novelas exemplares (o escandalosas)."

The Spanish list seems to be rather arbitrary, altered according to the translator's whimsy rather than adhering to a more serious principle of selection. For example, an important treatise on women's education, Juan Luis Vives's *Institutione feminae christianae*, translated into Spanish in 1528, is not on the list, perhaps because it was very rare, as Josefa Amar y Borbón notes in her own treatise on women's education (175, 322). Amar y Borbón's *Discurso sobre la educación física y moral de las mugeres* (1790) is not on the list either. However, despite the randomness of the selection, the intent to make Leonora a caricature of the romantic woman reader can be discerned in the choices and substitutions made by the translator.

The seventeenth-century French romances cited in the English version, such as La Calprenède's *Cleopatra*, D'Urfé's *Tales Tragical and Comical* and *Astraea*, and Madeleine de Scudéry's *Clelia* are accompanied by the same annotations in both the English and Spanish versions, even though the books themselves do not seem to have been published in a Spanish translation. For example, D'Urfé's name is not mentioned when citing a book obviously read and reread by Leonora, with favorite passages marked: "Cuentos en verso, encuadernados en tafilete, dorados por el canto y dobladas las hojas en varios pasages" (11) ("Tales in Verse by Mr. *Durfey*: Bound in Red Leather, gilt on the Back, and doubled down in several places" [156]). The *Grand Cyrus* is similarly marked, with "un alfiler clavado en una de las hojas de en medio" (10) ("a Pin stuck in one of the middle Leaves" [154]). Although the equivalent annotation is made in the Spanish version, the title has been replaced with that of the original classical text, "La *Cyropedia* de Xenephonte," suggesting that the Spanish translation of Scudéry was unknown, yet the book still has the pin stuck in its leaves. The Spanish list adds a description to La Calprenède's *Casandra* that does not appear in the English version, indicating that this volume at least was known to the translator: "[una] novela complicada, sin unidad, ni extensión competente" (10) [a complicated novel, without unity or adequate development].[7] Scudéry's *Clelia* is annotated in the same way in both versions: "que se abría de suyo en el lugar en que pinta dos amantes en un vergel" (11) ("which opened of itself in the Place that describes two Lovers in a Bower" [156]).

Although seventeenth-century French romances had been popular reading for women and men in England through the early eighteenth century (Doody xi–xviii), they were not as well known in Spain. La Calprenède's *Casandra* was translated into Spanish in 1792, but *Cleopatra* had not been published in translation.[8] Scudéry's *Cyrus*, for example, was translated from Tuscan to Spanish and published in Madrid in 1682, but her *Clelia* was never translated into Spanish (Mongrédien 546–51). Yet here *Clelia* appears in Leonora's library, opening by itself to the picture of two lovers in a bower. Similarly, Molière's *Les femmes savantes* was never translated into Spanish (Lafarga 410), although the original was well known in intellectual and artistic circles. The Spanish translator of Addison's piece who added "Las *Mugeres sabias* de Molière" to the list (11) perhaps meant that Leonora would have read the work in the French original, but it seems more likely that he added the paradigmatic satire of learned women in order to reinforce his ridicule of Leonora's intellectual pretensions. As the Marquise de Lambert observed in her *Réflexions nouvelles sur les femmes,* Molière's satire had the effect of attaching shame to women's knowledge, and it was generally understood "as a send up of female pretension" (Sheriff 113–15). Since this work does not appear on the English list, we must assume that the Spanish translator adds it to disparage women's learning.

The suggestion that the list of Leonora's books is part of the fictional portrait of Leonora, and by extension of women readers in general, is reinforced by other tongue-in-cheek annotations echoed in the Spanish text. The title *"Oración y Meditación,* y al lado un frasquito de agua de la Reyna de Hungría" (11) ("A Prayer Book: With a Bottle of *Hungary* Water by the side of it" [156]) implies in both versions the banality of women's religious devotions, which were carried out at their dressing table and so were reduced to the status of their cosmetics. Finally, the Spanish version simply translates the title of the English book *"Instrucciones de la Ferte* para las Contradanzas" (11) (*"La Ferte's* Instructions for Country Dances" [157]), written by the early eighteenth-century London dancing master, rather than substituting a native alternative, of which there were several. But tellingly, this final title immediately follows "Taylor's *Holy living and dying"* in both lists and so is meant to point out again, through humorous incongruity, the limited spiritual dimensions, the lack of intellectual seriousness, and the tendency toward romance of women's reading practices.

This comparative analysis shows that while the Spanish list was probably copied from Addison's list and the most obvious cultural incompatibilities smoothed over, the connection between women's reading and romance was as strong at the end of the century in Spain as it had been more than eighty years earlier in England. Lucienne Domergue points out that before the Revolution, Spanish censors treated novels like any other book. But after 1795 a wave of sentimental novels, known as *novelas inglesas,* began to make the censors uneasy and led to a prohibition of the publication of novels in 1799 (Domergue 489–91). Inmaculada Urzainqui observes that authors and editors were very aware of women's preference for novels and the commercial demand it created ("Nuevas" 489). Leonora's literary portrait was published, therefore, at a crucial moment in the history of the novel in Spain, when increasing literacy among women and the availability of sentimental novels ignited fears about the connection between women and novels and by extension about women's acquiring cultural power as authors.

Framing Doña Leonora's Library

Concluding the letter, the narrator describes his very brief meeting with Leonora and his friend's later observations about her. She is a childless widow who because of an unfortunate first marriage has decided to remain single and withdraw to the company of her books. She seems to eschew frivolous female pursuits and to prefer to correspond only with men, but "[c]omo su lectura se reduce casi a la de los Romances, le ha dado un modo particular de pensar y de conducirse, como se echa de ver en su casa, su jardín y sus muebles" (12) ("As her Reading has lain very much among Romances, it has given her a very particular Turn of Thinking, and discovers it self even in her House, her Gardens and her Furniture" [158]). She has engineered her country estate to look like "un palacio encantado" (12) ("a kind of Wilderness . . . a little Enchanted Palace" [158]). Although the Spanish version omits the idea of "Wilderness" (perhaps evidence of a different aesthetic of nature), Leonora has fashioned a romantic landscape for herself:

> Las peñas que hay alrededor figuran unas grutas cubiertas de madreselva y jazmines. Los bosques forman unos paseos cubiertos, enlazándose unos árboles con otros, y llenos de jaulas de tortolillas. Las fuentes corren entre guijas, y les enseñan a murmurar con agrado. Se recogen en un lago hermoso, habitado de dos Cisnes apareados, y se desaguan por un arroyuelo, que corre por un verde (prado) valle, y es conocido en la familia con nombre de *arroyo murmurador*. (12)

> The Rocks about her are shaped into Artificial Grottoes covered with Wood-Bines and Jessamines. The Woods are cut into shady Walks, twisted into Bowers, and filled with Cages of Turtles. The Springs are made to run among Pebbles, and by that means taught to Murmur very agreeably. They are likewise collected into a Beautiful Lake, that is Inhabited by a Couple of Swans, and empties it self by a little Rivulet which runs through a Green Meadow, and is known in the Family by the Name of *The Purling Stream*. (158)

She has imitated for herself, that is, the romantic landscape of her favorite tales. The narrator beholds her with both admiration and pity, seeing "lo extravagante que se ha vuelto esta Dama por su lectura" (13) ("how odly this Lady is impoved [sic] by Learning" [158]). In the Spanish, she is "extravagante," a more extreme criticism than "odly . . . improved." Because she is "susceptible de las impresiones de lo que lee" (13) ("so Susceptible of Impressions from what she reads" [158]), she would have been better served by "aquellos libros, que se dirigen a ilustrar el entendimiento, y enderezar las pasiones antes que por aquellos, que apenas tienen otro uso que el de dar rienda suelta a la imaginación" (13) ("such Books as have a tendency to enlighten the Understanding and rectify the Passions, as well as . . . those which are of little more use than to divert the Imagination" [158]). But the narrator has already undermined this assertion that Leonora could have been guided (presumably by him or some other enlightened man) to better reading, because the list of her library books shows that she had acquired the serious titles herself and yet had not read them. And in this conclusion we find also a significant difference between the Spanish and English versions: "En medio de los inocentes entretenimientos que se ha formado, cuánto más apreciable aparecería divertida en las ocupaciones de su sexo, que empleada en diversiones menos racionales, aunque más brillantes y singulares?" (13) ("Amidst these Innocent Entertainments which she has formed to herself, how much more Valuable does she appear than those of her Sex, who employ themselves in Diversions that are less Reasonable, tho' more in Fashion?" [158]). Although the phrasing is ambiguous, Addison seems to compare Leonora favorably with women occupied by more frivolous pursuits but not yet at the enlightened stage of learning. However, he may be equating her with frivolous women as well, implying that she is no more valuable than them. The Spanish version, on the other hand, asserts unambiguously that she would be better off following the traditional occupations of her sex than in more brilliant yet singular pursuits, eliding the difference between fashion and learning. The apparent confusion of terms—*traditional women, frivolous women, intellectual women*—in the English and Spanish versions of the article's conclusion points to the problematic Enlightenment vision of women: while they should be educated according to their social purpose as wives and mothers, there were lingering doubts about their capacity to exercise reason, as well as wariness regarding their inclinations and desires once the Pandora's box of reading had been opened.

The list of books in Leonora's library is framed by the description of the fanciful decoration and organization of her library and the description of her romantic landscaping. The "serious" titles on her library shelves remain opaque, resistant signs that serve to describe what Leonora is not, while the "romantic" titles open of themselves, show use and interest, and indeed lead the reader into the "vergel" or "Bower" of Leonora's copy of *Clelia,* into the grottos, paths, and wildernesses of her garden. If the teacups and bric-a-brac of the library are drawn from a rococo visual vocabulary of consumerism, display, and superficial adornment that is gendered as feminine, the winding paths and dead-end, concealed grottos deploy a different vocabulary of a feminized nature designed to cultivate the sentiments rather than to lead to a goal: sensibility, not science, is the governing principle. The titles of Leonora's books invite the reader to confront assumptions upon which writing— here, the production of the list of Leonora's books—deploys its power. Among these assumptions are gendered reading practices: a perceived feminine susceptibility to sentiment and solipsistic imagination in reading and an inability to enter the transcendent world of ideas. Rather than in writing or in study, Leonora's creative response to her books manifests itself in interior decorating and landscaping.

The list of books creates a static moment in the narration, and the titles are a concrete manifestation of writing itself. The list is a form of quotation, an intertextual technique that stalls the narration with the rhetorical trope of description and creates a tension between "assimilation and dissimilation," thus "permitting another world to radiate into the self-contained world of the [text]" (Meyer 6). The intertextual list of books calls attention to the duality of writing, to its nature as concrete medium and intangible signifier, as at once a creative practice and its receptive other, reading. The list of titles within the text creates a sudden opacity in the text that helps the reader "see" the material nature of writing.[9] The intradiagetic titles, therefore, bring before us the assumptions, such as those that concern gender and reading, that allow us to experience textuality as writing and as reading.

Outside the list's framing letter, an epigraph from Virgil, ". . . *Non illa colo, calathisive Minervae, / Femineas assueta manus . . .*" (152) ("Unbred to spinning, in the loom unskill'd" [152n]), describes the approach into battle of the marvelous warrior woman Camila, of the Volscian nation. The extradiagetic epigraph functions, perhaps, as the library catalog card for this piece: "Al uso femenil no acostumbrada / Ni tuerce el hilo, ni el coser le agrada" (9). The brief quotation from book 7 of the *Aeneid* omits the awe and amazement Camila inspired in those who saw her and focuses instead on her lack of skill in traditional feminine tasks. When Addison drew on his classical education to summarize Leonora's character (her classical texts were made of wood, we recall), was he blind to Camila's greatness, or did he purposely suppress that part of the description? According to Barker-Benfield, Addison considered political women "Amazons" (307), and in general in the eighteenth century the figure of the Amazon was used to criticize "gender-crossing" women who sought a public role or voice, especially after the French Revolution (351).

Amazons were women who shunned traditional female domestic roles to war with men on the battlefield. Leonora, we should remember, is a childless widow, a woman who is not identified by the traditional role of daughter, wife, or mother. Although she seems quite respectable, within Enlightenment ideology she can be criticized because she has no useful role in society and has withdrawn into a private world. She cultivates a sensibility, manifested in her house and grounds, that does not enhance any appropriate social role. She is not given the derogatory epithet *bachillera*, used to designate women who supposedly made a show of their learning. Indeed, she hardly speaks at all; she is merely an (imagined) woman reader. Leonora's portrait, then, asks about the ends and uses of women's intellect and subjectivity. Leonora's portraits appear early in the Enlightenment in England and then toward the end of the period in Spain, at moments of substantial change in women's literacy and reading practices and new developments in the literary marketplace. Leonora's portrait cannot tell us anything precise about the experience of real women readers. It is proof, though, that as women's literacy grew, as women gained knowledge of themselves and of the world through reading, as they began to express their thoughts and to shape their subjectivity in writing and to become authors, the social, cultural, and political consequences would be profound, and thoughtful people of the day realized this. Leonora, like other literate and learned women of her day, fit in neither a man's world nor a woman's, a difficult "place" to inhabit. She is, however, a text herself, and one that is read from a "spectator's" point of view and from (his) blind spots. Leonora and her library are signs of a gendered literary world in which enlightened thinkers were still trying to find a woman's place.

APPENDIX
Doña Leonora's Library

The lists of books in Doña Leonora's library appearing in the *Spectator* and the *Semanario de Salamanca* are reproduced exactly below. Publication information provided in the notes to the English edition of the *Spectator* appears in brackets below the English entries. Where possible, contemporary translations of the works in Spanish appear in brackets below the Spanish entries.

English (1711)	Spanish (1795)
Addison and Steele, *Spectator* 154–57	*Semanario de Salamanca*, 4 July 1795, 10–11
Ogleby's Virgil. [*Works*, trans. John Ogilby, 1649–54, reprinted 1711]	la *Eneyda de Virgilio* por Hernández de Velasco. [*La Eneida de Virgilio*, trans. Gregorio Hernández de Velasco and Maffeo Vegio, 1768]
Dryden's Juvenal. [*Satires*, trans. John Dryden, 1693]	
Cassandra. [by La Calprenède, 1642–45, trans. 1705]	La *Casandra*, novela complicada, sin unidad, ni extensión competente. [*La Casandra*, trans. Manuel Bellosartes, 1792–93]
Cleopatra. [by La Calprenède, 12 vols., 1647, trans. 1652]	
Astraea. [by Honoré d'Urfé, 1607–27, trans. 1657–58]	La *Astrea*.
Sir *Isaac Newton's* Works. [*Principia mathematica*, 1687; *Opticks*, 1704; *Aritmetica universalis*, 1707]	
	Las Obras de Franklin.
The *Grand Cyrus*: With a Pin stuck in one of the middle Leaves. [*Artamène*, by Madeleine de Scudéry, 10 vols., 1649–53]	La *Cyropedia* de Xenephonte, con un alfiler clavado en una de las hojas de en medio.
	La *Lógica de Condillac*. [*La lógica, o los primeros elementos del arte de pensar*..., trans. Bernardo María de Calzada, 1784]

Pembroke's Arcadia.
[*The Countess of Pembroke's Arcadia*, by Sir Philip Sidney, 1590]

Lock of Human Understanding. With a Paper of Patches in it.
[John Locke, *Essay concerning Human Understanding*, 1690; the 1711 edition is advertised in the *Spectator*]

A Spelling Book.

Ortografía Castellana.

A Dictionary for the Explanation of hard Words.
[*Cocker's English Dictionary*, 1704]

Diccionario Castellano.

Fr. Luis de Granada, introducción al Símbolo de la Fe.
[Fray Luis de Granada, *Obras espirituales del Padre Fr. Luis de Granada . . . Tomo segundo de la introducción del símbolo de la fe,* 1678]

La *Perfecta Casada.*
[by Fray Luis de León, 1583]

Sherlock upon Death.
[*A Practical Discourse concerning Death*, by William Sherlock, 1689, 1705]

The fifteen Comforts of Matrimony.
[trans. 1682 from *Quinze joies de mariage*]

Ensayos de Trublet.

Sir *William Temple's* Essays.
[*Miscellanea*, 1680, 1690, 1701]

Father *Malbranche's* Search after Truth, translated into *English*.
[Nicholas de Malebranche, *Recherche de la vérité* (1674–75), trans. 1700 as *Father Malebranche his Treatise concerning, The Search after Truth*]

A Book of Novels.

Malebranche, investigación de la verdad.

Novelas exemplares (o escandalosas) de Doña María de Zayas.

La *Optica del Cortejo.*
[by Manuel Antonio Ramírez y Góngora, 1774]

La *Pragmática de los lutos.*
[*Manda el rey nuestro señor y en su real nombre los alcaldes de su casa y corte: Que por cuanto en contraversión a lo prevenido en diferentes leyes reales y con especialidad en la pragmática sanción, expedida y publicada en diez y siete de noviembre de año passado de mil setecientos veinte y tres, en los lutos que se deben poner por muerte de personas reales,* 1760]

Las *Mugeres sabias* de Molière.

The Academy of Compliments.
[1705]

Culpepper's Midwifery.
[*A Directory for Midwives,* by Nicholas Cullpeper, 1651]

The Ladies Calling.
[by Richard Allestree, 1673]

Tales in Verse by Mr. *Durfey:* Bound
in Red Leather, gilt on the Back, and
doubled down in several places.
[*Tales Tragical
and Comical*, by Thomas D'Urfey, 1704]

Cuentos en verso, encuadernados en
tafilete, dorados por el canto, y dobladas
las hojas en varios pasages.

All the Classick Authors in Wood.

Toda la colección de Autores en veinte y
quatro a vo.

A Set of Elzivers by the same Hand.
[Dutch printers of elegant editions]

La colección Elzeviriana de Autores
clásicos.

Clelia. Which opened of it self in the
Place that describes two Lovers in a
Bower.
[by Madeleine de Scudéry, 1654–60,
trans. 1655–61]

El Romance de Clelia, que se abría
de suyo en el lugar en que pinta dos
amantes en un vergel.

Bakers's Chronicle.
[*A Chronicle of the Kings of England from
the Time of the Romans Government unto
the Raigne of King Charles*, 1643]

Advice to a Daughter.
[*The Lady's New-Years Gift; or, Advice to a
Daughter*, by George Savile, 1688]

Los *Mundos* de Fontenelle.
[Bernard le Bouyer de Fontenelle,
*Conversación sobre la pluralidad de los
Mundos*, 1796]

Educación de las niñas por Fenelón.
[François de Salignac de la Mothe
Fénelon, *Escuela de mugeres y educación
de niñas*, trans. Martín del Valle, 1770]

	Discursos filosóficos sobre el hombre, por Forner. [Juan Pablo Forner, *Discursos filosóficos sobre el hombre*, 1787]
	El *Buffon*, traducido. [Georges-Louis Leclerc, comte de Buffon, *Historia natural general y particular*, trans. Joseph Clavijo y Fajardo, 1785–1805]
	El *Censor*. [periodical published 1781–87.]
The New *Atalantis*, with a Key to it. [Mrs. Manley's *Secret Memoirs . . .* , 1709–10]	
Mr. *Steel's* Christian Heroe.	
A Prayer Book: With a Bottle of *Hungary* Water by the side of it.	*Oración y Meditación*, y al lado un frasquito de agua de la Reyna de Hungría.
Dr. *Sacheverell's* Speech. [1710, upon his impeachment before the House of Lords]	
Fielding's Tryal. [*The Arraignment, Tryal and Conviction of Robert Feilding, Esq; for Felony, in Marrying her Grace the Dutchess of Cleaveland, his first Wife, Mrs. Mary Wadsworth, being then alive*, 1707–8]	
Seneca's Morals. [by Sir Roger L'Estrange, 1678]	Las *Obras morales* de Séneca.

Taylor's holy living and dying.
[*The Rule and Exercises of Holy Living*
and *The Rule and Exercises of Holy Dying*,
1650–51]

La Ferte's Instructions for Country Dances.
[*A Discourse or Explications of the Grounds of Dancing*, 1711]

Instrucciones de la Ferte para las contradanzas.

NOTES

1. *Semanario Erudito y Curioso de Salamanca*, 4 July 1795, 9–13.
2. Bolufer Peruga studies this dynamic in "*Espectadores*" and *Mujeres*, ch. 7. See also Jaffe; Kitts; and Urzainqui, "Los espacios."
3. "Discours XIX," in Addison and Steele, *Le Spectateur*, 127–34.
4. Unless otherwise noted, the text and page from Addison's original essay (Addison and Steele, *Spectator* 152–59) follow the Spanish translation.
5. My translation.
6. See María Victoria López-Cordón Cortezo's discussion of the *cortejo* in chapter 6 of this volume.
7. My translation.
8. A translation was rejected by the censors in 1798 (Domergue 490).
9. Françoise Meltzer makes this point in regard to ekphrasis, the literary portrait, in *Salomé and the Dance of Writing*.

WORKS CITED

Addison, Joseph, and Richard Steele. *Le Spectateur, ou, Le Socrate moderne, où l'on voit un portrait naif des moeurs de ce siècle*. Vol. 8. Paris: Chez Merigot, 1754.

———. *The Spectator*. Ed. Donald F. Bond. Vol. 1. Oxford: Clarendon, 1965.

Aguilar Piñal, Francisco. *La biblioteca de Jovellanos (1778)*. Madrid: Centro Superior de Investigaciones Científicas, 1984.

Amar y Borbón, Josefa. *Discurso sobre la educación física y moral de las mugeres*. Madrid: Benito Cano, 1790.

Barker-Benfield, G. J. *The Culture of Sensibility: Sex and Society in Eighteenth-Century Britain*. Chicago: University of Chicago Press, 1992.

Bolufer Peruga, Mónica. "*Espectadores* y lectoras: Representaciones e influencia del público femenino en la prensa del siglo XVIII." *Cuadernos de Estudios del Siglo XVIII* 5 (1995): 23–57.

———. *Mujeres e Ilustración: La construcción de la feminidad en la Ilustración española*. València: Institució Alfons el Magnànim, 1998.

Demerson, Georges. *Don Juan Meléndez Valdés y su tiempo (1754–1817)*. Vol. 1. Madrid: Taurus, 1971.

Domergue, Lucienne. "Ilustración y novela en la España de Carlos IV." In *Homenaje a José Antonio Maravall*, ed. María Carmen Iglesias, Carlos Moya, and Luis Rodríguez Zúñiga, 483–98. Madrid: Centro de Investigaciones Sociológicas, 1985.

Doody, Margaret Anne. Introduction to *The Female Quixote*, by Charlotte Lennox, x–xxxii. Oxford: Oxford University Press, 1989.

Guinard, Paul-J. *La presse espagnole de 1737 a 1791: Formation et signification d'un genre*. Paris: Centre de Recherches Hispaniques, 1973.

Infantes, Víctor. "La mirada en la escritura: Una historia de la lectura y del lector." *Bulletin Hispanique* 100.2 (1998): 333–41.

Jaffe, Catherine. "Suspect Pleasure: Writing the Woman Reader in Eighteenth-Century Spain." *Dieciocho* 22.1 (1999): 35–59.

Kitts, Sally-Ann. *The Debate on the Nature, Role and Influence of Woman in Eighteenth-Century Spain*. Lewiston, NY: Edwin Mellen, 1995.

Kowaleski-Wallace, Elizabeth. *Consuming Subjects: Women, Shopping, and Business in the Eighteenth Century*. New York: Columbia University Press, 1997.

Lafarga, Francisco. *Las traducciones españolas del teatro francés (1700–1835)*. Barcelona: Universitat de Barcelona, 1983.

Meltzer, Françoise. *Salomé and the Dance of Writing: Portraits of Mimesis in Literature*. Chicago: University of Chicago Press, 1987.

Meyer, Herman. *The Poetics of Quotation in the European Novel*. Trans. Theodore Ziolkowski and Yetta Ziolkowski. Princeton, NJ: Princeton University Press, 1968.

Mongrédien, Georges. "Bibliographie des oeuvres de Georges et de Madeleine de Scudéry." *Revue d'Histoire Litteraire de la France*, 1933, 224–34, 412–25, 538–65.

Rodríguez de la Flor, Fernando. *El Semanario Erudito y Curioso de Salamanca (1793–1798)*. Salamanca: Diputación de Salamanca, 1988.

Rueda, Ana. "*Óptica del cortejo*: Panóptico para una comedia de bastidores." *Dieciocho* 27.2 (2004): 255–76.

Sarrailh, Jean. *La España Ilustrada de la segunda mitad del siglo XVIII*. Madrid: Fondo de Cultura Económica, 1992.

Sheriff, Mary D. *Moved by Love: Inspired Artists and Deviant Women in Eighteenth-Century France*. Chicago: University of Chicago Press, 2004.

Shevelow, Kathryn. *Women and Print Culture: The Construction of Femininity in the Early Periodical*. London: Routledge, 1989.

Soubeyroux, Jacques. "Niveles de alfabetización en la España del siglo XVIII: Primeros resultados de una encuesta en curso." *Revista de Historia Moderna: Anales de la Universidad de Alicante* 5 (1985): 159–72.

Urzainqui, Inmaculada. "Los espacios de la mujer en la prensa del siglo XVIII." In *Del Periódico a la Sociedad de la Información*, vol. 1, ed. Celso Almuiña and Eduardo Sotillos, 53–79. Madrid: Sociedad Estatal España Nuevo Milenio, 2002.

———. "Nuevas propuestas a un público femenino." In *Historia de la edición y de la lectura en España, 1472–1914*, ed. Víctor Infantes, François López, and Jean-François Botrel, 481–91. Madrid: Fundación Germán Sánchez Ruipérez, 2003.

"Virtue in Distress" in the Spanish Sentimental Novel
An Unsustainable Model of Rational Sensibility
ANA RUEDA

Sensibility of soul, which is rightly described as the source of morality . . . is the mother of humanity, of generosity; it is at the service of merit, lends its support to the intellect, and is the moving spirit which animates belief.
—LOUIS DE JAUCOURT, *Encyclopedia*

*I*n eighteenth-century studies, especially in the last two decades, the concept of sensibility has been the object of an ongoing critical and theoretical debate, yet it has not produced a critical consensus on the meaning of *sensibility*. Moreover, among Hispanists it has remained of marginal interest to literary critics and generally has been relegated to historians of the period. Since this concept underwent a remarkable change at the end of the eighteenth century across Europe, it is useful to examine from a historical and text-oriented point of view the changing meaning of the concept in Spanish culture at the turn of the century. The controversy surrounding the concept of sensibility is based on the fact that sentimental novels, with their trite love stories, their emphasis on emotions—"passions"—that are invariably accompanied by copious tears, their rhetoric of gesture, and the monotonous order of the epistolary mode, are dismissed as simple, banal, and negligible. When examined closely, however, sentimental novels reveal an amalgam of discourses that defy consensus on what sentimental fiction meant to readers in the eighteenth century. The lack of a precise understanding of what was meant by *sensibility* and *sentimental* toward the end of the eighteenth century prevents this fictional genre from fitting neatly into the rational systems of Enlightenment discourse and causes difficulties when one attempts to determine the political role that the genre played in the various constructions of sensibility. Because of the complexity of sentimental ideas in Spain, as in the rest of the Continent, I shall concentrate on one of the topoi that best illuminates the change the concept of sensibility underwent: "virtue in distress," or woman as the victim of man the libertine.

The problem of sensibility affects both male and female characters, but especially females because many novelists accepted the idea of a superior female sensibility and gave it a privileged status, even when it bordered on the excessive and morbid (Todd 120). The plots that most severely try the moral virtue of the female protagonist are those in which the man poses an extreme sexual threat, triggering her moral sensibility. This manifests itself though a complex system of "sensible" signs, physical and moral as well as aesthetic, sexual, religious, and other signs. In the Spanish novel, the woman's body offers a wide range of responses, following the rules of sentiment, from passive resistance (rejection) to efforts to reform the seducer. In such situations Spanish heroines exhibit an unshakable faith in verbal persuasion. Alternatively they might express their sensibility in a bodily way by means of tears, fainting, sudden fevers, or seizures, going to the extreme of inflicting irreparable physical harm on themselves. These extreme examples are read today as ambiguous reactions, perhaps as the neurotic manifestations of sexual derangement caused more by the rigors of the code of virtue than by a virtuous heart. The gratification that the sentimental female protagonist feels only when she sees herself as a victim and when she is suffering is puzzling and problematizes the notion of rational sensibility.

The arousal of the virtuous woman's passion produces an instability that puts her on the line between "virtue" and "vice" in such a way that she may incline toward either goodness or wickedness. In fact, the sexually harassed woman is the subject of sentimental scenes that appear more apt for arousing passions than for restraining them, since in sentimental rhetoric the word *virtue* immediately conjures up the word *vice*. The regularity of this juxtaposition situates sensibility on the threshold between humanitarian impulses and depraved ones. Examples of virtue are mixed with examples of depravity, as occurs in a collection of stories by Ignacio García Malo, *Voz de la naturaleza* (1787–1803), designed to make the reader "love virtue and abhor vice in light of the alternating examples that they contain" (1:ii). Nothing, of course, prevents the reader from seeing the negative examples as constituting a self-help manual. This dangerous combination of virtue and vice undermines the novel's claim that it provides instruction, though it may make such a claim either to calm contemporary doubts about the genre or to silence the censors. The praiseworthy objective of encouraging virtue and showing how vice is punished, often found in prefaces, was, as everyone knew, the justification required to elude censorship.

Such ambiguities in sensibility, which I hope to clarify, allow us to see the gap between the idealism and the social utilitarianism of the eighteenth century. An examination of the topos "virtue in distress" will reveal the contradictions in sensibility, which in some ways, but not all, overlap the changes the concept experienced in France and England, although with a certain time-lag. In addition to its symbolic significance, the topos "virtue in distress" offered practical solutions for situations that compromised woman's virtue. Thus, it provides insights into why strength of spirit, which made a woman virtuous, always caused her to suffer the consequences of her own virtue and led her to the nunnery, to death, or to marriage.

Although this is not the place to carry out a detailed historical and cultural survey of sensibility in Spain, it is useful to provide a context for it within the European debate over the new direction that sensibility took at the end of the eighteenth century, as we trace it in its Spanish context in the newspapers of the period, in essays, and novels. In the process we will examine (1) the change in the meaning of *sensibility* in Europe about 1800; (2) some key discourses that came together in the sentimental novel; and (3) the responses of Spanish heroines in distress and the disadvantages of being sensible. This inquiry will lead us to certain conclusions about the breakup of the sentimental novel and (4) the identification of new forms that channel sensibility.

The Change in the Meaning of Sensibility

The term *sentimental* became semantically contaminated in the literature of the end of the eighteenth century, undergoing a shift in meaning from "refined and elevated," in reference to such qualities as tenderness and long-suffering, to "superficially emotional" or even "excessively emotional" (Mullan, "Sentimental" 236; Brissenden 718). The sentimental novel, in spite of losing prestige because it was a formulaic genre, had its own internal dynamic and constituted an important link between Enlightenment concepts of moral philosophy and nineteenth-century ideas about the emotions, with origins in the first half of the eighteenth century.

In a detail of the famous political cartoon from 1798 entitled *The New Morality* (fig. 1) James Gillray depicts Sensibility next to Justice and Philanthropy as the three Muses or Graces of French radicals. Sensibility, dressed in an outlandish

FIG. 1. James Gillray, *The New Morality*, 1798. Library of Congress.

tunic and pileus with a revolutionary rosette, sheds huge tears over the body of a tiny dead bird while holding the works of "Rosseau" in her hand and unceremoniously squashing the head of Louis XVI beneath her foot. This distortion or misrepresentation of sentiment suggests that the cult of sensibility, which had exercised vital influence in Europe in the second half of the eighteenth century, right up to the French Revolution, had become by the end of the century a ridiculous, selfish, and morally irresponsible idea on account of its involvement in the measures of radical reform associated with the Jacobin Terror. Sensibility, until then considered the most refined of moral feelings and one of the most dynamic and fertile notions of eighteenth-century tradition, ended by being the object of attacks on various fronts that exposed the implications of the doctrine of sentiment and gave the *coup de grâce* to the ideal of benevolence, or of doing good indiscriminately.

Is it possible that hearts trained to believe in sensibility as a way of life were, in fact, destined to be a part of the violence and chaos that engulfed France? As the eighteenth century gave way to the nineteenth the Spanish felt the impact of the French Revolution, and they reacted to the French invasion with the War of Independence. In these turbulent years sensibility ceased to be a gift of nature that ennobles mankind, and it acquired a clearly undesirable look: Spanish conservatives associated it with liberal reformers, whom they considered to be infected with anti-Christian, pro-French sentiment, and liberals accused the conservatives of a sentimental longing for the *ancien régime*. Sensibility, when it was not seen merely as something passé, was held to be an erroneous, absurd, and demoralizing idea that threatened Spain with the same violent fate that France has suffered. In 1818 in Valencia there appeared a work that is significant in the development of the sentimental novel, *Amelia o los desgraciados efectos de la extremada sensibilidad*. Spanish sentimental heroes also warned of the potential dangers of sentimentalism. In Mor de Fuentes's *La Serafina* (1797) Alfonso says that "too powerful an emotion is dangerous for a sensible soul" (128), while the protagonist of Cosca Vayo's *Voyleano o la exaltación de las pasiones* (1827) has a propensity to uncontrolled passions that reveals the urgency to produce new languages of sociability. Tears, the indicator par excellence of sensibility, were not going to bring Spain out of poverty or provide a cure for the sufferings and injustices that the French invasion had caused. Francisco de Goya's engraving *Porque fue sensible* (Because she was sentimental) (fig. 2) depicts a tearful woman in prison. Was the painter satirizing the government's fear of sensibility? The *capricho* is an ambiguous example of "virtue in distress" and parodies sensibility, which could barely survive in a world where commiseration was rare and malevolence prevailed.

Through repetition of scenes such as that of "virtue in distress" and through the artificial treatment of this topos, the sentimental novel intimated that sentimentalism was flawed in some fundamental way. The scenes that trapped sentimental heroines in situations in which the libertine might gratify his lust not only cast doubt on the eighteenth-century fantasy that man acted with good will when the opportunity arose but froze the heroines in extreme circumstances in which the regulating mechanisms of social and private codes appeared to be temporarily suspended for the purpose of testing virtue. Rational sensibility usually did not come out on top in these tours de force, and the heroine lost her edge in her desperate attempts to check the unbridled passion of her seducer by proposing some reasonable solution, while in danger of exciting her offender even more.

FIG. 2. Francisco de Goya, *Porque fue sensible*, 1797-99. Reproduced with permission from Biblioteca Nacional de España, Madrid.

Establishing how sensibility gradually evolved in the postrevolutionary years is difficult. The main question is whether the polemic surrounding sensibility was embedded in the concept itself from its beginning or emerged after the concept became politically contaminated by the effects of the French Revolution.

Let us now feel the pulse of Spanish culture in the twenty years preceding the French Revolution. The writings of these two decades give us insights into the construction, out of various discourses, of the sentimental novel and help elucidate the debate over the ethics of sensibility. To understand the "virtue in distress" topos, one needs an ample context that does not reduce the scenes of confrontation to theatrical accounts of guilty seducers and innocent victims. We cannot understand fully the complex behaviors of these heroines in whom sensibility reaches its fullest development until we have examined the moral predicaments and the social and literary fantasies to which they respond. So let us establish parameters for the discussion of sensibility and its transformation at the end of the century.

The Sentimental Novel as an Amalgam of Discourses

Within the sentimental novel discourses from a range of sources converge around the central theme of sensibility in ways that are complementary yet also create conflicting tensions. The most intriguing discourses for the current study include moral philosophy, civility, and physiology and sexual morality. Markman Ellis, who provides a more elaborate scheme of these discourses, including theology, medicine, and sexuality, among others, stresses that "[t]he history of late eighteenth-century sensibility is not itself an enlightenment discourse but a philosophical nightmare of muddled ideas, weak logic, and bad writing" (7). He adds that none of these discourses alone can account for the sentimental novel: "Sentimentalism discovers its power in the novel's freedom to mix genres and discourses freely. In the novel, in other words, sensibility comes together" (8). Perhaps flaws in the wholeness of sensibility are detected in these discourses, and therefore the tensions between the different discourses, as well as within a given discourse, may well be the roots of the dissolution of the amalgam that is sensibility.

The postulates of moral philosophy had a decisive influence during the second half of the century with regard to the two central concerns of the period: how human beings should conduct themselves and what principles should guide their actions.[1] Hume's work *Of the Passions,* known in Spain as *Disertación sobre las pasiones* (1757), influenced, among others, Adam Smith, Rousseau, Voltaire, and Kant, the ancestors of twentieth-century ethics. Hume criticizes the rationalist theory of moral philosophy, which concedes absolute predominance to reason, and he emphasizes the dominant moral role of the passions, which provide the basis for his alternative ethical model opposed to rationalism. In order to bridge the gap between reason and sentiment, Hume introduces his concept of sympathy, the faculty that allows us to assume the sentiments of others. Hume, and later Adam Smith, John Mullan concludes, wanted to understand how experiences were communicated and how sentiments could be both intense emotions and moral judgments (249). For Hume, reason (which included the faculty of reasoning and the way in which truth was determined) was subordinated on a practical level to the passions and must "serve them and obey them" as their slave (14).[2] Thus the passions occupy a primordial place in moral behavior, ultimately determining conduct. Consequently, ethical judgments begin with an intuitive and aesthetic moral sense informed by the passions and are subject to empirical observation based on experience and analytical reasoning.[3] As a result, the promotion of ethical behavior may be intrinsically flawed by its reliance on the decidedly nonrational passions. But as we shall see, moral philosophy is not sufficient to explain, without the aid of other discourses, the negative destiny that awaits sensibility.

In his popular newspaper *Cajón de sastre* (1760–61) Mariano Nifo undertook an important project: to study man as a moral being, while recognizing the need to pay attention to the social contingencies of his own time.[4] In his discourse the journalist focuses his critical observation of customs on the ordinary experience of his fellow citizens. The *Cajón* is replete with edifying examples of moral actions taken mainly from the literature of the Spanish Golden Age. The case of the beautiful Doña María Coronel, the wife of Don Juan de la Cerda, must have seemed a rather extreme case. Nifo tells how this historical lady, in order to defend her virtue from the sexual advances of the lascivious king, Pedro el Cruel, poured boiling oil over her body and caused terrible blisters and injuries. The king, horrified when the woman exposed her disfigured body, allowed her to go away. The same could be said for the other exemplary ladies who parade through the newspaper, wounding themselves, throwing themselves out of windows, mutilating themselves, or cloistering themselves of their own free will when they fear that their virtue is in danger. Nifo asks whether the women of his day would tolerate such abuses and sacrifice their bodies on the altar of virtue: "There are countless women who would do this and much more if it were necessary; but experience tells us *je ne sais quoi*" (1:264). Nifo's ironical hesitation is important because it questions the supposed universality of rational sensibility, if not the concept per se. Nifo's *"je ne sais quoi"* undermines the possibility of timeless exemplars for the eternal feminine. He seems in tune with his readers, eager to leave behind the extravagant, antiquated models from Spain's glorious past to make way for personal experience (not reason) as the new regulator of conduct.[5]

About the middle of the eighteenth century, European writers began to inject into their fictions recently assimilated concepts from the scientific discourse of the period, thereby transforming the paradigm of sensibility in the novel from merely a mental activity to one that included the whole body. Sentimental novels adopted the vocabulary of medicine on the functioning of the nervous system in order to describe an expanded range of emotions and sentiments. This physiological discourse trained readers to pay attention not only to sensation as a way of knowing but also to the interior impulses associated with sensation. Novels described the ebb and flow of conscience and the portrayal of intense emotions by deploying a whole repertory of conventions associated with the sentimental rhetoric of the body: fainting, weeping, sighing, beating hearts, blushes, tears.[6] For novelists of the eighteenth century a woman's body provided an excellent experimental subject for studying the question of feminine virtue: "the woman's body is the mediator of the truth of sentiment; it is beyond her control yet displays her virtue," writes Mullan (*Sentiment* 113). But the problem was precisely that the novels started to depict this body language in such lurid colors and with such liveliness that virtue took on an erotic cast. Geoffrey Sill comments that Richardsonian heroines were not conscious of the concupiscent desires that animated their virtuous behavior, desires that tended to establish "a pattern of passive resistance and aggressive reproof.... By both raising and frustrating his [Mr. B's] passions, Pamela undesignedly erotizes her virtue" (174). In many cases, the harassed virtuous woman did not admit her amorous passion to herself. Seen in this light, her proclivity to fainting or to sudden fevers would not be a sign either of weakness or of strategy, as Sill points out, but a symptom of nervous sensibility associated with sexual anxiety.[7]

Writers and critics of the period agreed that the novel was instrumental in shaping sensible female readers, whom they considered communicating vessels between morality and corporal sensibility. Reading *insensibly* imparted moral values that manifested themselves in the reader in a physical and observable way, and other members of society would "read" the signs of it as evidence of interior sensibility. But the sentiments of fictional characters and the readers who shared their suffering or joy operated within complex relationships that did not guarantee sympathetic responses to the suffering of others. Indeed the virtuous capacity to share the feeling of another human being was in danger of provoking such emotional distress that it might upset the delicate balance between feeling and reason. Lady Bradshaigh told Richardson that while reading the last volumes of his *Clarissa* "I verily believe I have shed a pint of tears, and my heart is still bursting, tho' they cease not to flow at this moment, nor will, I fear, for some time" (qtd. in Mullan, "Sentimental" 247). How many Spanish women must have read *Clarissa* and other novels of the same sort and, convulsed with similar sensibility, added their own copious tears to the already overflowing European river of tears!

This emotional instability reveals that the sentimental novel fulfilled its objective of wringing the hearts of its female readers. But because these readers' emotions bordered on undesirable passions that were ultimately selfish, one wonders about the moral authority of their judgments and the ennobling character of their affections. In other words, it is not clear how these emotional effusions worked to advance the common good over the private good. Were these affections purely altruistic, or were the female readers in love with virtue itself?

This moral ambiguity emerges most notably in novels that intended to teach sensibility through scenes of "virtue in distress" that were manipulated to provoke a moral sentiment in the reader. But the ethical duplicity of the novel and contemporaries' clear awareness that people did not read novels for their moral principles complicate the picture. The claim of moralists and censors that the novel contributed to the moral degeneration of female readers was accompanied by ridicule of the idea that the novel might serve an educational purpose for young women. Josefa Amar y Borbón believed that careful upbringing was the only weapon against the passions, but she eliminated novels or romances from her educational plan because they taught intrigues and deceptions (185). Rodríguez de Arellano put his finger in the wound when he denounced the complacency of the sentimental novel when it painted moral corruption and then sold it as a preventative remedy for the very same thing (Rueda, *Cartas* 79).

Heroines in Distress, Complex Responses

In the history of the Spanish novel sexual harassment is a battle that the heroines must win with virtue as their only weapon. As a consequence, "virtue in distress" produces colorful and extraordinary solutions. Let us look closely at scenes of seduction that describe the protagonists' great emotional distress. They come from *La desventurada Margarita* (1803), by García Malo; *La prostitución,* by Castillo y Mayone (1833); and *La seducción y la virtud o Rodrigo y Paulina* (1829).[8]

In *La desventurada Margarita* the protagonist loses her virginity to Don Juan, who keeps up the pretense that he will marry her but leaves her when she becomes pregnant. After her father spends his entire fortune seeking justice for his daughter with useless appeals to various tribunals, Margarita and her child have no other option but to turn to begging. The heroine pays dearly for her "ill-placed trust" (71) in Don Juan, which causes her to endure further sexual abuse; even poverty conspires against her, her pallor making her more beautiful, and "the appearance of her son, a victim of penury, is very seductive" (58). A libertine sends her a message in which he offers to take her out of her poverty if she will accede to his "vile lust." Margarita, her character strengthened by maternal love and extreme poverty, tears up the note; although she has lost her honor, she still has her virtue. She chooses virtue and goes out to beg for alms. Prostitution continues to be a tempting prospect, but thanks to her virtue, she succumbs only to hunger. After a scene that the narrator describes as "sublime and sensible" (88) she dies embracing the body of her child.

Another story following the model in which the world demands the suffering and death of the heroine as the price of her virtue/chastity and offers her no way to fit into the machinery of society is the more well known *Cornelia Bororquia*, by Luis Gutiérrez. But there is an important difference: Cornelia is a character who knows nothing of sex, but Margarita has experienced it and lost her innocence (as the character of the child underscores). The recovery of virtue demands total abstinence from sexual activity, but in the end chastity and innocence have an equally destructive effect on the sensible woman, as when Margarita refuses to betray her principles. Neither of the heroines is capable of perceiving intuitively the danger that threatens her (from the archbishop in the case of Cornelia and from Don Juan in the case of Margarita) until it is too late. It is significant that Cornelia's imprisonment occurs before the novel begins, as does Margarita's seduction by Don Juan. Both novels are constructed around the tribulations that result from these unfortunate occurrences in order to emphasize that the heroines are victims of their own virtue.

Gutiérrez's denunciation of the social institutions in his novel (e.g., the Inquisition) seems to be more far-reaching than García Malo's indirect criticisms, implied in the heroine's death by starvation, which he converts into a sublime spectacle of sensibility.[9] Nevertheless, although Margarita does not succumb to prostitution in her effort to recover her virtue, we should not forget that her sentimentalized character is constructed on a social and literary foundation that reveals tensions present in the period. The virtue of the heroine is condemned by the judicial system that eats up her savings, and prostitution, a new danger, puts her to the test. The introduction of these social ills gives the novel an important political dimension. How were the novels that tackled these issues related to the structure of society and the political interests of the nation? Do those novels that touch on the subject of prostitution fit the Enlightenment scheme to reform prostitutes by persuading them to repent, as Markman Ellis argues (ch. 5) in the case of the British sentimental novel? Did *La desventurada Margarita* move its readers, male and female, to perform acts of charity in support of hospitals and rehabilitation centers for "fallen women" or to propose reforming the judicial system? Though we do not yet have answers to such questions, I suggest that these novels led readers to examine the usefulness of sensibility with regard to serious social problems.

Was it an effective means for achieving the goals of social utilitarianism, or was it nothing more than a useless feeling?

In *La seducción y la virtud*, an anonymous epistolary novel that concludes with the marriage of the heroine and her seducer, Paulina's end appears to be more optimistic and is explicitly indebted to the Richardsonian model (although this "Pamela" arrives twenty years late): "Lovelaces do not exist only in Richardson's mind" (xii).[10] Rodrigo is a charming Lovelace, a Don Juan newly arrived in Granada who tries to seduce the virtuous and incorruptible Paulina. Paulina, who has received a careful upbringing from her aunt, reading precepts drawn from Fénelon, Bossuet, Ducreux's history of the church, and the Bible (3:258–59), is well prepared to resist Rodrigo's numerous hare-brained efforts to seduce her. Eventually she unmasks and triumphs over the seducer, turning him by means of virtue and marriage into a civic-minded and morally upright person. The "reformed seducer," though his repentance is late and appears unconvincing to today's readers, is common in the Spanish sentimental novel (*La Luciana*, by Antonio Farigola y Domínguez; *Cornelia Bororquia*; *Adelaida o el suicidio*, by Joaquín del Castillo y Mayone; and *Voyleano*, to name a few), and José Zorrilla would consecrate it later with his romantic version of the myth in *Don Juan Tenorio* (1844). As Sylvia Truxa explains, in the Spanish sentimental novel the woman "saves" the man from his Don Juanism and becomes the civilizing agent. Reason, not passion, is the key to Paulina's heart: "It is not declarations of love from an ardent and overheated imagination that succeed in winning a heart like mine. It is the use of sound reason [and] the practice of virtue that earn the right to enthrall me and to capture it" (3:33). The novel, with its struggle between seduction and virtue, confirms that the Richardsonian theme was well assimilated and that it still found a receptive audience in Spain, although its connection with the old Spanish myth of the seducer seduced should not be overlooked.

The model of sensibility that Paulina provides is tinged with ambiguity. Paulina is virtuous because she represses the amorous desire she feels for Rodrigo from the first moment she sees him. This is clearly inconsistent with sentimental fiction's objective of finding personal happiness. Paulina writes to her confidante: "He is always on my mind. I feel the stirring of vague, indefinable desires . . . [yet] this same painful anxiety in which I live has a certain something agreeable and delicious that would make me happy if your scruples and fears did not cloud the bright future that it seems to promise" (2:78–79). In the face of Rodrigo's aggressive behavior Paulina must exercise constant vigilance, and though she is perpetually at war with herself, her self-control is reinforced by the codes of behavior in force (the restraints of religion, the desire for public esteem, the slow rhythm of a Spanish-style courtship).

The climactic scene of the novel takes place in a barn to which Rodrigo has taken Paulina after kidnapping her. Rodrigo declares his love and moves as if to put his arm around her waist. This gesture unleashes in the heroine a fit of trembling, screaming, and declamatory gestures in stark contrast to her usual reserved behavior. Beside herself with apprehension, she falls on her knees and raises her eyes and hands to heaven. She takes the penknife that is lying on the chest where Rodrigo writes to his confidant and points it at her heart, threatening to kill herself if Rodrigo takes advantage of her: "Rodrigo, if you take another step, you will be responsible for my death" (164). Rodrigo moves away and backs up to the wall of the barn, and Paulina, fleeing, throws the penknife, which is "quite bloody" (165) because she has cut her finger, to him from the staircase. As I have observed elsewhere, the penknife is the tool most often used by the heroines of epistolary novels to inscribe the limits of sexuality on their own bodies (*Cartas* 396). Paulina makes use of this piece of writing equipment to defend her virtue and to educate the man as a social being, that is, by inscribing on her own body and with her own blood the rules of her moral virtue.[11]

Paulina seems to have won. The bloody penknife is, however, a sign that the damage is already done, from the point of view of the heroine of the epistolary novel, who up to now has barricaded her virtue behind her letters, and the spilled blood is symbolic of "penetration/rape" by Rodrigo through his letters of seduction (Rueda, *Cartas* 395–96).[12] Paradoxically, it is Rodrigo who has triumphed, since he has managed to engage Paulina in a correspondence that leads to the dangerous physical encounter in the barn, which ultimately causes her to lose her composure. The novel also undermines the heroine's triumph by softening the threat to her virtue, because Rodrigo's version of the facts exculpates him from evil intentions. He explains to his confidant: "I was afraid that people might hear us, and I approached the door to see whether there was anyone there. She apparently thought that I was doing something else" (163). Paulina congratulates herself on having turned her seducer into an honorable man, but the symbolic levels and the circumstantial details that Rodrigo contributes indicate that this man was, as a seducer, quite harmless.

The central idea of the novel, the triumph of virtue over seduction, becomes illusory. Paulina, with optimistic faith in marital bliss with a reformed libertine and in her capacity to correct Rodrigo's sentiments (which are essentially good) only circumvents the problem that she appears to solve. In the end, she faces (without any suggestion in the narrative that it is problematical) life with an exseducer who does not really need to give convincing proof of social rehabilitation, because after all Rodrigo is no Lovelace. If the efforts of the virtuous heroine do not appear laughable, her self-complacency does not give her any moral superiority. Furthermore, the reader must wonder whether the reward (Rodrigo) is equal to the distress that the heroine has endured in the prolonged battle of the sexes throughout the three volumes that make up the novel. Perhaps the readers of the period enjoyed seeing the reformed seducer reintegrated into a domestic economy, and perhaps they even believed that virtue could protect against seduction. The book's instruction in sensibility is, nevertheless, questionable, because the fields of virtue and vice are ambiguous: the victim suffers from pride, and the seducer reveals sincere love. The moral project of *La seducción y la virtud* had to contend with the reasoning of readers who could easily come to opposite conclusions on the basis of the same imaginary facts.

What is wrong with being sensible? The two heroines reveal different effects that weaken sensibility. Each, in her own way, made the reader question the limits of virtue and the price of a refined sensibility. Sensibility demanded a high price of the woman. On the one hand, it offered the pleasure of doing good, as in the case of "virtue in distress," where it appeared as an effort to reform her attacker, softening him and humanizing him. On the other hand, it subjected women to the tortures of love, pain, and suffering, something like the mixed and unsettled state between life and death described by Saint Teresa's "Muero porque no muero" (I am dying because I do not die). The victims of men's passions acquired a touch of the sublime that separated them from worldly considerations. For example, Cornelia, the virgin sacrificed at the stake, sorrowfully "raises her eyes to heaven" (141) until "at last her spirit flew to the bosom of the Eternal One" (143). In view of these immolations to sensibility that separated the heroines from the social plane, we ought to ask ourselves what type of sensibility were they supposedly teaching, and what type of sexual instruction did readers, male and female, derive from these tableaux of seduction. How did these glorified heroines foment social sensibility? To what extent was this genre effective in educating women, when refined emotion met nothing but hostility in the world and happiness required heroines to suffer before they flew to the celestial spheres?

Both models of virtue in reality dramatized the failure of sensibility as a pattern of behavior for life. Virtue itself, and not their suffering, which was always marked by ambiguity, placed them in a situation of weakness and powerlessness. The harassed heroines suffered because they were virtuous. Therefore, the central message of the paradigm of "virtue in distress" was not that virtue was rewarded but that "virtue invited its own punishment" (Brissenden 94). And the readers of the novels in which these episodes occurred could not avoid asking themselves whether their feelings for these damsels in distress might possibly be contaminated with the negative aspects of sensibility, such as the questionable pleasure of watching the suffering of others.

The gulf between these models of female conduct and historical reality reduced them to uselessness, even if readers had been able to extract valid principles for life from their readings. The exemplary models of feminine conduct were impossible to follow in practice, and as Nifo suspected, neither the women of his day nor those of the beginning of the nineteenth century were inclined, in real life, to become sublime tragic victims like Margarita, or helpless sacrificial figures like Cornelia, or spotless heroines who suppressed their amorous impulses on the altar of virtue like Paulina. The stories of the fictional characters suggested that to feel more deeply was not the privilege of a sensible soul but a curse that led to suffering and self-destruction.

The architecture of sensibility, constructed of different discourses (moral philosophy, civility, physiology, sexual morality), collapsed under the weight of its own concept of a "reasonable sentiment." In the first place, moral sentiments, however exquisite and elevated they might be, were not automatically reasonable. In the second place, such spontaneous emotions were absolutely useless, as we have seen, and as Brissenden points out (29), they were contaminated with pessimistic ideas about the nature of the world and of society that easily destroyed the humanistic optimism of the eighteenth century.

New Directions for Sensibility

The eighteenth century aspired not to extinguish undesirable (selfish) passions, symbolized by the common metaphor of the "runaway horse" *(caballo desbocado)* but to control them. "Without love there is no virtue," claims Voyleano in the novel of the same name (1:56). But a man exercises virtue by holding his capacity for feeling in subjection to reason. The refined and chivalrous lover of *La Serafina* is no longer a model to emulate. The male protagonists of Cosca Vayo's *Voyleano*

(1827), Cortina y Roperto's *Teresa* (1835), and Boix's *El amor en el claustro* (1838) love ardently and do not manage to restrain their passions, but they do not harass the women whom they love, and the women do not barricade themselves against sex. Voyleano's benevolence toward Roberta's family unleashes uncontrollable feelings against the French, which the novel makes no effort to defend even as a patriotic gesture. In *Teresa* the tearful Isaac, a victim of his own passions, disinters his beloved, in romantic fashion, with the deranged purpose of sexual gratification. The intensely passionate Eduardo in *El amor en el claustro* seduces Adelaida in the monastery in which he is a monk, and he lives to regret, in letters, the moral ruin that his uncontrolled sexual desires have brought upon his beloved and himself. With one foot in eighteenth-century sensibility and the other in romanticism, their divided consciences do not succeed in maintaining the difficult balance required of a "sensible man." They are unable to avoid moral pitfalls. And the authors seem unable to sew the various discourses into a seamless whole. The novels unravel formally because the epistolary exchanges are interrupted in order to alternate with third-person narration. The letters are incomplete and inadequate to sustain the emotional equilibrium that once characterized rational sensibility.

Just as the letter eventually ceased to be an efficient defense in liminal situations between seduction and virtue, disintegrating in the hands of epistolary novelists, so also feelings ceased to be communicable. Feelings became more and more impotent, and commiseration (sensibility) no longer managed to elevate them. Was this the beginning of the end of a type of novel that sympathized with the afflicted and sought a sensibility balanced with reason? Or was it a change that was predictable because of the way in which the concept had been formulated at its inception? I fear that until there is more research, we Hispanists are not yet in a position to offer a categorical answer to these questions. But we can affirm that sensibility did indeed linger for a while before it could be pronounced dead and that there was at least one indicator of the changing focus of sensibility in the first decades of the nineteenth century. I refer to the politicization of sensibility with regard to *lo español* and what was considered quintessentially Spanish. In other words, sentimentality shifted from social to political concerns and to modern nation formation.

Without straying too far from the topos of "virtue in distress," new models set the tone in works that are interesting because of political revolutions in the sentimental novel. These novels—*Voyleano*, *Teodora* (1832), *El senador mexicano* (1836), *La sombra del religioso* (1836), and others—radically modified universal sensibility and benevolence by developing national themes as part of an effort to unify the community of the peninsula. The War of Independence created an awareness of the need for such a project, as José Antonio Maravall has shown. As the locus shifted to the state, sexuality ceased to project the private realm of intimate and bodily sensations as a means of stabilizing the boundaries between public (social norm) and private (subjective experience). The citizen's private life and the potential influence of an individual's opinion were subsumed under the pressures of the polity. And sensibility, seen now as a false and superficial response to real problems, lost its sovereignty.[13]

In these novels, the thrust of historical fact altered the makeup of the sentimental man and woman, requiring the invention of heroines of moral and bodily fortitude, which would not allow them to succumb to the promptings of their sensibility.[14] An illuminating case is *Teodora* (1832), a novel about the War of Independence in which the heroine, with the strong, fearless personality of an Agustina de Aragón during the siege of Zaragoza, decides not to give in to her love for Rodophe, a French colonel on Spanish soil, because it is more important to defend the fatherland. The politics written into the novels reveal the cracks in the dam erected by refined sensibility that could not be preserved in the face of the urgent need to find, in the new political frame, solutions for human problems such as the old tensions between duty to society and personal liberty. Eventually the crisis of sensibility would force virtue to give in to the passions, to madness, and to the newly fashionable cult of the longing for death after having tested the voluptuous pleasures of love, as occurs in numerous plots from the 1830s, such as *Irene y Clara*, *Adelaida o el suicidio*, *Teresa*, and *El amor en el claustro*.

Tears ceased to be morally admirable, but they did not disappear; instead, they became part of a new conceptual paradigm, a new aesthetics of suffering divorced from the pleasures of suffering for the sake of virtue and from the illusions created by the moral superiority of "virtue in distress." Was it possible for what the Marquis de Sade called "the sweetness of virtue's tears," in his dedication to *Justine*, to maintain credibility after the attack that Sade himself mounted in this novel against the illusions of virtue, using the very model of virtue in distress?[15] Dissatisfaction with the optimism of the sentimental novel came to the surface and finally demolished the self-congratulatory value of virtue, to be replaced by feelings of desperation, malaise, and anger. Innate principles and instinctive morality no longer had the social and cultural context that had supported them. As the heroine of *Teodora* proves as she wages war against France, sensibility no longer had anything to do with social reform and should be separated from benevolence and from humanitarianism. In spite of the repudiation of sentimental ethics, the sentimental novel did not disappear from the map. The form lived through the rise of realism, even though ethical dilemmas surrounding personal freedom and the collective good ceased to rouse feelings of sympathy in the reader.

Translated by Joseph R. Jones and revised by Matthew Feinberg. The author is very grateful for their expertise and for their editorial suggestions.

NOTES

1. Works like *Sistema físico y moral del hombre* (1825), a translation of Pierre Roussel's 1805 work, were also influential.

2. This passage from Hume's *Treatise of Human Nature*, bk. 2, pt. 3, "Of the Will and Direct Passions"—"Reason is, and ought only to be the slave of the passions, and can never pretend to any other office than to be the slave and obey them"—has often been misunderstood. Hume did not mean to say that the act of reasoning was inferior to sentiments or emotions, but that sentiment was the primary, fundamental element in the process by which we produce moral sentiments. He also wanted to emphasize that this was a private and subjective matter.

3. Álvarez Barrientos confirms that this applies to the Spanish novel.

4. The *Cajón de sastre*—literally "Tailor's Chest"—was a weekly publication. The seventy issues of the first edition (1760–61), the edition I follow, were later collected into seven volumes. There were several later collected editions (Enciso Recio 215–16).

5. For a more elaborate argument on Nifo's discourse on civility see Rueda, "El *Cajón de sastre* de Nifo."

6. Anne Vila examines works that incorporate biomedical models of sensibility, such as Denis Diderot's *La religieuse* (1796), Jean-Jacques Rousseau's *La nouvelle Héloise* (1761), Pierre Choderlos de Laclos's *Les liaisons dangereuses* (1782), and the Marquis de Sade's *Justine, ou les malheurs de la vertu* (1791), in conjunction with medical texts of the period.

7. See also Pinch; and Van Sant.

8. For a detailed analysis of these novels from an epistolary point of view, see Rueda, *Cartas*, 301–13; 389–90 and 403; and 323–32 and 393–403, respectively.

9. The sublime touch associated with sensibility is due to Burke and Kant. For their classic definitions, see Monk, 8, 58, 84–85).

10. The anonymous author combines Richardson's models freely. Pamela resists her master's efforts to seduce her by subduing him and testing the morals of the repentant suitor after they are married. In contrast, Clarissa resists her family's pressure to marry a suitor she hates, and she dies dishonored by Lovelace, the seducer whose proposals of marriage she has refused On the impact of Richardson in Spain, see Coé.

11. Paulina's psychology originates in the senses. The scene relies on the theories of Helvetius, whose fatalist view of physical sensibility connects the blood not only to critical judgments and ideas

but also, by means of pleasure and pain, to the passions, virtue, vices, self-interest, happiness, sociability, and power (O'Neal 4–5).

12. In this view I follow Ruth Perry, who establishes an equation between the letter and the female body, by virtue of which the seducer who opens a woman's letter is committing mental rape.

13. Burgett's study on the literary and the political history of sentimentalism in the post-Revolutionary United States is relevant.

14. See Janis Tomlinson's discussion of the new artistic model of heroic women as a result of the War of Independence in chapter 13 of this volume.

15. *Justine or The Misfortunes of Virtue* (1790) is about the continuous assaults endured by the virtuous Justine. Sade dedicated the work to an anonymous lady. Undoubtedly sweetness and mortification (the pleasure of doing good and of suffering) had ceased to be Sade's objective.

WORKS CITED

Álvarez Barrientos, Joaquín. *La novela del siglo XVIII*. Madrid: Júcar, 1991.
Amar y Borbón, Josefa. *Discurso sobre la educación física y moral de las mujeres*. Madrid: Benito Cano, 1790.
Amelia o los desgraciados efectos de la extremada sensibilidad: Anécdota inglesa traducida por D. J. F. S. Valencia, 1818.
Boix, Vicente. *El amor en el claustro o Eduardo y Adelaida: Cartas eróticas*. Valencia: Jacinto Talamantes, 1838.
Brissenden, R. F. *Virtue in Distress: Studies in the Novel of Sentiment from Richardson to Sade*. London: Macmillan, 1974.
Burgett, Bruce. *Sentimental Bodies: Sex, Gender, and Citizenship in the Early Republic*. Princeton, NJ: Princeton University Press, 1998.
Castillo y Mayone, Joaquín del. *Adelaida o el suicidio: Novela original, sacada de la historia verdadera de la heroína*. Barcelona: D. Ramón Martín Indar, 1833.
———. *La prostitución o consecuencias de un mal ejemplo: Novela original*. Barcelona: Ramón Martín Indar, 1833.
Coé, A. M. "Richardson in Spain." *Hispanic Review*, 1935, 56–63.
Cortina y Roperto, Ibo de la. *Teresa o las víctimas de la codicia: Novela sentimental*. Barcelona: J. Rubio, de M. Sauri, 1835.
Cosca Vayo, Estanislao. *Voyleano o la exaltación de las pasiones*. 2 vols. Valencia: Ildefonso Mompié, 1827.
Ellis, Markman. *The Politics of Sensibility: Race, Gender, and Commerce in the Sentimental Novel*. Cambridge: Cambridge University Press, 1996.
Enciso Recio, Luis Miguel. *Nipho y el periodismo español del siglo XVIII*. Valladolid: Universidad de Valladolid, Secretariado de Publicaciones, 1956.
Farigola y Domínguez, Antonio. *La Luciana en cinco periodos: Novela escrita en verso castellano*. Madrid: D. Francisco Martínez Dávila, 1819.

García Malo, Ignacio. *La desventurada Margarita: Anécdota tercera*. In García Malo, *Voz de la naturaleza*, vol. 2.

———. *Voz de la naturaleza*. 2 vols. Madrid: Aznar, 1787–1803.

[Genlis, condesa de]. *Adelaida o el triunfo del amor*. Trans. María Jacoba Castilla Xarava. Madrid: Aznar, 1801.

Guijarro Ripoll, Antonio. *Teodora, heroína de Aragón. Historia de la Guerra de la Independencia o Memorias del Coronel Blok, escritas (y no publicadas) en francés por Mr. Rodolphe, y traducidas al castellano por.* . . . Valencia: Cabrerizo, 1832. Also attributed to Francisco Brotons or anonymous.

Gutiérrez, Luis. *Cornelia Bororquia o la víctima de la Inquisición*. 2nd ed. 1800. Ed. Juan Ignacio Ferreras. Madrid: Vosa, 1994.

Hume, David. *Disertación sobre las pasiones*. Ed. and trans. José Luis Tasset Carmona. Madrid: Anthropos, 1990.

———. *A Treatise of Human Nature*. 1739–40. Bk. 2, "Of the Passions." Pt. 3, "Of the Will and Direct Passions." http://www.class.uidaho.edu/mickelsen/ToC/hume%20treatise%20ToC.htm#** (accessed April 2008).

J. S. y C. *La sombra del religioso o Corsino y Malvina en el convento incendiado: Novela original española por J. S. y C.* Barcelona: Agustín Roca, 1836.

La seducción y la virtud o Rodrigo y Paulina. 3 vols. Valencia: José Gimeno, 1829.

Maravall, José Antonio. "Espíritu burgués y principio de interés personal en la Ilustración española." *Hispanic Review* 47 (1979): 291–325.

Monk, Samuel Holt. *The Sublime: A Study of Critical Theories in XVIII-Century England*. New York: Modern Language Association of America, 1935.

Mor de Fuentes, José. *La Serafina*. 1797. Ed. Ildefonso Manuel Gil. Zaragoza: Universidad de Zaragoza, 1959.

Mullan, John. "Sentimental Novels." In *The Eighteenth-Century Novel*, ed. John Richetti, 236–54. Cambridge: Cambridge University Press, 1996.

———. *Sentiment and Sociability: The Language of Feeling in the Eighteenth Century*. Oxford: Clarendon, 1988.

Nifo, Francisco Mariano. *Cajón de sastre o montón de muchas cosas buenas, mejores y medianas, útiles, graciosas y modestas, para ahuyentar el ocio sin las rigideces del trabajo o, antes bien, a caricias del gusto*. 7 vols. Madrid: don Gabriel Ramírez, 1760–61.

O'Neal, John C. *The Authority of Experience: Sensationist Theory in the French Enlightenment*. University Park: Pennsylvania State University Press, 1996.

Perry, Ruth. *Women, Letters, and the Novel*. New York: AMS, 1980.

Pinch, Adela. *Strange Fits of Passion: Epistemologies of Emotion, Hume to Austen*. Stanford, CA: Stanford University Press, 1996.

Richardson, Samuel. *Pamela Andrews o la virtud recompensada: Escrita en inglés por Thomas [sic] Richardson; Traducida al castellano, corregida y acomodada a nuestras costumbres por el traductor, Ignacio García Malo*. 4 vols. Madrid: Antonio Espinosa, 1794.

Robledo, María de las Nieves. *El senador mexicano o Carta de Fermín a Tlaucolde*. Madrid: Colegio de Sordo-Mudos, 1836.

Rodríguez de Arellano, Vicente. *El decamerón español o colección de varios hechos raros y divertidos*. 5 vols. Madrid: Gómez Fuentenebro, 1805.

[Rousseau, Jean-Jacques]. *Julia o la nueva Heloisa: Cartas de dos amantes habitantes de una ciudad pequeña al pie de los Alpes.* Bayona: Lamaignière, 1814.

[Roussel, Pierre]. *Sistema físico y moral del hombre: Ensayo sobre la sensibilidad y nota sobre las simpatías.* París: Masson e Hijo, 1825. Originally published as *Système physique et moral de la femme, suivi du système physique de l'homme, et d'un fragment sur la sensibilité* (Paris: Crapart, Caille et Ravier, 1805).

Rueda, Ana. *Cartas sin lacrar: La novela epistolar y la España Ilustrada, 1789–1840.* Frankfurt: Iberoamericana Vervuert, 2001.

———. "El *Cajón de sastre* de Nifo: Ropería y gabinete de acciones ilustres para el gran Teatro del Mundo." In *Actas del Congreso Internacional de Periodismo y Literatura Mariano Nifo.* Alcañiz: Instituto de Estudios Turolenses, forthcoming.

Sade, Marquis de. *Justine or The Misfortunes of Virtue.* 1790. Reprint, New York: Castle Books, 1964.

Sill, Geoffrey. *The Cure of the Passions and the Origins of the English Novel.* Cambridge: Cambridge University Press, 2001.

Salvá, Vicente. *Irene y Clara, o La madre imperiosa.* Paris: Librería Hispano-Americana, 1930.

Todd, Janet. *Sensibility: An Introduction.* London: Methuen, 1986.

Truxa, Sylvia. "L'eroe nel romanzo sentimentale spagnolo ed in altre letterature europee." In *Il romanzo sentimentale, 1740–1815,* ed. Giuliano Baioni, Paolo Amalfitano, Francesco Fiorentino, and Giuseppe Merlino, 143–70. Pordenone, Italy: Studio Tesi, 1990.

Van Sant, Ann Jessie. *Eighteenth-Century Sensibility and the Novel: The Senses in Social Context.* Cambridge: Cambridge University Press, 1993.

Vila, Anne C. *Enlightenment and Pathology: Sensibility in the Literature and Medicine of Eighteenth-Century France.* Baltimore: Johns Hopkins University Press, 1998.

13

Mothers, *Majas,* and *Marcialidad*
Faces of Enlightenment in Spain
JANIS A. TOMLINSON

*T*he artist Francisco Goya y Lucientes (1746–1828) is more readily associated with depictions of war and atrocity than with images of women. That this is so shows how critical reception can skew our view of an artist's work, for certainly his portrayals of women of his time far outnumber his portrayals of atrocity and war. Yet it is these latter works that are so frequently reproduced, as images such as *The Disasters of War* seem so germane to modern society. In contrast, his images of women—often types of women no longer familiar to us or portraits of women known mainly as Goya's sitters—seem to have lost their immediacy.

The 2002 exhibition Goya: Images of Women offered a unique opportunity to gather and appreciate the breadth of Goya's imagery of women.[1] Unlike the exhibition held in Madrid, which included religious and allegorical figures, the North American version focused on portrayals feasibly inspired by Goya's experience from his arrival at the court of Madrid in 1775 to his death in Bordeaux in 1828. This chronological survey of paintings, drawings, and prints illustrated how the artist's imagery broadened and matured to reflect the increased and wide-ranging visibility of women in society and in urban spaces in late eighteenth- and early nineteenth-century Spanish society—from the select few who were members of the Economic Society of Madrid to spouses of important men, street vendors, streetwalkers, and actresses.

Goya's interest in contemporary female types is apparent from the first works he painted upon arriving at the court of Madrid. These early paintings were designs for tapestries, which would be delivered to the Royal Tapestry Factory of Santa Barbara, where they would be transformed into tapestries to decorate royal residences outside of Madrid. They illustrate types popularized by comic interludes at the theater *(sainetes)* and in popular prints. In these designs—or tapestry cartoons—Goya represented subjects that would have been familiar to his patrons the Prince and Princess of Asturias, depicting pastimes on the outskirts of Madrid, the annual fair of Madrid, the feast day of Saint Isidore (the city's patron saint), and such traditional themes as the four seasons. The women portrayed, from fruit vendors to dames accompanying men in French dress, represent a wide variety of social classes.

Perhaps the single most important trend in late eighteenth-century Spain that influenced the imagery of women presented in Goya's tapestry cartoons was a new visibility of women on the urban stage, in clear defiance of the customs of their mothers and grandmothers, enclosed in their houses, the most daring of them occasionally venturing to the window or balcony. This stage was defined in part by the reforms of King Carlos III, who patronized such projects at the Paseo del Prado and the city Puerta de Alcalá, still known to visitors today. The new visibility of women in these settings was accompanied by a new mode of behavior, defined by a very worldly young girl who explains this behavior to the narrator of the 1774 satire *Óptica del cortejo:*

> What good is a good dress if not displayed in a *marcial* manner? Freedom in dress and in conversation is what makes us well seen, for without *marcialidad* a woman is an Image without movement.
> And what is *marcialidad*? I asked my Nymph. She answered: *Marcialidad* is to speak freely, to treat all with liberty, to throw away the affectation of honesty, for all that about having your skirt to the floor, of hiding your face behind a veil, of speaking with a shameful blush . . . was only the custom of Spanish Ladies of old, back when Spain was closed to all commerce. (Ramírez y Góngora 6–7)

The mention of commerce in relation to this new attitude, *marcialidad*, was not serendipitous, but relates to another concern of enlightened minds: the harmful obsession with luxury goods, often imported, which undermined the national economy. The embodiment of such excessive indulgence was the *petimetra*, the affected coquette who was a slave to foreign fashion and customs, principally French (Bolufer Peruga 186). The *petimetra* was a stereotype often ridiculed in sainetes and by writers on contemporary customs; her antithesis was the *maja*, a streetwise woman of brazen manner who might earn her living as a street vendor or maid.

FIG. 1. *The Haw Seller (La Acerolera)*, 1779, oil on canvas, 259 x 100 cm. Reproduced with permission from Museo del Prado, Madrid.

This juxtaposition is illustrated by two cartoons for tapestries in a series painted from January 1778 to January 1779 to decorate the bedchamber of the Prince and Princess of Asturias, *The Haw Seller (La Acerolera)* and *The Militar and the Lady (El Militar y la Señora)* (figs. 1 and 2). Throughout this suite, Goya portrays anecdotes illustrating the open atmosphere of the annual fair in Madrid, where men and women of all classes mingled and flirted. In these two complementary scenes Goya shows the *maja* as *The Haw Seller* and the *petimetra* escorted by her gentleman in military garb, hence, the term *militar*. Dressed in bright primary colors, the *maja* turns her basket laden with ripe fruit toward the viewer and away from the crowd of caped *majos* who stand behind, apparently trying to get her attention. In the second cartoon the *petimetra*, in black overskirt and pastel bodice, daintily extends her hand to an older companion, whose gaze is unfocused, in contrast to the younger male in a tricorne, who clearly directs his gaze toward the woman. She, in turn, ignores both of these men, as well as viewers of the tapestry design, as she turns and looks upward, extending her arm and fan in the direction of a figure once seen looking over the wall behind. Goya's pairing of these two popular types, who compete for our attention, mirrors their competition in many of the *sainetes* of the day. But one popular refrain suggests that ultimately it would be the *maja* who conquered our hearts:

> A slap in the face from any *maja*
> is worth more
> than all the compliments
> from the *madamas*;
> for it is said that
> the first is all tenderness,
> and the second, deception.
> —(Martín Gaite 97–98)

Although presented so often as antitheses, both the *maja* and the *petimetra* enjoyed their new freedom, sharing a forthright demeanor and acting and dressing to attract attention, preferably male. The *petimetra* embodied the Enlightenment only in its most banal form, by her adoption of French manners, which she would justify as being ahead of her time; the *maja* gained fame as her necessary and nationalistic antithesis.

During the 1780s Goya continued to paint tapestry cartoons but also won his

FIG. 2. *The Militar and the Lady (El Militar y la Señora)*, 1779, oil on canvas, 259 x 100 cm. Reproduced with permission from Museo del Prado, Madrid.

earliest commissions for portraits of the aristocracy, including *The Duke and Duchess of Osuna and Their Children (Los duques de Osuna y sus hijos)* painted in 1787–88 (fig. 3). From this point onward, his reputation as a portrait painter would grow, as would his range of female sitters, which eventually encompassed members of Spain's most elite aristocratic families, the Queen María Luisa (who came to power in 1789), actresses, family members, and women whose identity remains unknown to us.

Is it possible to relate the women painted by Goya to the Enlightenment world that paralleled, if it did not influence, their lives? Perhaps it is best to proceed with caution as we look at these images within the context of this volume, in its desire to document Hispanic women's experience of the Enlightenment. The constraints imposed upon a portrait or even a "genre" image intended to represent everyday life are many, making it a highly mediated report of experience. Commissioned portraits are mute representations of a sitter who presents herself to the artist, who in turn translates that presentation to contemporaries and to posterity. She is stilled, adorned, and in Goya's portraits passive (in contrast to French portraiture of the age, in which she might be portrayed among her books, instruments, or other accoutrements of her culture). Who controls this representation? The artist, to be sure, although his own expression might be tempered by the demands of whoever is paying for the portrait—possibly the female sitter but also very possibly her spouse or father. The portrait, then, becomes a projection of the desires of multiple participants, adjudicated by the painter. Multilayered, it cannot be read as a transparent rendering of any individual's will or experience.

FIG. 3. *The Duke and Duchess of Osuna and Their Children (Los duques de Osuna y sus hijos)*, 1787-88, oil on canvas, 225 x 174 cm. Reproduced with permission from Museo del Prado, Madrid

Complicating the matter further is the nature of the Enlightenment as translated in Spain, which had a very practical aspect, closely allied with the absolutist monarchy. As such, its initiatives could be championed or spurned according to the desires of the king. As I have stated elsewhere, "To represent late eighteenth-century Spain as a coherent succession of reforms is historically inaccurate: rather than Enlightenment, this was a period of sparks, a few of which caught fire but most of which burned out quickly of their own accord" (Tomlinson, *Goya in the*

Twilight 18). Goya's images of women reflect the changing social and historical situation of his period, projected as a combination of the patrons' desires and the artist's intent, a complex facet of the Enlightenment in its broadest sense.

The most widely acknowledged female incarnation of the Enlightenment in Goya's art is the Duchess of Osuna, whose character and relationship with the painter were the subject of a recent article by Andrew Schulz. María Josefa de la Soledad Alonso Pimentel (1752–1834), the twelfth Duchess of Benavente, married her cousin Pedro Alcántara Téllez Girón (1755–1807) in 1771. During the engagement he unexpectedly inherited the title of Marquis de Peñafiel, heir to the house of Osuna, and would become the ninth Duke of Osuna following his father's death in 1787. The duchess is remembered for her own involvement in Enlightenment projects of her day: one of fourteen women elected to the newly created women's section (Junta de Damas) of the Economic Society of Madrid in 1787, she participated in their initiatives for social reform. The duchess was very possibly the instigator for the patronage of the arts in the Osuna household and also the hostess of a *tertulia* (the Spanish equivalent of the salon) that included artists and writers, among them Tomás de Iriarte, Leandro Fernández de Moratín, and Gaspar Melchor de Jovellanos. It may well have been the duchess, rather than her husband, who commissioned several works from Goya, including portraits, decorative genre scenes, and a series of witchcraft scenes. The duke and duchess were also among the earliest purchasers of the series of aquatint etchings titled *Los Caprichos*, published in 1799.

But to contemporaries the most important duty of the enlightened woman in Spain was to educate herself in order to raise and educate her children. The volumes in the Osuna library dealing with the upbringing and education of children, by the abbé de Condillac, Josefa Amar y Borbón, Lenglet du Fresnoy, and others, clearly attest to the duke and duchess's interest in these matters (Schulz 273). And the duchess's hard-won position as a mother—after early miscarriages and the deaths of four of her children by the age of four—undoubtedly reinforced her maternal devotion to the children who survived, depicted by Goya in *The Duke and Duchess of Osuna and Their Children* (see fig. 3). Often used to anchor discussion of the duchess as the enlightened mother, the portrait shows her surrounded by three of her children: from left to right, Francisco de Borja, the future tenth Duke of Osuna; Pedro de Alcántara, the future prince of Anglona (seated on a cushion); and Joaquina, the future Marquesa of Santa Cruz. Holding the hand of her father is Josefa Manuela. The boys hold toys appropriate to their gender, a stick horse and a toy carriage; and each girl hold a fan, an important accessory to adult female comportment. The presence of toys in this and other paintings by Goya is a sign of recognition of the distinction between childhood and adulthood that we also find in American portraiture from this time. Costumes reinforce the gender and youth of the boys, who wear skeleton suits, a recent innovation that replaced the earlier robe or frock, comprised of long trousers and a short attached jacket worn over a wide-collared shirt. The girls wear a less ornate version of their mother's dress, and their simple hairstyles also underscore their youth.[2]

Family portraits are scarce in Spanish painting: with the exception of portraits of the royal family, we can think only of Juan Bautista Martínez del Mazo's *The Family of the Painter* (1664–65) and Goya's *The Family of the Infante Don Luis* (1784) (Portús Pérez cat. nos. 44, 45). Yet these portraits clearly aspire to more than a family portrait, with children and grandchildren present in Mazo's portrait and in the presence of a household cortège in that of the family of Don Luis. Limited to parents with children, the portrait of the Osuna family introduces a new subject undoubtedly desired by the patrons: the nuclear family.

Rarely discussed in relation to the Osuna family portrait is how very restrained its representation of the family is: its very austerity might betray the artist's struggle to adapt a novel theme. Perhaps Goya or his patrons—well-known Anglophiles—were inspired by prints after paintings of British families or conversation pieces. Yet British (and American) family groups are often set in their houses or on the grounds, given some hints of domesticity. In contrast to these, the Osuna family is isolated from daily experience against a tonal background perhaps inspired by Velázquez, whose works in the royal collection were known to Goya: no domestic setting, no glimpse into the inner sanctum, is offered. Nor is there any hint of familiar love: like the infantes of Velázquez's portraiture, they exude the decorum basic to their class. By the late 1770s we find examples in English and American portraits of children taking center stage, sometimes displacing their fathers, as they reach, clamor, and laugh; such mirth is absent from Goya's depiction. And certainly there is no room for expressing the exuberance about motherhood seen in contemporary French paintings, where motherhood implied virtue as well as sexual fulfillment (Duncan 570–83). Such overt allusions to joy or to the connection between motherhood and physical love were clearly alien to the representation of the Spanish aristocracy. More than a direct reflection of

Enlightenment experience, Goya's portrait of the Duke and Duchess of Osuna and their family betrays an attempt to represent enlightened ideals of the family in a manner suitable to traditions of aristocratic portraiture in Spain, in which the decorum of portraiture seems to have won out.

To find images of motherhood less constrained than that seen in the portrait of the Osuna family, we turn to Goya's drawings, although even here the images are few. From the mid-1790s on, the artist created drawings, independent of paintings, in which he recorded images either seen or imagined and which were collected in several albums. Working in ink, chalk, or crayon on paper, the artist could formulate images far less labored or refined than those seen in paintings; moreover, in his drawings he had no patron to please. An early drawing in the first album of these drawings, thought to have been done during a visit to the Alba estate in Sanlúcar in 1796, shows a dark-haired woman, usually assumed to be the Duchess of Alba, holding her adopted black child, María de la Luz, on her lap. It is a very simple image, with forms broadly defined in India ink wash. The theme is revisited over a decade later in a ca. 1810 drawing of a woman holding an infant in her lap and gazing over the child's head. The inscription reads "Buena mujer, parece" (A good woman/wife, it seems) and perhaps explains the paucity of images of motherhood in Goya's imagery. For the ironic "parece" suggests the artist's own distrust of the image of ideal motherhood he depicts.

In fact, although Goya explores a range of women in his prints and drawings, positive images of women are often offset, if not outnumbered, by the negative images of women as prostitutes, bad mothers, witches, or grotesques. These women are involved in folly, deceit, and treachery more often than in virtuous practices. His portrayals of such negative examples dominate the series of eighty satirical etchings known as Los Caprichos, in which he parallels the writers of the day, who, "more than describing the conduct of contemporary women . . . sought to reform them, and in censuring them expressed the concerns and desires of enlightened men" (Bolufer Peruga 114).[3]

But we would be wrong to categorize this imagery as misogynist in any way, since in Los Caprichos no one is shown to best advantage. Scenes of courtship between aging suitors and young demoiselles, of flirtation between streetwalkers and potential customers, of the accused and accusers of the Inquisition—all are caught in an elaborate dance illustrating human folly. Nevertheless, etchings within the series such as capricho 3, Que viene el Coco! (Here comes the bogeyman!), in which the mother encourages the superstitious beliefs of her children, perhaps in order to meet her lover, or *capricho 25, Si quebró el Cantaro* (If he broke the jug), in which an old woman thrashes a child, suggest that Goya's own belief in unenlightened behavior was perhaps stronger than his faith in pristine stereotypes. *Parece.*

With the possible exception of the Osuna family portrait, we do not find among Goya's commissioned representations of women a single image that reflects a clear desire to provide an unequivocal image of Enlightenment principles, whether the artist's or those of his patron and/or sitter. Yet the changes he introduces in portraying women bespeak his awareness of changing social customs during the late eighteenth century. One of these—continuing the theme of family—is that of pregnancy. To be sure, pregnancy had appeared in early Spanish portraits; specifically, pregnant princesses were depicted in celebration of the happy event in a country always eager for an heir to the throne (Serrera 50). Yet it was only in the later eighteenth century that pregnancy was celebrated as the realization of the woman's mission, toward which all her physical care was aimed, just as the goal of her education was the upbringing of her children. Josefa Amar y Borbón opens her *Discurso sobre la educación física y moral de las mujeres* (Discourse on the Physical and Moral Education of Women), published in 1790, with a chapter titled "Care That Should be Taken during Pregnancy," which is followed by a section on childbirth and nursing (Amar 86–95). Lifestyle, as well as fashion, might harm the unborn infant, and in fashion one of the most dangerous practices was the use of stays that impeded the growth of the infant and so might result in birth defects. Such constraints also caused a variety of respiratory problems in the mother (Amar y Borbón 86–88).[4]

Both the prestige and recent theories of pregnancy may underlie Goya's innovative portraits of two pregnant women, the full-length *Countess of Chinchón (La Condesa de Chinchón)* (fig. 4) and the half-length portrait *Josefa Castilla Portugal de Garcini* (1804; Metropolitan Museum of Art, New York,).[5] Both women are portrayed in white Empire-style gowns—free of the stays and restrictive garments that might harm the unborn child—with their hands crossed over their stomachs, far more obvious here than in earlier royal portraits of expectant mothers. Wearing no shawl or overcoat, both women are dressed for confinement. And both portraits refer to the lineage of the child: the countess wears on her right hand a large miniature that we assume depicts her husband, Manuel Godoy, the Prince of Peace; the less ambitious portrait of Josefa was intended as a pendant to that of her husband, Ignacio Garcini, of the Brigade of Engineers. The countess's dress, a fine muslin with small flowers and a blue border, is clearly far more elaborate

FIG. 4. *The Countess of Chinchón (La Condesa de Chinchón)*, 1800, oil on canvas, 174 x 144 cm. Reproduced with permission from Museo del Prado, Madrid.

than the simple one worn by Josefa. And while the wife of the engineer appears with her long hair loose over her shoulders, the aristocratic countess (cousin to the king) wears hers in a bonnet decorated with sprigs of wheat, a traditional symbol of fertility.

These images reinforce the dominant idea of womanhood that accompanied the Spanish translation of Enlightenment: that the most important goal of an enlightened woman was to be an enlightened mother. Noteworthy is that women with attributes of learning are absent from Goya's pictorial vocabulary; although young women might read letters, as in the large image entitled *Young Women* (ca. 1812; Musée de Beaux-Arts), they never seem to pick up a book. Only in one late lithograph does Goya show a woman reading, but she is again the benevolent caregiver, reading to two children at her knees. Three portraits of aristocratic women in the Museo del Prado include attributes of the arts. The first, of Doña Joaquina Téllez-Girón y Pimentel, Marquesa de Santa Cruz (1805), shows her in a white

Empire-style gown, extended upon a divan. Wearing a wreath of grape leaves and grapes, she holds a lyre, the traditional attribute of the Muse of lyric poetry, Erato. But she is clearly assuming airs. Very different is the 1816 portrait of her younger sister, Doña Manuela Girón y Pimentel, the Duchess of Abrantes (who, born only in 1794, does not appear in the portrait of the Osuna family discussed above). Although she too wears a crown, hers is a crown of flowers that a fashionable woman might have worn, particularly if she was about to perform. That seems to be the case here, as she holds a score in her right hand and looks toward her listener. The *Marquesa de Villafranca Painting Her Husband* introduces the attributes of painting. The aristocratic sitter, an honorary member of the Real Academia de Bellas Artes de San Fernando, sits in an armchair, comfortably resting before the portrait of her husband. She could not paint from this position, nor would she paint in the dress she wears; once again, the woman seems to assume the attributes of an art rather than actually practice it. That she was nevertheless pleased with the portrait is suggested by its inclusion in the Real Academia exhibition of 1805.

As Mónica Bolufer Peruga has discussed, the woman who took her learning for its own sake was a figure of ridicule in contemporary literature (145–51). Such women, known as *bachilleras*, transgressed social boundaries by taking learning beyond what was desirable for fulfilling the social role as mother and even ventured into subjects considered appropriate for men only. We can only guess that by the time Goya began to paint female subjects, in the later 1780s, this stereotype had fallen into such disrepute that neither the artist nor his patrons would suggest painting a woman among books because of the possibly pejorative connotations.

So how would the modern woman be defined? One trait that comes into play here is that of *marcialidad*, mentioned above in relation to Goya's tapestry cartoons. I have written elsewhere that it is this attitude that marks the modernity of Goya's *Naked Maja* (*Goya in the Twilight* 120). But I would like to suggest here that this forthright manner of the modern woman also made possible a series of full-length portraits of the 1790s that culminates in an image of 1799 embodying strength, nationalism, and female sexuality: that of María del Rosario Fernández (1755–1803), or *La Tirana* (fig. 5).

Standing before the railing and fountain of a garden landscape, *La Tirana* wears "a dress of white spangled muslin, decorated at the hem in typically Spanish fashion with a border of gold lace or embroidery, and she is swathed in a long, fringed Indian shawl" (Ribeiro 76–77). The shawl was a required accessory to the white Empire-style gown, here made of silk (rather than the cashmere that was popular in France) and thus appropriate for Spain's moderate climate. Despite her Empire

FIG. 5. *La Tirana*, 1799, oil on canvas, 206 x 130 cm. Reproduced with permission from Museo de la Real Academia de Bellas Artes de San Fernando.

gown, this woman could not be more different from such coquettish neoclassical counterparts as Madame Récamier: she stands proudly, with arm akimbo, and directly confronts the viewer, her eyes set off by dark hair and heavy brows. Her personal presence is reinforced by her painterly substance, as the masterful broad strokes defining the shawl and the gold impasto of its fringe enliven the surface of the painting. Her attitude seems appropriate to her popular name *La Tirana* (The Female Tyrant), although some say it was given to her because of her husband, the actor Francisco Castellanos, who was called "the Tyrant" because of the tragic roles he played. Goya presents the actress at the age of forty-four, when talent and self-awareness have displaced the charms of the coquettish youth. There is no pendant to the portrait representing her well-known husband, although he may have commissioned the work.

This portrait culminates a decade of production of standing female figures that include the Marquesa de Solana as well as two full-length portraits of the Duchess of Alba. But in portraying these members of the aristocracy Goya may have been visually keeping a respectable distance, as was demanded by decorum. The figures seem more fragile, set back within the surrounding space, their elegant dresses carefully rendered.[6] This is not so with *La Tirana*. Her commanding presence parallels the presence she assumed on stage in Spanish translations of French neoclassical dramas such as Pierre Laurent de Belloy's *Zelmire*, one of the most often performed, introduced in 1781 and repeated in 1782, 1785, 1787, and often in the final decade of the eighteenth century. Her role is described in a review of Celmira in the *Memorial literario* of September 1785:

> This tragedy translated from the French of Mr. Du [sic] Belloy and performed in 1762 is a success in our theater, because of the marvelous piety of a daughter for her father, the contrast of effects that result from the various changes in fortune of the characters and appropriateness of the characters. Add to this the strength of the acting by the Actress that plays the role, supported equally by the rest of the cast to the pleasure of the audience in the frequent performances of this Tragedy. (qtd. in Qualia 151)

But this painting of *La Tirana* goes beyond paying homage to a talented actress. It betrays an acknowledgment of female power unencumbered by fashion or female decorum, betraying the growing acceptance of *marcialidad* raised to a new level. And just as the actress is not diminished by her femininity, so the artist is not constrained by details of fashion. The bold handling of the paint seen in the broad strokes that play over the surface to form and enliven the actress's magnificent salmon/orange shawl seems to reinforce the power of her personality while at the same time holding it in check. She seems as closely related to de Kooning's *Women* of the 1950s as she does to the relatively timid Duchess of Osuna, portrayed only eleven years earlier.

In the years following 1800 Goya began to paint portraits of less well know women—family members or women whose identity is unknown, or perhaps known only from an inscription. These are also more modest portraits, half- or three-quarters-length rather than the full-length portraits of the 1790s. The beauty and quiet dignity of many of these portraits, such as *Antonia Zárate* (ca. 1806; National Gallery of Ireland, Dublin) or *Young Lady Wearing a Mantilla and Basquiña* (ca. 1800–1805; National Gallery of Art, Washington, DC), cannot be disputed, yet without any further information about the sitters these portraits remain impenetrable in their mute beauty.

The imagery of the empowered female, embodied first in the flirtatious *maja* and evolving into the figure of *La Tirana*, would undergo one last major transformation in Goya's art. In 1808 French troops occupied Spain, leading to a war fought throughout the peninsula that would last until 1813. In March 1808 a crowd rose up against the royal favorite, Manuel Godoy, forcing the abdication of his patrons, King Carlos IV and Queen María Luisa. Their son, Fernando VII, came to power, and Goya was commissioned by the Real Academia de Bellas Artes de San Fernando to paint a portrait of the new king. Months later, on 2 October, the artist wrote to his academic colleague Don Josef Munárriz:

> I have finished the painting of the King, our Lord, Fernando VII, which the Royal Academy graciously commissioned of me, which once dry will be hung at my request by D. Josef Fol, as I cannot do it in person since I have been called by His Excellency Don Josef Palafox to go this week to Saragossa to view the ruins of that city with the aim of painting the glorious deeds of her citizens, from which I cannot excuse myself as I am so much interested in the glory of my native land. (qtd. in Sayre 126)

Goya went to Zaragoza, and according to an account of 1830, he had to leave the besieged city to take refuge in the town of his birth, Fuendetodos, in November. Zaragoza fell to the French on 21 February 1809; by May Goya had returned to Madrid, where he would remain throughout the remaining years of the war (Sayre 126–27). It was in Madrid that he would etch the series of prints that would become known as *The Disasters of War*. The date 1810 is etched on the earliest plates of this series, suggesting that these images were inspired by the artist's own recollections and by his translations of contemporary accounts of the war rather than by eyewitness testimony.[7]

In *The Disasters of War*, women play a far more important role than in any previous imagery of battle. In fact, the siege of Zaragoza provided the background for perhaps the most famous story of female heroism to emerge from the war, that of Agustina of Aragón, cited in an English account of 1809:

> The Sand-bag battery before the gate of the Portillo, was gallantly defended by the Aragonese.... Agustina Zaragoza, about 22 years of age, a handsome

FIG. 6. *And this too (Y esto también)*, ca. 1812, etching and aquatint, 16.5 x 22 cm, Collection Desastres de la Guerra. Reproduced with permission from Biblioteca Nacional de España, Madrid.

woman, of the lower class of the people, whilst performing her duty of carrying refreshments to the gates, arrived at the battery of the Portillo, at the very moment when the French fire had absolutely destroyed every person that was stationed in it. The citizens, and soldiers, for the moment hesitated to re-man the guns; Agustina rushed forward over the wounded, and slain, snatched a match from the hand of the dead artilleryman, and fired off a 26-pounder, then jumping upon the gun, made a solemn vow never to quit it alive during the siege, and having stimulated her fellow-citizens by this daring intrepidity to fresh exertions, they instantly rushed into the battery, and again opened a tremendous fire upon the enemy. (Sayre 133–34)

Although Agustina was perhaps the best-known heroine of this struggle, she was not the only one. Contemporary accounts drew attention to the bravery of women in battle and to the atrocities they suffered. Popular prints were struck honoring the women of Zaragoza, Agustina and another heroine, Casta Álvarez (Calcografía cat. nos. 98–100). With bodies developed by physical labor, wearing working-class dress, their skirts ending mid-calf and arms bared, these women are ready for battle.[8]

It is this type that inhabits the war scenes of Goya's etchings, where in images such as plates 4, *The women give courage (Las mugeres dan valor)*, and 5, *They are like wild beasts (Y son fieras)*, women engage in hand-to-hand combat to save themselves, their honor, or their children. They suffer the ravages of war that have no respect for the niceties of gender distinction in plates 19, *There is no more time (Ya no hay tiempo)*, and 30, *Ravages of War (Estragos de la Guerra)*. With determined expressions, they stand tall over a low horizon as they escape the front with children, livestock, and few domestic items in tow in *And this too (Y esto también)* (fig. 6). The women who populate *The Disasters of War* bring to a heroic culmination the roles for women that emerged in Goya's earlier works. Like the *majas* who populate the tapestry cartoons, these are working-class women unafraid of confrontation; like the Duchess of Osuna or the expectant Countess of Chinchón, they are mothers whose mission is to protect their children and family; and like *La Tirana*, they are heroic in stature.

Do they reflect an experience of the Enlightenment? Perhaps it would be more appropriate to say that the Enlightenment as it was formulated in Spain made their appearance possible. Without the opening up of Spain to French products as well as ideas, the *petrimetra* and her nemesis, the *maja*, might never have been formulated. The Enlightenment brought a new value to women's lives—at least in word—as protectors of national traditions, as mothers, as heroines. Did these words play out in daily experience? That is not the question here. What is certain is that they did affect the perspective of Goya and of his patrons and are mirrored by the dozens of female figures who populate his works.

NOTES

1. The exhibition was held at the National Gallery of Art, in Washington, DC, from 10 March to 2 June 2002. See Tomlinson, *Goya: Images.*

2. The significance of toys and of the skeleton suit is discussed in Calvert, 105–11.

3. A full scholarly treatment of the portrayal of women in Goya's many prints and drawings has yet to be undertaken. On *Los Caprichos*, see Alcalá Flecha, as well as Tomlinson, "Images of Women." For the images cited here, see Gassier and Wilson, cat. nos. 360, 1251, 1699.

4. See Morant's discussion of Amar's *Discurso* in chapter 3 of this volume.

5. See Gassier and Wilson, cat. no. 821.

6. The exception here is the well-know "solo Goya" portrait of the Duchess of Alba at the Hispanic Society of America, New York. However, it is noteworthy that this portrait remained in the artist's studio in 1812 and thus was either never offered to or rejected by its patron.

7. The best summaries of the events portrayed by Goya available in English are Sayre, 125–94; and the entries by Jesusa Vega on these images in Sayre and Pérez Sánchez, 185–210.

8. See Ana Rueda's discussion of the effect of the War of Independence on the representation of women in sentimental novels in chapter 12 of this volume.

WORKS CITED

Alcalá Flecha, Roberto. *Matrimonio y prostitución en el arte de Goya*. Cáceres: Universidad de Extremadura, 1984.

Amar y Borbón, Josefa. *Discurso sobre la educación física y moral de las mujeres*. 1790. Madrid: Cátedra, 1994.

Bolufer Peruga, Mónica. *Mujeres e Ilustración: La construcción de la feminidad española*. Valencia: Institució Alfons el Magnànim, 1998.

Calcografía Nacional. *Estampas de la Guerra de la Independencia*. Madrid, 1997. An exhibition catalog.

Calvert, Karin. "Children in American Family Portraiture, 1670–1810." *William and Mary Quarterly*, 3rd ser., 39.1 (1982): 87–113.

Duncan, Carol. "Happy Mothers and Other New Ideas in French Art." *Art Bulletin* 55.4 (1973): 570–83.

Gassier, Pierre, and Juliet Wilson. *The Life and Complete Work of Francisco Goya; with a Catalogue Raisonné of the Paintings, Drawings, and Engravings*. New York: Morrow, 1971.

Martín Gaite, Carmen. *Usos amorosos del dieciocho en España*. 1972. Barcelona: Lumen, 1981.

Portús Pérez, Javier. *The Spanish Portrait: From El Greco to Picasso*. London: Scala, 2004. An exhibition catalog.

Qualia, Charles B. "The Vogue of Decadent French Tragedies in Spain, 1762–1800." *PMLA* 58.1 (1943): 149–62.

Ramírez y Góngora, Antonio. *Optica del cortejo: Espejo claro en que con demonstraciones practicas de el entendimiento se manifiesta lo insubstancial de semejante empleo*. Córdoba: Juan Rodríguez, 1774.

Ribeiro, Aileen. "Fashioning the Feminine: Dress in Goya's Portraits of Women." In Tomlinson, *Goya: Images of Women*, 71–87.

Sayre, Eleanor. *The Changing Image: Prints by Francisco Goya*. Boston: Museum of Fine Arts, 1974. An exhibition catalog.

Sayre, Eleanor, and Alfonso E. Pérez Sánchez. *Goya and the Spirit of Enlightenment*. Boston: Museum of Fine Arts, 1989. An exhibition catalog.

Schulz, Andrew. "Goya's Portraits of the Duchess of Osuna: Fashioning Identity in Enlightenment Spain." In *Women, Art, and the Politics of Identity in Eighteenth-Century Europe*, ed. Melissa Hyde and Jennifer Milam, 263–83. Burlington, VT: Ashgate, 2003.

Serrera, Juan Miguel. "Alonso Sánchez Coello y la mecánica del retrato de corte." In *Alonso Sánchez Coello y el retrato en la corte de Felipe II*, 38–63. Madrid: Museo del Prado, 1990. An exhibition catalog.

Tomlinson, Janis A., ed. *Goya: Images of Women*. Washington, DC: National Gallery of Art, 2002. An exhibition catalog.

———. *Goya in the Twilight of Enlightenment.* New Haven: Yale University Press, 1992.

———. "Images of Women in Goya's Prints and Drawings." In Tomlinson, *Goya: Images of Women,* 51–69.

Contributors

MÓNICA BOLUFER PERUGA is *profesora titular* at the Universitat de València, where she received her PhD in early modern European history. She is a cultural historian specializing in the Spanish eighteenth century and its European context, with an emphasis on gender and the Enlightenment.

REBECCA HAIDT is associate professor of Spanish at Ohio State University. She holds a PhD in Spanish and comparative literature from Washington University in St. Louis, with a specialty in eighteenth-century literature and culture, especially as they deal with gender issues.

LUCY D. HARNEY is associate professor of Spanish at Texas State University–San Marcos. She holds a PhD in comparative literature from the University of Texas at Austin and a master's of music from Texas Tech University. Her research interests include eighteenth- and nineteenth-century Spanish and Latin American literature and cultural studies and the *zarzuela*.

CATHERINE M. JAFFE is professor of Spanish at Texas State University–San Marcos. She holds a PhD in comparative literature from the University of Chicago, and her research interests include women writers, gender and reading, and the history of women's reading in eighteenth-, nineteenth-, and twentieth-century Spain.

ELIZABETH FRANKLIN LEWIS is associate professor of Spanish at the University of Mary Washington. She holds a PhD in Spanish literature from the University of Virginia and researches women writers and gender issues in eighteenth- and early nineteenth-century Spain.

MARÍA VICTORA LÓPEZ-CORDÓN CORTEZO is *catedrática* in the Department of Modern History at the Universidad Complutense de Madrid, where she received her PhD. Her research has focused on Spanish and European history, with a special emphasis on gender and the eighteenth century.

FRÉDÉRIQUE MORAND obtained her PhD in Hispanic studies from the Université Paris VIII Vincennes-Saint-Denis. She is an independent researcher and an expert on the life and poetry of María Gertrudis Hore.

ISABEL MORANT DEUSA is *profesora titular* of early modern history at the Universitat de València, where she completed her PhD. Her research interests include women's history and the history of marriage.

MARÍA JOSÉ DE LA PASCUA SÁNCHEZ is *profesora titular* of early modern history at the Universidad de Cádiz, where she earned her PhD. Her research interests include women's history and sociocultural history, and to that end she directs the research group Género e Historia.

BEATRIZ QUINTANILLA-MADERO is *profesora titular* of psychiatry and medical psychology at the School of Medicine of the Universidad Panamericana, Mexico, and the director of the Department of Psychiatry there. She holds a medical degree from the Universidad Autónoma Metropolitana–Xochimilco and a PhD in psychiatric medicine from the Universidad de Navarra. Her areas of research interest include the history of psychiatry, personality and mood disorders, and ethics in psychiatry.

ANA RUEDA is professor of Spanish literature at the University of Kentucky. She received her PhD from Vanderbilt University. Her areas of research interest include the eighteenth-century epistolary and sentimental genres.

MARÍA A. SALGADO is professor emeritus of Spanish and Spanish American literature at the University of North Carolina, Chapel Hill. She holds a PhD in Spanish literature from the University of Maryland. She has published books and articles on various topics of eighteenth-, nineteenth-, and twentieth-century literature from Spain and Latin America.

ELISA SAMPSON VERA TUDELA is lecturer in the Department of Spanish and Spanish American Studies, King's College, University of London. She holds a PhD in history from the European University Institute (Italy). Her main research interests include the history and literature of colonial and nineteenth-century Latin America.

JANIS A. TOMLINSON is the director of university museums at the University of Delaware. She received her PhD in art history from the University of Pennsylvania. She is an expert on the art of Francisco de Goya, and served as guest curator of the 2002 exhibition Goya: Images of Women at the National Gallery of Art, Washington, DC.

Index

Ablitas, Countess of, 113n7
Abrantes, Doña Manuela Girón y Pimentel, Duchess of, 229
La Academia del Buen Gusto (Academy of Good Taste), 111, 113n7
Addison, Joseph, 178–80, 185, 187–89, 190. See also *Spectator*
Adelaida o el suicidio (Castillo y Mayone), 213
Adultery, 41, 43–44
Aeneid (Virgil), 188
Africa, 136, 169, 173
Agency of women, 9, 119, 121, 126, 131–33
Ágreda, Madre, 48n18, 88
Aguirre, Cayetana de, 26–27
Aguirre, Juan Antonio, 62
Agustina of Aragón, 213, 232–33
Alba, Duchess of, 111, 226, 231, 234n6
Alcántara, Pedro de, 88
Alcedo, Antonio de, 173–74
Alfonso X, King, 3, 44
Allestree, Richard, 192
Alumbrados (enlightened ones), 131
Álvarez, Alonso, 21
Alzate, José Antonio de, 147, 149, 155n6
Amar y Borbón, Josefa: contributions of generally, 1–2; on Eve, 1, 3; on health, 56; identity of, as writer, 23, 25; on learned woman as cultural icon, 18–19; on moral education, 53–59, 206; on needlework by women, 118; on predominance of passion and its effects on women, 10; on pregnancy and childbirth, 227; on Rousseau, 12n11, 61n4; on sentimental novels, 206; translation of Lampillas's essay on Spanish literature by, 23; on vices of women, 58; on women's admittance to Economic Society of Madrid, 6, 23, 51–52; on women's conflicted and limited experiences, 6; on women's curiosity, 1, 3, 11n9; on women's desire for attention and praise, 104; on women's education, 6, 9, 12n11, 15, 52–60, 184, 224; writings by, 1, 6, 15, 18–19, 23, 51–60, 184, 227

Amayuelas, Countess of, 21
Amazons, 188–89
Amelia o los desgraciados efectos de la extremada sensibilidad, 201
Les Américaines (Mme Le Prince de Beaumont), 24–25
El amor en el claustro (Boix), 212, 213
Amorous discourse. *See* Love
Andromaque (Racine), 62, 63, 66–67
Antonia Zárate (Goya), 231–32
Anxiety hysteria, 144
"Apología de las mujeres" (Joyes y Blake), 27, 47n7
Aranda, Count of, 110
Arcos, Duchess of, 113n7
Arenal, Electa, 89
Arenas, Reinaldo, 161
Aristotle, 147
Ars Amatoria (Ovid), 64, 70
Artamène (Scudéry), 190
Artisan-class women, 118
Astraea (D'Urfé), 184, 190
Asturias, Prince and Princess of, 219, 221

Bachillera (learned woman), 8, 21, 25, 35, 47n5, 189, 229
Barker-Benfield, G. J., 5, 188–89
Barreto, Isabel, 132
Barthes, Roland, 34

Bartolache y Díaz de Posadas, José Ignacio, 10, 101–2, 143, 146–54
Battle hysteria, 144
Beattie, James, 172–73
Bellosartes, Manuel, 190
Belloy, Pierre Laurent de, 231
Benavente, Countess-Duchess, 111, 224
Berwick, Duchess of, 109
Bigamy, 136–38
Birriel Salcedo, Margarita María, 132
Boccaccio, Giovanni, 18
Body: Amar y Borbón on, 55; exercise for, 149, 153; letter associated with, 215n12; link between moral character and, 171; opposition between mind/spirit and, 95; in sentimental novels, 198, 204–5, 209, 213; Sor Sebastiana on, 95–96; weakness of women's bodies, 155n12; women's association with, 5. *See also* Hysteria; Uterus
Boix, Vicente, 212
Bolufer Peruga, Mónica, 2, 7–9, 12n11, 15, 17–32, 35, 85, 96, 117–19, 178–79, 183, 195n2, 219, 226, 229, 237
Books. *See* Library; Reading audience
Bourbon dynasty, 10, 20, 86–87, 105–6
Bradshaigh, Lady, 205
Braganza, Bárbara de, 105, 106, 107
Brissenden, R. F., 199, 211
Britain: ancient inhabitants of, 173; and body viewed as indicator of identity, 171; china acquisition in, 182; convents in, 84; Enlightenment in, 84, 86; hysteria in, 149; portraiture in, 225; sensibility as concept in, 199; sentimental novels in, 207; women writers in, 22, 28; women's reading preferences in, 185
Buffon, Georges-Louis Leclerc, comte de, 183, 194
Burgett, Bruce, 215n13

Caballero, Fernán, 43, 163
Cabarrús, Francisco de, 117
Cajón de sastre, 204, 214n4
Calavesani, Francisco, 135

Calprenède, Gaultier de Coste, seigneur de La, 184, 190
Calzada, Bernardo María de, 190
Campomanes, Pedro Rodríguez, Conde de, 117–18
Cañas, Gonzalo de, 37
Cantigas de Santa María (Alfonso X el Sabio), 3
Los Caprichos (Goya), 201, 224, 226–27
Carbonell Esteller, Montserrat, 121–22
Carlos I, King, 138
Carlos III, King, 10, 106, 107, 111, 174, 219
Carlos IV, King, 111, 232
Carpentier, Alejo, 161
"Carta de la traductora a sus hijas" (Letter to her daughters; Joyes y Blake), 27
Carvajal y Lancáster, José de, 111
Carvajal y Mendoza, Antonia Luisa de, 131
Casandra (La Calprenède), 184, 190
Castellanos, Francisco, 230
Castillo y Mayone, Joaquín del, 206, 208
Castrillo, Marquise of, 113n7
Catastro de Ensenada, 123, 132, 140n1
Catastros, 123–24, 132, 140n1
Catherine of Bologna, 88
Catherine of Siena, 97n20
Catholic Church, 3, 4, 86–96, 151–52, 174. *See also* Convents and nuns
Cavallo, Sandra, 130
Cecilia Valdés: o La Loma de Ángel (Villaverde), 161–63, 167–74, 174–75n1, 175n4
El Censor, 179, 194
Censorship, 23–24, 26, 38, 47n10, 88, 179, 198–99, 206. *See also* Inquisition
Censos, 123–24
Cepeda, María del Rosario, 24, 34–36
Cernuda, Luis, 33
Cerrutti, Simona, 130
Cevallos, General, 63, 82n2
The Cheese and the Worms (Ginzburg), 133
Chichisveo (intimate and personal conversation between a man and a woman), 110
Children in family portraits, 222–26

China, 181–82
Chinchón, Countess of, 227–28, 234
Choderlos de Laclos, Pierre, 214n6
Chojnacka, Monica, 123
A Chronicle of the Kings of England from the Time of the Romans Government unto the Raigne of King Charles, 193
Cienfuegos, Beatriz, 21
Clarissa (Richardson), 205, 214n10
Clelia (Scudéry), 82n8, 184, 188, 193
Cleopatra (La Calprenède), 184, 190
Clothing: Amar y Borbón on, 58; of children, 225; corsets as cause of hysteria, 148, 149; and household economy, 101, 116, 119, 121, 122, 124–26; of *maja*, 221, 222; of *petimetra*, 221, 223; of pregnant women, 227–28; of women in Goya's paintings, 221–23, 227–31, 233. *See also* Textiles
Colonial period. *See* Spanish America
Comedies (plays), 20–21
Common Sense (Paine), 167
Condillac, abbé de, 183, 190, 224
Confessional letters by religious women, 16, 85–96, 102
Convents and nuns: aristocratic women as nuns, 151–52; condition of, in Mexico, 87; confessional letters and hagiography of Sor Sebastiana, 16, 85–96, 102; Diderot on, 84; exclusion of, from study of Enlightenment, 85–86; Feijoo on, 84; Hore as nun, 24, 33, 42–47; hysteria and nuns, 151–52, 153; in Mexico, 86–96, 96n8; nun's marriage to Christ, 75–76; patrons of convents, 152; reform of convents, 86–87, 151–52; servants for, 152; Sor Sebastiana as nun, 85–96; in Spanish American Enlightenment, 84–96, 96n8; as women alone, 131
Conversación sobre la pluralidad de los Mundos (*Entretiens sur la pluralité des mondes*; Fontenelle), 183, 193
Copernicus, 183
Cornaro, Luigi, 149

Cornelia Bororquia (Gutiérrez), 207, 208
Coronel, Doña María, 204
Cortejo, 70, 83n15, 110, 183
Cortina y Roperto, Ibo de la, 212
Cosca Vayo, Estanislao, 201, 211–12
Costumbrismo, 162–63, 169
Countess of Chinchón (*La Condesa de Chinchón*) (Goya), 227–28, 234
The Countess of Pembroke's Arcadia (Sidney), 191
Court: etiquette of, 107–8; ladies-in-waiting and other female attendants at, 105–6; as model of sociability, 104–7; queen's role in, 105, 106–7
Credit, 124
Criada (maid), 118
Criollo, 87, 97n10
Cristobalina, 63
Cuba: entrepreneurial ethic in, 169; hypergenation in, 168; iconic *mulata* of, 8, 10, 161–74; ideology of *cubanidad* (Cubanness) in, 162; independence for, 162; race in, 171; slavery in, 162, 169; upward mobility in, 167–68. *See also* Spanish America
Cuba intelectual, 175n2
Cueto, Leopoldo Augusto de, 42, 43, 47–48nn10–11, 63
Cullpeper, Nicholas, 192
Cyrus (Scudéry), 184, 190

D'Amelia, Marina, 130
Davis, Natalie Zemon, 133
De Genlis, Mme, 21
De Hostos, Eugenio, 171
De Institutione feminae christianae (Vives), 183–84
De Kooning, Willem, 231
De la Cerda, Cayetana, Countess of Lalaing, 24
De la Cerda, Don Juan, 204
De la Coste, Hilarion, 19
De la Cruz, Isabel, 131
De la Cruz, Magdalena, 131
De la Cruz, San Juan, 83n16

De la Cruz, Sor Juana Inés, 81n1, 82n8, 97n12
De la Pascua Sánchez, María José, 8, 9, 10, 101, 128–42, 132, 238
De mulieribus claris (Boccaccio), 18
"Defensa de las mujeres" (Defense of Women; Feijoo), 1, 3, 4–5, 27, 62, 81n1
Defoe, Daniel, 182
Dekker, Rudolf, 133
Demerson, Paula, 2
Los desastres de la guerra/*The Disasters of War* (Goya), 10, 160, 218, 232–34
La desventurada Margarita (García Malo), 206–8
Diderot, Denis, 84, 95, 214n6
"Discurso en defensa del talento de las mujeres" (Discourse in Defense of the Talent of Women; Amar), 1, 6, 23, 51–52
Discurso sobre la educación física y moral de las mujeres (Discourse on Women's Moral and Physical Education; Amar y Borbón), 15, 18–19, 23, 25, 51–60, 61n2, 184, 227
Discursos filosóficos sobre el hombre (Forner), 183, 194
Disease. *See* Hysteria
Divorce, 44
Docta ignorantia, 97n19
Doctors. *See* Medical discourse
Documentation. *See* Research sources
Domergue, Lucienne, 185
Domestic working women, 116–17, 118, 126
Don Juanism, 81, 166, 206–11. *See also* Sentimental novels
Drama. *See* Plays and playwrights
Dryden, John, 190
The Duke and Duchess of Osuna and Their Children (Los duques de Osuna y sus hijos) (Goya), 222–26
Dupuy La Chapelle, N., 57
D'Urfé, Honoré, 183, 184, 190, 193

Economic Society of Madrid, 6, 22, 23, 51, 107, 116, 117, 218, 224
Education: and *bachillera* (learned woman), 8, 21, 25, 35, 47n5, 189, 229; Feijoo on, 4–5; Jovellanos on, 4; Lambert on, 60, 61n3; moral education, 53–59; and motherhood, 224, 228, 229; Rousseau on, 9, 60, 61n4; of royal children, 108; of women, 6, 8, 9–10, 12n11, 15, 18–19, 22, 52–60, 179, 183–84, 224
Egodocuments, 133
Elasticity of social position, 138
Elias, Norbert, 138
Ellis, Markman, 203, 207
Émile (Rousseau), 5, 9, 12n11, 60, 61n4
Emotions. *See* Hysteria; Passions; Sentimental novels; Sensibility
Empson, William, 166
Enfilade, 111
England. *See* Britain
Enlightenment: characteristics of, 2, 19–20, 85, 234; empirical orientation of, 4–5; exclusion of nuns from study of, 85–86; in France, 85; literary characteristics of, 164; and meaning of *ilustrar*, 86; and modern curiosity, 3, 11n9; and modernity, 85; political and social theory of, 166–69, 174; records of, 8–9, 115–16, 119–23; scholarly neglect of Hispanic Enlightenment, 1–2; and secularization, 85, 86, 96n3; sentimental rhetoric of, stressing gender differences, 9–10. *See also* Gender; Spain; Spanish America; and specific writers
Enseñar deleitando (teaching while delighting), 63
Entretiens sur la pluralité des mondes (Fontenelle), 183, 193
Epilepsy, 146, 153, 155n18
Erauso, Catalina de, 132
Escobar, Marina, 88
Escuela de mugeres y educación de niñas (Fénelon), 183, 193
Essay Concerning Human Understanding (Locke), 4, 191
Estepa, Marquise of, 113n7
Estrado (elevated platform), 109
Eve, 1, 3–4, 7, 155n12

Fabián y Fuero, Francisco, 151

Fabulistas, 164
Families. *See* Marriage
The Family of the Infante Don Luis (Goya), 225
The Family of the Painter (Martínez del Mazo), 225
Family portraits, 222–26
Farfán, Agustín, 149
Farnesio, Isabel de, 105, 106–7, 111
Fauve-Chamoux, A., 132
Feijoo, Benito Jerónimo, 1, 3, 4–5, 27, 62, 81*n*1, 84, 147, 179
Feilding, Robert, 194
Felipe II, King, 105
Felipe V, King, 105, 106, 108
Feminist history, 12*n*12
Les femmes savantes (Molière), 184–85, 192
Fénelon, François de Salignac de la Mothe-, 52, 183, 193, 208
Fernández de Moratín, Leandro, 66, 224
Fernández, María del Rosario, 229–30
Fernando VI, King, 63
Fernando VII, King, 232
Fiction. *See* Reading audience; Sentimental novels; and specific authors
Fischer-Homberger, Esther, 146
Fontenelle, Bernard le Bouyer de, 183, 193
Forner, Juan Pablo, 183, 194
Forradellas, Joaquín, 34
France: ancient inhabitants of, 173; astronomers and scholars from, in Spain, 37; and body viewed as indicator of identity, 171; *enfilade* system in, 111; Enlightenment in, 84–86; and French Revolution, 9, 10, 189, 199–201; literacy in, 179; motherhood in paintings in, 225; portraiture in, 222; romances from, 184–85; sensibility as concept in, 199–201; and Spanish War of Independence, 232; women writers in, 22, 28. *See also* Rousseau, Jean-Jacques
Fuerte Híjar, Marquise of, 21, 107, 111

Galen, 144–45
Gálvez, María Rosa, 1–2, 23–24, 112
García de la Huerta, Vicente, 62, 112
García Malo, Ignacio, 198, 206–8
Gay, Peter, 96*n*3
Gelpí, Juan, 171
Gender: Amar on, 6, 53, 54–56, 59; and china, 181–82; Doña Leonora's library, 181–82; education of women, 6, 8, 9–10, 12*n*11, 15, 18–19, 22, 52–60, 179, 183–84, 224; and Enlightenment generally, 2–11, 19–20, 85, 228; etiquette between men and women, 108–12; Eve as symbol of women, 1, 3–4, 7, 155*n*12; Goya's images of women, 160, 218–34; and hysteria, 143–54; learned woman as cultural icon, 17–20, 23–24, 28; limitations of records for documentation of women's contributions, 115–16, 119–24; and literacy, 179; and motherhood, 160, 222–26, 234; natural law on, 82*n*10; and public versus private spheres, 116, 117–20, 124, 125; Rousseau on gender roles, 5, 9, 60, 61*n*4; sentimental rhetoric of Enlightenment on gender differences, 9–10; sexuality of women, 133–35, 229–30; stereotypes of women, 3, 5, 7–8, 56, 65, 153–54, 155*n*12, 211; and vices, 58; women's association with the body and beauty, 5; women's household work, 116–26. *See also* Convents and nuns; Marriage; *Mulata*; Reading audience; Sentimental novels; Women alone
Gillray, James, 199–200
Ginzburg, Carlo, 133
Glendinning, Nigel, 65, 82*n*9
Godoy, Manuel, 110, 227–28, 232
Goldmann, Lucienne, 166
Gómez de Castro, Mercedes, 26
Góngora, Luis de, 64
Goya, Francisco de: aristocratic women portrayed with attributes of arts by, 228–29; *Los Caprichos* by, 201, 224, 226–27; *Los desastres de la guerra/The Disasters of War* by, 10, 160, 218, 232–34; full-length portraits of women by, 229–32; motherhood portrayed by, 160, 222–28, 234; patrons of, 219; as portrait

Goya, (continued)
  painter, 222–32, 234n6; pregnant women portrayed by, 227–28; women's images by, 9, 160, 201, 202, 218–34
Goya: Images of Women exhibition (2002), 218–34, 234n1
Graffigny, Mme de, 26
Granada, Fray Luis de, 191
Great Britain. *See* Britain
Grimaldo, Marquise of, 108
Los gritos de Madrid, 120, 121
Guillén, Nicolás, 161
Gutiérrez, Luís, 207

Hagiography, 84–96, 97n13
Haidt, Rebecca, 7, 9, 101, 115–27, 171, 237
Harney, Lucy, 8, 10, 159, 161–77, 237
The Haw Seller (La Acerolera) (Goya), 220, 221
Health: Amar on, 56; environmental causes of poor public health, 149–50, 153; habits promoting, 149. *See also* Hysteria; Medical discourse
Helmont, John Baptista van, 146
Helvetius, 214–15n11
Hernández de Velasco, Gregorio, 190
Hickey y Pellizoni, Margarita: biographical information on, 62–63; compared with Hore, 36; contributions of generally, 1–2; criticism of men by, 76–79, 81; criticism of women by, 79–80; identity of, as writer, 25, 27; on love, 8, 15–16, 42–43, 62–81; on marriage, 70, 76–79, 81, 82n11; poetry by, 8, 15–16, 25, 47n6, 62–81; at *tertulias* (social gatherings), 22, 112; translation of Racine's *Andromaque* by, 62, 63, 66–67; as widow, 62, 66
Hidalguía (lower nobility), 22
Hippocrates, 144, 152
Hispanic Enlightenment. *See* Enlightenment; Spain; Spanish America
Honor code, 101
Horace, 65
Hore, Sor María Gertrudis de la Cruz: adultery by, 43–44; books owned by, 44, 48n18; and Cepeda's public examination, 34–36; compared with Hickey, 36; contributions of generally, 1–2; intellectual development of, 37–38, 46; on love, 38–43; marriage of, 33, 41, 101; as nun, 24, 33, 42–47; parents of, 33; poetry by, 9, 15, 34–47; religious writings by, 24; at *tertulias* (social gatherings), 22, 37–38
Horta, Pedro de, 147, 150, 152, 153–4
Household work by married women, 116–26
Hufton, Olwen, 128, 132
Hume, David, 172–73, 203, 214n2
Hurtado, Escolástica, 21
Hypochondria, 144
Hysteria: anxiety hysteria, 144; Bartolache on, 101–2, 143, 148–54; battle hysteria, 144; beginning of hysterical attack, 150; causes of, 145–49, 151, 152, 154; chocolate as cause of, 148–49, 153; definition of, 144; exercise as treatment for, 153; Galen on, 144–45; Hippocrates on, 144, 152; mass hysteria, 144; and menstruation, 145, 150–51, 153; in Middle Ages, 145; as nervous disease, 146; and nuns, 151–52, 153; and problems with uterus, 144–46, 152, 154, 154nn3–4; remedies for, 153, 156n26; in Renaissance, 145; statistics on, 151; symptoms of, 150–51, 154–55n5, 155nn17–22

Ignatius of Loyola, St., 88, 97n13
Illness. *See* Hysteria
La Ilustración Americana, 162
Iluminismo, 86, 88
Ilustración, 2, 4, 11n6, 86, 178, 179
Imbille, Luis de, 117–18
Industria (industry), 117
Inferiority of women. *See* Stereotypes of women
Information sources. *See* Research sources
Inquisition, 12n11, 131, 136–37, 179, 207, 226
Irene y Clara (Salvá), 213
Iriarte, Tomás de, 164, 224

Jaffe, Catherine M., 1–14, 159, 178–96, 237

Jaucourt, Louis de, 197
Johnson, Samuel, 27, 47n7
Johnson, Sherry, 162
Josefa Castilla Portugal de Garcini (Goya), 227–28
Jovellanos, Gaspar Melchor de, 4, 84–85, 180, 224
Joyes y Blake, Inés, 22, 27, 36, 42–43, 47n7
Juan, Jorge, 37
Juan Manuel, Don, 164
Judicial records, 133–40
Junta de Damas, 10, 22, 24, 51, 107, 111, 117, 224
Justine (Sade), 213, 214n6, 215n15
Juvenal, 190

Kant, Immanuel, 5, 172, 203, 214n9
Kish, Kathleen, 65
Knott, Sarah, 11n8
Kowaleski-Wallace, Elizabeth, 181–82
Kutzinski, Vera, 161

La Bruyère, Jean de, 164
The Ladies Calling (Allestree), 192
The Lady's New Years-Gift (Savile), 193
Lalaing, Cayetana De la Cerda, Countess of, 24–25
Lambert, Anne Thérèse de Marguenat de Courcelles, Marquise de, 24–25, 52, 57–60, 61n3, 185
Lamore, Jean, 161, 174–75n1
Lampillas, Xavier, 23
Lanser, Susan Snider, 82n4
Larra, Mariano José de, 162, 163
Latin America. *See* Cuba; Mexico; Spanish America
Lavater, Johann Caspar, 171
Lavrin, Asunción, 2, 96n8
Le Prince de Beaumont, Mme, 21, 24–25
Learned women: *bachillera* as, 8, 21, 25, 47n5, 189, 229; as cultural icon, 17–20, 23–24, 28; Molière's satire of, 185; and women of letters in eighteenth-century Spain, 17–28. *See also* Education; Women of letters; and specific women

Leclercq, Cécile, 167–69
Lenglet Du Fresnoy, Pierre Nicolas, 224
León, Fray Luis de, 58, 183, 191
Leonora, Doña, 178–95
Lerner, Isaías, 174
L'Estrange, Sir Roger, 194
Lettres de Mme de Montier, 21
Lettres d'une péruvienne (Graffigny), 26
Lewis, Elizabeth Franklin, 1–14, 43n13, 43n19, 237
Les liaisons dangereuses (Choderlos de Laclos), 214n6
Library: of Doña Leonora, 178–95; Osuna library, 224; of Sor María Gertrudis de la Cruz Hore, 44, 48n18. *See also* Reading audience
Linné, Carl von, 172
Literacy, 10, 85, 179, 183, 185, 189. *See also* Education; Library; Reading audience
Locke, John, 4, 12n10, 167, 183, 191
Lope de Vega, 63, 64
López, María, 136–37
López-Cordón Cortezo, María Victoria, 2, 8, 9, 10, 101, 103–14, 160, 237
Lorenzana, Francisco Antonio, 151
Louis XIV, King, 106
Louis XVI, King, 200
Love: courtly love, 64, 70, 75, 81; and family portraits, 225; Hickey on, 8, 15–16, 42–43, 62–81; Hore on, 38–43; Ovid on, 64, 70; and Plato's theory of hysteria, 154n3; Scudéry on, 82n8; Zayas on, 82n8. *See also* Sentimental novels
Lovejoy, Arthur O., 172
Lucena, María, 134–35
Luis, William, 174n1
Luzán, Ignacio de, 65
Lynch, Deidre, 171

Mack, Phyllis, 7
Madrid Secondhand Dealers' Guild, 122–23
Maffei, Giovanni Pietro, 97n13
Maids. *See* Domestic working women

Maja (lower–class Spanish woman), 8, 10, 160, 219–21, 232, 234
Maldonado y Ormaza, Catalina, 113n7
Malebranche, Nicholas de, 192
Manrique, Josefa, 111–12
Maravall, José Antonio, 213
Marchante, Sebastiana, 135–36
Marchese, Angelo, 34
Marcialidad (uninhibited, outspoken manner), 160, 219, 229–31
María, Madre, La Antigua, 88
María Luisa, Queen, 105, 106, 107, 110, 222, 232. See also Parma, María Luisa de
Marinelli, Lucrezia, 19
Marquesa de Villafranca Painting Her Husband (Goya), 229
Marriage: and adultery, 41, 43–44; Amar on, 54–55; arranged marriages, 33, 41; and bigamy, 136–38; and *cortejo*, 70, 83n15, 110, 183; and divorce, 44; emigration of married men to Spanish America, 137–40; Hickey on, 70, 76–79, 81, 82n11; and natural law, 82n10; as norm in Spanish culture, 66; nun's marriage to Christ, 75–76; problems of, 101,133, 134–35; and women of letters, 21, 27; and women's household work, 116–26
Marriage contract, 8, 101, 138
Martí, José, 161
Martín, Andrés, 88
Martín Gaite, Carmen, 2, 6, 83n15, 113n6, 221
Martínez Alier, Verena, 168, 169, 171
Martínez del Mazo, Juan Bautista, 225
Mary, Queen, 182
Masones de Lima, Ana María, 113n7
Mass hysteria, 144
Matilla Tascón, Antonio, 122
Maya, Miguel de, 87
McKendrick, Melveena, 65, 82n10
McKnight, Kathryn Joy, 97n17
Medical discourse: on hysteria, 101–2, 143–54; in Renaissance, 145. See also Health
Meléndez Valdés, Juan, 180

Meltzer, Françoise, 195n9
Mena, Beatriz de, 137
Mendoza, Catalina de, 131
Menstruation, 145, 150–51, 153
El Mercurio Volante, 101–2, 143, 147–54, 155n7, 155n9
Mesonero Romanos, Ramón de, 162–63
Mexico: Bourbon reforms in, 86–87; convents and nuns in, 86–96, 96n8; hysteria in, 101–2, 143, 146–54. See also Spanish America
Mexico City, 149–51
Midwifery, 192
The Militar and the Lady (El Militar y la Señora) (Goya), 221, 222
Molière, 60, 184–85, 192
Montesquieu, Charles–Louis de Secondat, baron de, 167
Montiano Circle, 62
Montiano y Luyando, Agustín, 22, 25, 111–12
Montijo, Countess of, 111
Mor de Fuentes, José, 201
Moral education, 53–59, 206
Moral philosophy, 199, 203–4
Morand, Frédérique, 9, 10, 15, 33–50, 101, 238
Morant Deusa, Isabel, 2, 9, 15, 51–61, 119, 238
Moreri, Luis, 44, 48n18
Mother tongue, 89
Motherhood, 12, 55–56, 160, 222–29, 234
Las Mugeres sabias (Les femmes savantes; Molière), 184–85, 192
Mujer esquiva (aloof woman), 65
Mujeres de carpinteros, 88–89
Mulata: characteristics of, 173–74; as Cuban symbol, 10, 161–74; definition of, 173; in fiction, 161–74; innocence of, 167, 168–69; physical appearance of, 170–72; relationships between white men and, 167–70, 173; social climbing by, 167–68; as victim, 8, 164, 168–70, 174
Mulierum virtutes (Plutarch), 18
Mullan, John, 203, 205
Munárriz, Don Josef, 232

Naked Maja (Goya in the Twilight) (Goya), 229
Nervous disorder, 146. *See also* Hysteria
The New Morality (Gillray), 199–200
New Spain. *See* Spanish America
Newton, Sir Isaac, 183, 190
Nifo, Mariano, 19–20, 204, 211
La nouvelle Clarice (Le Prince de Beaumont), 21
La nouvelle Héloise (Rousseau), 214n6
Novelas exemplares (o escandalosas) (Zayas), 180, 183, 192
Novelas inglesas (sentimental novels), 185
Novels. *See* Sentimental novels; and specific authors
Nuns. *See* Convents and nuns

Obras espirituales (Granada), 191
Observations on the Feeling of the Beautiful and the Sublime (Kant), 5
Of the Passions (*Disertación sobre las pasiones*; Hume), 203
Ogilby, John, 190
Olavide, Pablo de, 84–85
Óptica del cortejo (Ramírez y Góngora), 183, 192, 219
Osuna, Duchess of, 21, 27, 111, 222–26, 231, 234
Osuna, Duke of, 222–26
Outram, Dorinda, 7
Ovid, 64, 70

Pacheco, Isabel, 136
Padrón of 1773, 132, 140n2
Paine, Thomas, 167
Palazzi, Maura, 132
Pamela (Richardson), 205, 208, 214n10
Paracelsus, 146, 147
Parma, María Luisa de, 105, 106, 107, 110, 222, ,232
Passions: Amar y Borbón on, 10, 58, 206; and Don Juanism, 206–11; ethical nature of, 211–13; Helvetius on, 214–15n11; Hume on, 203–04, 214n2; and hysteria, 145, 149, 150; of love, 43, 71; and reading, 187, 205; signs of, 197–98, 201; of Sor Sebastiana, 10, 90. *See also* Sensibility; Sentimental novels
Pastoral, 20, 39, 65, 67, 83n16, 166
Pawnbroking, 124–25, 126
Pedro el Cruel, 204
Peñafiel, Marquis de. *See* Osuna, Duke of
El Pensador, 179
La Pensadora gaditana, 21
Pérez, Juana, 139–40
Pérez Magallón, Jesús, 2, 11n9
La perfecta casada (León), 58, 183, 191
Periodicals, 9, 19, 21, 28, 101–2, 143, 147–54, 159, 162, 178, 179. *See also* specific periodicals
Perry, M. E., 131
Perry, Ruth, 215n12
Peru, 156n25
Petimetra (fashionable woman), 8, 10, 219, 221
Philanthropic societies, 22
Physicians. *See* Medical discourse
Pimentel, María Josefa de la Soledad Alonso. *See* Osuna, Duchess of
Pintura del talento y carácter de las mujeres (Painting of the Talent and Character of Women; Gómez de Castro), 26
Pisan, Christine de, 19
Plagiarism, 26
Plato, 154n3
Plays and playwrights, 20–21, 23–24, 66, 91, 110–11, 231
Plutarch, 18, 19
Pocock, J. G. A., 16, 96n4
Poesías varias (Hickey), 25, 47n6, 63–81, 82n2, 112
Poetry: Cernuda on lyric poetry, 33; by Hickey, 8, 15–16, 25, 62–81; by Hore, 9, 15, 34–47; mystic poetry, 43, 83n16; pastoral form in, 65, 83n16; Spanish neoclassical poetry, 65; women of letters and, 22–23, 111
Pópoli, Duchess of, 21
Porque fue sensible (Because she was sentimental), 201, 202
Portraiture, 222–32, 234n6
Portugal de Garcini, Josefa Castilla, 227–28
Poverty of women, 118, 129–30, 138, 140

A Practical Discourse concerning Death (Sherlock), 191
Pragmática de los lutos, 192
"La primitiva 'Cecilia Valdés'" (Villaverde), 159, 161–68, 170–72, 174, 174–75nn1–2
Private versus public spheres, 116, 117–20, 124, 125. *See also* Public versus private spheres
Productivity, 124
La prostitución (Castillo y Mayone), 206
Prostitution, 117, 206–7, 226
Public education. *See* Education
Public versus private spheres, 6, 17, 20–28, 51, 86, 89, 97–98n26, 101–12, 116, 117–20, 124, 125, 126, 213
Pueblo, 162
Purcell, John, 155n19

Quijano, Benito, 139–40
Quintanilla-Madero, Beatriz, 7, 8, 9, 10, 101–2, 143–57, 238

Race, 8, 10, 159, 161, 168, 170–74. *See also* Mulata
Racine, Jean, 62, 63, 66–67
Ramírez y Góngora, Manuel Antonio, 183, 192
Rasselas, Prince of Abissinia (Johnson), 27, 47n7
Raulin, Joseph, 154–55n5
Reading audience: books owned by Sor María Gertrudis de la Cruz Hore, 44, 48n18; for confessional letters by religious women, 88, 89; Doña Leonora's library, 178–95; for French romances, 184–85; for periodicals, 21, 178, 179; for sentimental novels, 184–86, 205, 211; women as, in eighteenth-century Spain, 17, 20–22, 25–26, 28, 44, 57, 104, 111, 159. *See also* Library
Recherche de la vérité (Search after Truth; Malebranche), 192
Réflexions nouvelles sur les femmes (Lambert), 185
La religieuse (Diderot), 84, 214n6
Religious women. *See* Convents and nuns
Religious writing, 16, 22–24, 85–96, 102
Renaissance, 18, 138, 145, 166

Requisitorias a Indias (Warrants to the Indies), 137–40
Research sources: censuses and registries, 123–24, 132, 133, 140nn1–2; egodocuments, 133; judicial records, 133–40; limitations of, for documentation of women's contributions, 115–16, 119–24; variety of, 8–9
The Return of Martin Guerre (Davis), 133
Rial García, Serrana, 118–19, 132
Ribadeneira, Pedro de, 97n13
Ribera, Paolo, 19
Richardson, Samuel, 205, 208, 214n10
Risse, G. B., 155n23
Rita, 75–76
Roche, Daniel, 125
Rodríguez, Pedro, 117, 124
Rodríguez de Arellano, Vicente, 206
Roldán, Josepha, 136
Romanticism, 163–64, 212
Romero Masegosa y Cancelada, María Rosario, 26
Rousseau, Jean-Jacques: Amar y Borbón on, 12n11, 61n4; on civil state, 167; on education, 9, 60, 61n4; on gender roles, 5, 9, 60, 61n4; Hume's influence on, 203; influence of, on Villaverde, 162, 167; and *New Morality* political cartoon, 200; writings by, 5, 9, 12n11, 60, 61n4, 214n6
Roussel, Pierre, 214n1
Rowlands, Alison, 130
Rueda, Ana, 8, 9, 10, 159, 197–217, 238
Rull, Enrique, 65

La sabia indiscreta, 20–21
Saboya, María Luisa Gabriela de, 105, 106
Sade, Marquis de, 213, 214n6, 215n15
Sainetes (comic theatrical interludes), 218–19, 221
Saint-Simon, duc de [Louis de Rouvroy], 106, 108–9
Sainthood, 86–96
Sajonia, María Amalia de, 106, 107

Salgado, María, 8, 15–16, 62–83, 238
Samaniego, Félix María de, 164
Sampson Vera Tudela, Elisa, 8, 10, 16, 84–100, 102, 238
Santa Cruz, Doña Joaquina Téllez-Girón y Pimentel, Marquesa de, 224, 228–29
Sanz, F. J., 132
Savile, George, 193
Schlau, Stacey, 89
Scholarly sources. *See* Research sources
Scholasticism, 162
Schulz, Andrew, 224
Schurmann, Anna Maria, 19
Scott, Joan W., 12, 94
Scott, Walter, 162
Scudéry, Madeleine de, 19, 82n8, 184, 190, 193
Sebastiana Josefa de la Santísima Trinidad, Sor: autonomy of, from her confessors, 93–94; confessional letters by, 16, 85–96, 102; on convent life, 90; emotional states of, 91–96, 97n16; on evil and devil, 93; hagiography of, 87, 89; mystical experiences of, 10; saintliness of, 87–88, 90, 92; self-doubt of, 92–93; on writing, 91
Sebold, Russell, 163–64
La seducción y la virtud, 206, 208–10, 214–15n11
Seixo, Vicente del, 21, 24
Semanario de Salamanca, 44, 178–90
El senador mexicano (Robledo), 212–13
Seneca, 194
Sensibility: and amalgam of discourses in sentimental novel, 203–6; change in meaning of, 9, 95–96, 159–60, 199–202; and education, 57; European debate on, 197, 199–202; lack of precise meaning of, 197–98; and models of virtue, 210–11; new directions for, 211–14; and novels, 9; and political concerns, 212–14; and reading, 188–89; rhetoric of, 8; signs of "virtue in distress," 198; spectacle of, 207; and women's bodily experience, 5. *See also* Sentimental novels
Sentimental novels: and aesthetics of suffering, 213; as amalgam of discourses, 203–6; Amar y Borbón on, 206; and censors, 198–99, 206; and cult of longing for death, 213; and French romances, 184–85; letters in, 212; male virtue in, 211; and meanings of term *sensibility*, 197–202; moral ambiguity of, 205–6; moral philosophy discourse in, 203–4; and new directions for sensibility, 211–14; physiological discourse in, 204–5; political revolutions in, 212–14; reading audience for, 184–86; sexual harassment in, 198, 206–11; "virtue in distress" in, 159–60, 197–214
La Serafina (Mor de Fuentes), 201, 211
Serrano y Sanz, Manuel, 6, 62, 66
Sexuality: discourses of, 203; in Goya's images of women, 229–30; and the private sphere, 213; in sentimental novels, 198, 206–11; of women, 133–35, 161, 229–30
Sherlock, William, 191
Sherwood, Joan, 118, 126n2
Sidney, Sir Philip, 191
La Siempreviva, 175n2
Sill, Geoffrey, 205
Single women. *See* Women alone
Sistema físico y moral del hombre (Roussel), 214n1
Slavery, 162, 169, 173, 174, 175n3
Smith, Adam, 124, 203
Smith, Theresa Ann, 2, 11, 29n8, 86, 97–98n26
Sociability: and academic gatherings, 110–11, 113n7; and *chichisveo* (intimate and personal conversation between a man and a woman), 110; court as model of, 104–8; and entertainments, 110; and *estrado* (elevated platform) for women, 109; and etiquette between men and women, 108–12; languages of, 201; practices of, 9, 178, 180; and *tertulias* (social gatherings), 19, 22, 37–38, 111–12, 224; women in society in eighteenth-century Spain, 103–12
Sociedad Económica Matritense (Economic Society of Madrid), 6, 22, 23, 51, 107, 116, 117, 218, 224

Socrates, 147
Solana, Marquesa de, 231
Solis, Josepha, 135
La sombra del religioso, 212–13
Sorkin, David, 16, 96n4
Spain: Bourbon dynasty in, 10, 86–87, 105–6; Catholic tradition of, 3, 4; conceptions of gender difference in, 5; censuses and registries in, 123–24, 132, 133, 140nn1–2; Enlightenment in, and meaning of *ilustrar,* 86; judicial records in, 133–40; limitations of records for documentation of women's contributions in, 8–9, 115–16, 119–24; literacy in, 179; periodicals in, 178, 179; reading audience in, 21; scholarly neglect of Enlightenment in, 1–2; sentimental novels from, 159–60, 197–214; War of Independence in, 9, 10, 160, 201, 213, 232–34; women alone in, 128–40; women in society in, 103–12; women of letters in, during eighteenth century, 17–28; women's household work in, 116–26. *See also* Court; Enlightenment; specific monarchs; and specific Spanish women
Spanish America: Bourbon reforms in, 86–87; Catholic tradition of, 3, 4; conceptions of gender difference in, 5; confessional letters by religious women and hagiography in, 84–96; debate over religion and gender in, 16; emigration of married men to, 137–40; hysteria in, 151; *mulata* in, 8, 10, 161–74; saintly cults in, 88; scholarly neglect of Enlightenment in, 1–2. *See also* Cuba; Enlightenment; Mexico; and specific Spanish American women
Spanish War of Independence, 9, 10, 136, 160, 201, 213, 215n14, 232–34, 235n8
Spectator (Addison and Steele), 178–80, 190
Spell, J. R., 12n11
Spiritual discourse. *See* Confessional letters by religious women
Spiritual Exercises (Ignatius of Loyola), 88
Steele, Richard, 179, 190. *See also Spectator*
Stereotypes of women, 3, 5, 7–8, 56, 65, 103, 132, 153–54, 155n12, 159, 211, 227
Street vendors, 116–17, 120, 121, 126, 163, 218–19. *See also Maja* (lower–class Spanish woman)
Subirats, Eduardo, 2, 16, 86, 96
Sugar's Secrets (Kutzinski), 161
Sullivan, Constance A., 28–29n4, 62
Sur les femmes (Diderot), 95
Sympathy, 102, 203; of reader, 214; relation to hysteria, 145; as response, 205

Tadeo González, Friar Diego, 45
"Tales in Verse" (D'Urfé), 183, 184
Tales Tragical and Comical (D'Urfé), 184, 193
Taylor, Barbara, 11n8
Taylor's *Holy living and dying,* 185, 195
Téllez Girón, Pedro Alcántara. *See* Osuna, Duke of
Temple, Sir William, 191
Teodora (Guijarro Ripoll), 212–14
Teresa (Cortina y Roperto), 212, 213
Teresa of Ávila, 75, 76, 81n1, 83n16, 88, 97n14, 97n22, 131, 210
Tertulias (social gatherings), 9, 22, 37–38, 111–12, 224
Textiles, 9, 101, 116–26
Theater. *See* Plays and playwrights
Thomas, Antoine–Léonard, 26
Timaeus (Plato), 154n3
La Tirana (The Female Tyrant; Goya), 229–31, 232, 234
Tomlinson, Janis, 8, 9, 10, 160, 218–35, 239
Tour through Great Britain (Defoe), 182
Townsend, Joseph, 109, 110
Traité de l'education des filles (Fénelon), 183
Traité des affections vaporeuses du sexe (Raulin), 154–55n5
Translations, 21, 22, 23, 24, 26–27, 28, 34, 47n7, 62, 63, 66–67, 149, 178–80, 183–85, 231
Treatise on Human Nature (Hume), 214n2

Ulloa, Antonio de, 22, 37–38
Unmarried women. *See* Women alone

Urzainqui, Inmaculada, 185
Uterus, 144–46, 152, 154, 154nn3–4, 155n19
Utilidad (usefulness), 117, 147

Valdés, Fernando de, 88
Valdés, José Eugenio, 87–89, 95–96, 97n9
Varela, Félix, 162
Vegio, Maffeo, 190
Les veillées du château (de Genlis), 21
Velasco y Ayala, Leonor de, 113n7
Velázquez, Diego, 225
Vice, 58, 64, 174, 198–99, 210; and Helvetius's theories, 214–215n11. *See also* Sentimental novels
Vila, Anne, 214n6
Villaverde, Cirilo, 159, 161–74, 174–75nn1–2, 175n4
Virgil, 183, 188, 190
Virginia, la doncella cristiana, 26–27
Virtue: domestic virtue, 107; feminine virtue, 59, 167; and Helvetius's theories, 214–15n11; human virtue, 63, 65, 169, 174, 183; male virtue in sentimental novels, 211–12; meaning of "virtue in distress," 198; models of, 210–11; and motherhood, 225; signs of "virtue in distress," 198; vice versus, 58, 198–99; "virtue in distress" in sentimental novels, 9, 159–60, 197–214; women's virtue, 68, 79, 168
Vives, Juan Luis, 58, 183–84
Voltaire, 203
Voyleano o la exaltación de las pasiones (Cosca Vayo), 201, 208, 211–12
Voz de la naturaleza (García Malo), 198

Wall, Richard, 132
Weakness of women. *See* Stereotypes of women
Wet nurses, 118, 124–25, 126n2
Widows, 26–27, 62, 66, 111, 122–24, 129–37, 155n23, 178, 186, 189. *See also* Women alone

Women. *See* Gender
Women (de Kooning), 231
Women alone: and bigamy, 136–38; businesses of unmarried women, 123; factors impacting, 131–32; as heads of families, 132; judicial records on, 133–40; and life cycle, 130–31; meaning of term, 128–32; petitions for certificates of widowhood, 8, 135–36; poverty of, 129–30, 138, 140; sexuality of, 133–35; in sixteenth-century Seville, 131; theoretical approaches to, 130–32. *See also* Convents and nuns; Widows
Women of letters: as aristocrats, 24–25; in eighteenth-century Spain, 17–28; genres of women writers, 22; learned woman as cultural icon, 17–20, 23–24, 28; of lower social position, 25–27; meaning of term, 20; merit and respectability of, 25; as middle-class women, 25; as playwrights, 23–24; as readers, 21; religious writing by, 22–23; strategies of, 24–28; translations by, 22, 23, 26–27; as writers, 20, 21–27
Working-class women, 56, 116–17, 118, 124–25, 233–34. *See also* Maja (lower-class Spanish woman)
Wright, Anthony, 96n8
Writers. *See* Women of letters; and specific women

Young Lady Wearing a Mantilla and Basquiña (Goya), 231–32
Young Women (Goya), 228

Zaragoza, siege of, 213, 232–34
Zayas, María de, 20, 26, 81n1, 82n8, 180, 183, 192
Zelmire (Belloy), 231
Zúñiga y Castro, Josefa, 111